GAMECHANGERS
& RAINMAKERS

GAMECHANGERS & RAINMAKERS

How Sport Became Big Business

David Stubley

First published by Pitch Publishing, 2025

Pitch Publishing
9 Donnington Park,
85 Birdham Road,
Chichester,
West Sussex,
PO20 7AJ
www.pitchpublishing.co.uk
info@pitchpublishing.co.uk

© 2025, David Stubley

Every effort has been made to trace the copyright.
Any oversight will be rectified in future editions at the
earliest opportunity by the publisher.

All rights reserved. No part of this book may be reproduced,
sold or utilised in any form or transmitted in any form or by
any means, electronic or mechanical, including photocopying,
recording or by any information storage and retrieval system,
without prior permission in writing from the publisher.

A CIP catalogue record is available for this book
from the British Library.

ISBN 978 1 80150 930 5

Printed and bound on FSC® certified paper in line with
our continuing commitment to ethical business practices,
sustainability and the environment.

Typesetting and origination by Pitch Publishing
Printed and bound by CPI Group (UK) Ltd, Croydon, CR0 4YY

Contents

Introduction 9
Part One: Flat Caps and Blazers (1850–1914)
  1 The Football Split 20
  2 The Creation of the Modern-Day Olympic Games . 26
Part Two: The Madmen (1920–1960) 29
  3 Coast-to-Coast Cable 38
  4 The Matthews Cup Final 41
  5 The TV Boycott of the Melbourne Olympics 44
**Part Three: You Say You Want a Revolution? (The
        Swinging 60s)** 49
  6 Collective Bargaining of TV Rights 56
  7 Mark McCormack and IMG 61
Part Four: Shamateurism (The 1970s) 67
  8 'Welcome to Monday Night Football on ABC' ... 71
  9 Bernie Ecclestone Buys Brabham 73
  10 The Women's Pro Tennis Breakaway Tour 75
  11 New FIFA President 80
  12 Free Agency 82
  13 The Goddess of Victory 86
  14 The Official Partner 90
  15 The Superstation 92
Part Five: Made for TV (The 1980s) 95
  16 The Launch of ESPN 100
  17 New IOC President 104
  18 The Concorde Agreement 107
  19 The Creation of ISL 110
  20 The End of Amateurism 112
  21 Calgary TV Rights Auction 114
  22 Apple and the 1984 Superbowl 116
  23 The NBA Play-Off Finals 118
  24 The Los Angeles Olympics 121
  25 Michael Jordan and Nike 126

Part Six: Media Fragmentation (The 1990s) 131
   26 The Launch of BSkyB 133
   27 The Premier League 136
   28 The Premier League TV Contract......... 143
   29 Rugby Union (Finally) Turns Professional 146
   30 The UEFA Champions League 161
   31 The Rise of Team GB 172
   32 Salt Lake City Scandal............... 174

Part Seven: Going Global (The New Millenium).... 177
   33 The Premier League Goes Global 183
   34 The Bahrain Grand Prix.............. 193
   35 The Glazer Family Buy Manchester United 196
   36 The Launch of the IPL............... 208

Part Eight: An Ocean Full of Change 214
   37 London 2012 Olympics............... 218
   38 'FIFA-Gate' 221
   39 Sunderland Till I Die............... 226
   40 The Lionnesses.................. 228

Part Nine: What Lessons Can Sporting History Teach Us? 233
Conclusions....................... 234

Part Ten: The Sports Marketing Hall of Fame 273
Epilogue 281
Selected Bibliography.................. 284

Rainmaker: *'A person who generates income for a business or organisation by brokering deals or attracting clients or funds.'*

Introduction

The Battle of Old Trafford – 21 September 2003

OLD TRAFFORD held its breath. Manchester United were playing Arsenal during a period in Premier League history when there was always fireworks between these two teams. This game proved to be no different, after Patrick Vieira received a second yellow for a ghost lunge on Ruud van Nistelrooy which infuriated his team-mates. The Stretford End waved Vieira goodbye and urged their team on with cries of 'attack, attack, attack' but as the game entered injury time, the famous Arsenal back four were holding firm. Gary Neville then floated a hopeful cross into the box towards Diego Forlan as Arsenal defender Martin Keown stooped low to try and knock him off his stride. Over he went, Old Trafford erupted and cue Sky's Martin Tyler: 'Oh penalty, the controversy hasn't finished yet, Arsenal cannot believe it, in stoppage time and you know who's going to take it.' He continues, knowing he has us in the palm of his hand, 'This for four points. This to beat their fiercest rivals. This to go top of the Premiership tonight. The responsibility rests with Ruud van Nistelrooy.'

The United striker carefully placed the ball on the spot and Tyler paused for maximum effect before gasping, 'Oh, he's missed it, he's hit the bar. Arsenal can't believe it, it's the final whistle and Arsenal do get their draw, but it's not finished yet, they're all around Ruud van Nistelrooy

... there are people off the bench trying to pull the players apart ... if you ever doubted the intensity of the rivalry here, for maybe 75 minutes it was a football match, then it became a feud. Vieira went off, Van Nistelrooy suddenly lost the magic touch from the penalty spot, and he wasted the chance to win the game, but it was the ball that knocked against the bar and came out that was the decisive moment ... right at the end of the game.'

Breathless stuff, and when Steve Bennett blew his whistle for full time, he'd ended up awarding 38 fouls and handed out one red and eight yellow cards. A subsequent FA inquiry therefore charged eight players with misconduct and fined Arsenal £175,000 for failing to control their players. In the final game of the season the significance of that missed penalty kick became clear, when Arsenal beat Leicester City 2-1 to become the champions of England, and the first (and last) team to play an entire season in the Premier League without losing a game. A few years later Sky produced a documentary which told the story of this campaign, and the interviewer asked the coach of that title-winning team, Arsène Wenger, for his reflections on that autumn afternoon in Manchester. The film was called *The Invincibles,* and before answering Wenger paused, smiled wryly and then uttered a few sage words which provide the perfect runway for this book: 'Life,' he said, 'is about millimetres and timing.'

Why do we care so much?

I recently found myself trying to explain to someone why I love Crystal Palace Football Club so much. A lad from the New Forest who is now 'South London and Proud'. But how did that happen? I was born 138 miles away from Selhurst Park, own no shares in the club and pay to sit in a stand that hasn't seen much love since it was first built in 1924. It's true, though, I do love everything about this

Introduction

football club: our badge, our kit, the seats we sit in, and singing 'Glad All Over' by the Dave Clark Five when things are going well. As for following England. Well, don't get me started because I'm not ashamed to say I actually cried when we made it through to the final of Euro '20 with a shocked Mrs S asking quizzically, 'What's the matter?' At the time I struggled for answers but in hindsight what I should have said is this:

World Cup 1978	'We couldn't even qualify'
World Cup 1982	'If only Keegan had been fit'
World Cup 1986	'I'll give you the Hand of God'
World Cup 1990	'Bloody Germany'
World Cup 1994	'Didn't qualify'
Euro '96	'Has Southgate ever taken a penalty?'
World Cup 1998	'What was Beckham thinking of?'
Euro 2000	'Out in the group stages'
World Cup 2002	'What was Seaman doing off his line?'
Euro 2004	'Out on penalties – Portugal'
World Cup 2006	'Penalties – Portugal, again'
Euro 2008	'Didn't qualify'
World Cup 2010	'Bloody Germany (and why wasn't there VAR?)'
Euro 2012	'Penalties – Italy'
World Cup 2014	'Out in the group stages'
Euro 2016	'How many people even live in Iceland?'
World Cup 2018	'Croatia in the semis!'

The more I thought about my devotion to CPFC and England, the more I struggled to find rational reasons why they've become so important to me. Although those 15 minutes of real-life drama that played out in Manchester in September 2003 do at least provide a few clues: another chapter in the long-running rivalry between two football teams who really didn't like each other very much and with something unpredictable usually happening when they found themselves on the same pitch together. Will it kick off between Vieira and Roy Keane? Will the managers shake hands? Will pizza be thrown? Another episode of 'The Premier League' with neutrals feeling sorry for the victim and hating the pantomime villain who, on this occasion, was Dutch and wore the number ten shirt of Manchester United.

If we're feeling philosophical, 'The Battle of Old Trafford' (as Sky billed it) was a kind of Shakespearean improv, but to understand why, we need the help of Howard Jacobson, who writes about sport's role in society and concludes this: 'We give up our weekends to be part of the unrelenting hysteria of species survival, but at a safe distance.' What Jacobson is therefore saying is that sport plays to our natural urge to fight or flight: feelings that have been hard-wired into us for over 65 million years but suppressed through living in a civilised society. So next time you find yourself screaming at the TV when there's an obvious VAR mistake, or England make it to the final of a major competition, simply tell those around you it's your survival instinct kicking in and there's nothing much you can do about it.

Ellis Cashmore is another deep thinker on the sociology of sport and provides valuable additional context in his book, *Making Sense of Sport*, where he suggests that sport has become a modern form of religion. 'Sports fans do pursue a faith, albeit in their own way ... sport has become a functional substitute [for religion], supplying for the follower a meaningful cause, an emblematic focus, and a source of allegiance, even belonging.' I hear you, Ellis, and for anyone who thinks this is nuts, I encourage you to sit in a pub in Newcastle or Liverpool on matchday. In the words of Palace legend, DJ Maxi Jazz, 'This is my church. This is where I heal my hurt,' with many of us more emotionally invested in sport than any other form of entertainment. No one stands up, do they, in a West End theatre and screams abuse at Kenneth Branagh when he's playing King Lear; or tries to lob things at the TV when Logan Roy is once again being mean to his kids in an episode of *Succession*. And the reason, according to *Sunday Times* columnist Matthew Syed, is that they're going through 'the sociological equivalent of a psychoactive high'. He goes on, 'I have been to an Old Firm match [Celtic v Rangers] and watched as staid seemingly ordinary people start to transmogrify as they come into the perimeter of the ground. They adopt a new persona and then wallow in an orgy of cold hatred for an hour and a half before shapeshifting back again on the way home.'

Richard Gillis, presenter of *The Unofficial Partner* podcast agrees with Syed, although his is a far gentler take on what those Glasgow folk were experiencing: 'Football serves as an alibi for intimacy, an excuse we sometimes need to be together. The matchday rituals represent certainty, comfort, and hope in an increasingly complex world. We can orient ourselves and sometimes anchor ourselves by sharing the same experiences and spaces. It's a chance to do something and nothing together for a few hours each week.'

Millimetres and Timing

During the Covid lockdowns, the importance of sport came into sharp focus when, on 23 March 2020, Boris Johnson brought the industry to a standstill by telling everybody to stay at home. It then resumed a few months later in empty venues and against the backdrop of computer-generated cheering. Over the coming weeks – like everybody else – I really missed going to watch live sport and spent a lot of time remembering the good times, such as the maddest game of football I've ever seen in my life, at the Ataturk Stadium, Istanbul, when Liverpool came from 3-0 down at half-time to beat AC Milan on penalties in the 2005 Champions League Final. Then there was the joy of being with my girls at Wembley in 2014 when Palace were promoted to the

Premier League and a surreal day at Lords in the summer of 2019 when England won the cricket World Cup during a final 'super-over'.

As I thought about all this, I increasingly asked myself why it is that humans love sport so much and, as someone who makes a living from sports marketing, how did it become such big business? In search of answers, I subsequently found I needed to wind back to the 1850s and that thereafter, most of sport's most decisive moments happened quite by chance: flip-of-a-coin events like that penalty at Old Trafford, or when Nike nearly went bankrupt in 1975 after the bank closed its account for regularly exceeding its overdraft facility. Sky also came close to going out of business, before a single vote swung the lifesaving Premier League TV contract their way, and there's an argument that Gulf States wouldn't be so keen on sport if Sir Jackie Stewart hadn't had a chance encounter with someone onboard Concorde in the noughties.

The objective of this book is therefore to identify the pivotal moments in the history of sports marketing and it will conclude that the idea of thinking about sport as a serious business proposition only really began 40 years ago, and that many of the critical decisions that have since shaped the business of sport have been made by a small group of rainmakers whose business plans were largely written on the back of an envelope. Take Bernie Ecclestone for example, who was handed a £2bn lottery ticket when he bought the Brabham F1 team in 1971, and the Olympic Games, which were saved from ruin following a wild TV rights auction that took place over 48 hours in a swish Swiss five-star hotel.

So welcome to *Gamechangers & Rainmakers*. The story of how our deep passion for sport has created a fast-growing entertainment business which now generates billions of dollars of advertising, sponsorship and subscription revenue. And persuades us to part with hard-earned cash

Introduction

to buy pricey matchday tickets and premium branded merchandise. It's an industry that was born in the USA, but shaped in Tokyo, Bavaria, Sydney, London, Hamburg and Lausanne, and is a tale of skullduggery, chance, chancers, big personalities, big bets, big money, bad behaviour and 40 people and 40 game-changing moments.

PART ONE

Flat Caps and Blazers

'Sport – an activity involving physical exertion and skill in which an individual or team competes against another or others for entertainment' –
The Oxford Dictionary

1850–1914

Old Etonians. William Webb-Ellis.
Pierre de Coubertin.

HUMANS HAVE participated in sport for millions of years. Neanderthal man were expert archers, the Romans raced chariots, and 'kolfers' hit a pebble around the west coast of Scotland with a bent stick. The game of football has also been around for centuries and was originally known as 'mob football' with hundreds of villagers trying to transport an inflated pig's bladder from one end of their town high street to the other.

If we fast forward to the mid-Victorian era, it was a time of growing conflict across Europe. Britain's top public schools were therefore keen to teach students the values of teamwork in order to prepare them for the likelihood of military service. Quite soon, an unwritten hierarchy formed which favoured the boys who were good at sport and with the leg-up continuing on to university, with a rowing blue from Oxbridge often impressing employers far more than anything academic these young men could point to.

Something else the top schools liked about team sports was that learning to play by the rules imbued in their students the values of behaving like a gentleman: an odd British concept which a Swedish friend once asked me to describe and which I found hard to define. We therefore Googled it together and words like 'chivalrous, courteous and honourable' came pinging back at us. Although my favourite description came from *The Life of Pi*, with the lead protagonist describing an English gentleman as 'someone who still uses a butter knife even when dining alone'.

Whatever definition we go with, the reason this one word matters so much to this story is that for years it was weaponised by the privileged few as private sports clubs emerged as safe spaces where 'the old boys' could carry on enjoying their top-dog status. To gain entry you first needed to get proposed and then seconded by other old boys, which acted as perfect filters to keep out the riff-raff. Once elected you then swapped your old school uniform for the new club blazer and tie and were welcomed into the inner sanctum. Today, people complain their clubs are run by 'the old-boys' network' but in the 1800s they literally were, as private member clubs such as the Jockey Club and Marylebone Cricket Club (MCC) took it upon themselves to codify the rules of sport and decide who could and could not take part.

As their economy prospered, wealthy Americans soon became interested in how they too were perceived in society but unlike in Britain there was no convenient class system to put them in their place. Getting involved in sport was therefore an excellent way to show everyone how well you were doing. Take John Cox Stevens, for example: a successful steamboat entrepreneur from New Jersey who in 1821 offered $1k to anyone who could run ten miles in under an hour. He went on to establish the New York Yacht Club (NYYC), which 30 years later challenged the Royal Yacht Squadron to a race around the Isle of Wight after his members had built an elegant 93ft schooner to represent their club. They christened her *America* and in the summer of 1851 she proceeded to trounce Britain's fastest sailboats in their home waters. As the fleet neared the finish line off Cowes, Queen Victoria who was watching onboard the royal yacht, turned to her signal-master and asked him who was in the lead. 'The *America* your Majesty,' he replied. She then asked who was coming second and received an answer Nike's ad agency would have been proud of: 'Ah, your Majesty, there is no second.'

Back in the day, if you wanted to run, row, bat or sail for your club or country, then you needed to be a member of one of these clubs. Oh, and also be expert at using a butter knife.

#1 THE FOOTBALL SPLIT
(London, October 1863)

JC Thring was the headmaster of Uppingham School and in 1863 wrote *The Basic Rules of Football*, which included how to score a goal, how to take a goal kick and, wait for it, ... the first offside rule. However, many clubs at this time preferred playing by rules invented by Rugby School, which not only allowed players to kick the ball but also to pick it up: hence our first rainmaking moment, which took place at the Freemasons Arms in Covent Garden in 1863 and involved ten clubs from the London area who wanted to agree a common set of rules for football so they could all play each other fairly.

At their first meeting they decided to call themselves the Football Association of London (FA) and voted Ebenezer Morley, the founder of Barnes FC, as their secretary. Over the next 44 days and four follow-on meetings, it was agreed the group would go with Rugby's version of the game: handling was therefore now going to be OK, along with Rugby's other odd rule that allowed players to 'hack' opponents in the shins. All was therefore well until Morley arrived at the sixth meeting and told his colleagues he'd changed his mind and couldn't get comfortable with either hacking or handling. The supporters of Rugby's rules were furious and, since they were also unwilling to back down, there was only one possible solution: to form two codes, with one allowing its players to pick up the ball, run with it and hack one another. And another which did not.

Morley wasted no time putting his legal skills to work and within days had written the 13 rules of Association Football, which included how big the pitch should be, outlawed handling, and my personal favourite which stated that 'no player shall wear projecting nails, iron plates, or gutta percha on the soles or heels of his boots'. Meanwhile, Edwin Nash – the secretary of Richmond FC – called another meeting at the Pall Mall restaurant for clubs like his who wanted to carry on playing the 'rugby-type of game'. The gathering attracted 21 clubs who decided to call themselves the Rugby Football Union (RFU) and over lunch voted unanimously to play by the rules developed by their namesake. However, the bust-up up with Morley had obviously left its mark on some of them too, since they surprisingly voted to also ban hacking. This decision must have seriously hacked off Morley when he heard about it but undeterred he went on to serve as president of the FA for seven years and left behind him an enduring legacy which included introducing the FA Challenge Cup with its first final played at the Kennington Oval in 1872, won by the old boys of Harrow.

Congratulations, therefore, to our first rainmaker, Mr Ebenezer Cobb Morley, who gifted us the FA Cup, a spherical ball to kick and a crossbar for Ruud van Nistelrooy to hit. As for the Freemason's Arms? Well, you can still enjoy a pint in there today as it celebrates its rightful place in history with FA memorabilia on the walls and multiple plasma screens showing Sky Sports on a loop. You can also watch both codes of football in the Ebenezer Morley pub in Hull and the William Webb Ellis in Twickenham, whom legend tells us was the student at Rugby who was the first to pick up the ball and run with it.

North v South

The Industrial Revolution was led by a cohort of northern mill and factory owners who worked their employees hard, usually seven days a week, and often in unpleasant conditions. In the late 1800s, workers therefore formed trade unions to fight for their rights, which soon led to the Factory Act of 1874, which was a pivotal moment for this story, since it ruled that workers must be given time off at weekends to rest. Employers subsequently encouraged their staff to set up works teams since they saw it as a good way for them to keep fit. In 1878 the carriage workers of the Lancashire and Yorkshire Railway formed Newton Heath FC, who a few years later changed their name to Manchester United and began playing at a ground called Old Trafford. Meanwhile, other clubs such as Everton FC, Derby County and Burnley FC formed as offshoots of local cricket clubs and some grew out of English pub culture, with one in north London formed by regulars of The White Hart who played on a pitch down the lane.

During this prosperous period in history, towns across the north competed ferociously with one another for the honour of having the most elegant town hall or most attractive park. The idea of civic pride therefore became important to Victorians and expressing it on the football pitch soon became part of the rivalry. Local businessmen then started to get interested in the game, but not to make money (since the FA rules only allowed dividend payments up to five per cent), but for the kudos of being associated with something the people living and working in their community cared passionately about. Like club directors, players weren't allowed to be paid either, although that was easily solved by ambitious clubs like Blackburn Rovers paying their players through the owner's private company and was a loophole that led to regular complaints. One of these involved Notts County, who complained to the FA that Rovers' star striker Jimmy Douglas had been paid to play in the 1884 cup semi-final, although a subsequent FA inquiry discovered that Douglas was in fact listed on the payroll as a mechanic at the owner's mill.

As the motivation to win increased, the policy of self-regulation was clearly not working and so a few clubs joined in the Notts County chorus and threatened a breakaway competition unless changes were made, with historian Simon Heffer explaining the pressure this placed on football's governing body: 'The FA had to capitulate to survive, which it did on 20 July 1885. It decided to allow payment of players provided they had been born or had lived for two years within six miles of the club's ground. Football's evolution into a predominantly working-class sport would soon be complete.' This was a good start, but the big clubs were still unhappy since now there was an expectation from their players that they would be paid to play, which meant the owners faced the new challenge of having to fund a sizeable wage bill which could only be covered by selling matchday tickets. The big clubs therefore turned on the FA again and accused them of prioritising FA Challenge Cup matches over scheduling more lucrative derby games that would sell out and therefore help them pay the bills.

In 1888, William McGregor, a director of Aston Villa FC, wrote to 11 of the top English clubs to propose a new Football League competition. However, he wasn't looking for a revolution, just the opportunity to play more games that would attract big crowds. His suggestion was thus that the new league should continue playing under FA rules but that two home and away fixtures should be scheduled each season between league teams. That way, Villa would be guaranteed two games against their arch-rivals West Bromwich Albion and their fans could also jump on the new railway network to enjoy a day trip to Wolverhampton and Nottingham. It all made sense, and so in May 1888 the English Football League was formed with six founding teams from Lancashire (Blackburn Rovers, Bolton Wanderers, Preston North End, Burnley, Accrington and Everton) and West Bromwich Albion, Derby County, Notts County, Stoke and Wolverhampton joining Villa as the six founding clubs from the Midlands.

As Association Football started to get organised, interest in rugby football was growing fast too, especially amongst the working people of the north, with the catalyst being the launch of the Yorkshire Challenge Cup, which held its first final in 1877 between Halifax and York, attracting a huge crowd of 9,000 fans. With growing excitement around this competition, towns like Batley and Leeds set up their own clubs and, as gate receipts grew, money started to become available to pay players for the wages they were missing out on when representing their club. However, this development didn't go down at all well with the southern clubs, who feared the direction of travel was to follow Association Football towards the pathway to professionalism. With the growth in the north, the RFU sensed their control of the game was slipping away and so a new rule was introduced which stipulated that rugby football could only be played by amateur clubs and that fines would be issued to anyone found to be paying their players to play. A game of cat and mouse then ensued until the RFU upped the stakes in 1898 by announcing that any game which was played at a ground charging an entrance fee would have the result declared void. These latest 'establishment punishments' were a step too far for the northern clubs, who didn't have wealthy benefactors to lean on like their southern cousins, so losing gate receipts would make it impossible for them to survive. A meeting of the top clubs in Yorkshire and Lancashire was therefore hastily arranged at the George Hotel in Huddersfield to discuss the idea of a new breakaway league codenamed 'The Northern Rugby League'. A unanimous vote then decided players would be paid and that new rules would also be introduced to make this league more exciting, which included scrapping the line-out, changing the scrum format and reducing the number of players on the pitch to 13.

'Take Me Down to the Ballgame'

John Higham wrote a fascinating book called *The Reconstruction of American History*, which analysed the transformation of North America from a continent of just seven million people to a population of over 70 million. He believes sport played an important part in shaping modern America as German settlers imported their love of gymnastics and the Irish brought with them their passion for prize fighting and horse racing.

Towards the end of the 1800s football was introduced by British workers and was soon adopted by America's elite colleges, who again couldn't decide whether or not to pick up the ball. Harvard liked the rules of rugby, McGill preferred Morley's, and so the two teams alternated the rules whenever they played one another. As the game's popularity grew, Walter Camp, a former Yale alumnus, phased in a new set of 'American' rules and, just like the northern rugby clubs, decided to introduce new ideas to make the game more exciting, which included the touchdown and allowing players to throw a forward pass.

In 1892, the success of American football helped create another new sport that would emerge as the nation's third power sport and also have a profound impact on the lives of young people living in urban America. It was the idea of Dr James Naismith, a PE instructor from Springfield College, Massachusetts, who was looking for an indoor activity to help keep his footballers fit during the winter months. He therefore nailed two peach baskets to each end of his gym and told players to try and score a 'basket'.

If football was emerging as the most popular game to play in England, then its equivalent in America was a game which evolved as a hybrid of rounders and softball and one that Higham believes played a big part in helping to galvanise immigrant communities. As wealth and leisure time increased, baseball fans soon became happy to pay to watch the top players, which in 1876 led to the creation of Major League Baseball (MLB) featuring the Boston Red Stockings, Chicago White Stockings, Cincinnati Red Stockings, Hartford Dark Blues, Louisville Gray's,

Mutual of New York, Philadelphia Athletics, and the St Louis Brown Stockings.

#2 THE CREATION OF THE MODERN-DAY OLYMPIC GAMES
(Paris, June 1896)

In 1886, a 23-year-old French baron visited Rugby in search of inspiration to help restore his country's broken morale after the humiliation of the Franco-German war. After a guided tour of the school, he was impressed with how competitive sport had been integrated into the curriculum and so when Pierre de Coubertin returned to Paris, he decided it was a model the top French schools could benefit from in order to strengthen the character of their own young men. He therefore created the *Union des Societies Francaises des Sports Athletiques* (USFSA) which he briefed to tour schools across the country and teach students about the values of competitive sport.

Like many Europeans of this era, De Coubertin had developed a deep fascination with Ancient Greece and a personal interest in the Olympic Games, which was a religious festival created to honour the Greek god Zeus and involved hundreds of cities competing against each other in a range of athletic events. In 1894 De Coubertin was then invited back to England by William Penny Brookes to watch the Olympian Games, which was an event he'd created in the small Shropshire village of Much Wenlock. He was a doctor and was convinced playing sport could help improve the health of young people, and when he heard about the Frenchman's interest in using sport to drive societal change, he wanted him to experience the Olympian Games and to discuss the idea of creating an international version.

In June 1896, De Coubertin was invited to attend an international sports conference in Paris and seized the opportunity to pitch the idea. These were tense times in Europe, and the notion of using sport as a platform to unite the world therefore landed well with delegates, who agreed they would create an organisation to make it happen. They called it the International Olympic Committee (IOC) and felt it would be symbolic if the first event was staged at its spiritual home. They also devised an Olympic flag with five interlocking rings to personify the world's five continents, and chose black, red, blue, green and yellow so each athlete could identify with at least one colour from their national flag. Two years later the first modern Olympic Games took place in Athens with 200 athletes representing 13 individual nations.

Despite dedicating his entire life to developing the modern Olympic movement, unlike many of the rainmakers we'll meet in this book, De Coubertin did not profit personally from his work. In fact, he died almost penniless, although as the IOC's website explains, this man's motivation was never to make money for himself: 'Baron Pierre de Coubertin was only 1.62m (5ft 3in) tall, but by many measures, he was a giant of the 20th century. Born into the French aristocracy on 1 January 1863, he became a champion of the common man, embracing the values of France's Third Republic – liberty, equality, fraternity.'

PART TWO
The Madmen

'Although I'm not saying that this is its primary role, we have yet to find a more effective means of financing a free, varied, and democratic media' –
Jean-Marie Dru, TBWA

1920–1960

Matthews. The Yankees. Chicago Bears

ONE OF the key themes of this book is the alchemy that has developed over the years between sport and the media: a relationship that began in the 1850s after Prime Minister Palmerston abolished tax on newspapers, resulting in a rise in literacy rates. As readership soared, manufacturers like Cadbury and Lipton Tea subsequently bought newspaper ads to expand their sales and introduced distinctive packaging and slogans to make products stand out from the crowd. The brand was born and so too the advertising industry which was created to build them.

In search of our next rainmaker, we therefore head to New York City to meet Albert Lasker, who was born in Freiburg, Germany, but raised in Texas by his parents. He was a highly creative man and regarded by many as the father of the advertising business after inventing the idea of an agency which employed both creative and media people. It was called Lord and Thomas and made money from charging newspapers 15 per cent commission on the client bookings they sent their way. This first generation of 'Madmen' honed their copywriting skills during the Great War by producing hard-hitting posters for the war effort, such as the famous one of Uncle Sam pointing his finger threateningly and barking, 'I want YOU for the US Army'. When the war was over, and newspapers became cluttered with messages, ad agencies were challenged by their clients to come up with equally impactful creative work and some started to believe products needed to be differentiated to cut through. One of these was Claude Hopkin, who when working on a campaign for Schlitz beer discovered its bottles were steam-cleaned. This was standard practice in the beer industry at the time, although none of its competitors had pointed this out to the consumer, and so Hopkin penned the famous headline 'Schlitz bottles are washed with live steam', which inferred his client cared far more about hygiene than its competitors. Sales took off and the unique selling proposition (USP) had been invented, which is a concept we shall hear much more about in later chapters of this book.

The Growth of Radio

In 1894, a young Italian inventor called Guglielmo Marconi started work in the UK on an idea to create a long-distance wireless transmission system and in 1922 the British Broadcasting Company (BBC) was formed. On the other side of the Atlantic, the BBC was joined by WEAF, who later changed their name to the National Broadcasting Company (NBC), and United Independent Broadcasters, which was created by a New York talent agent. Both were funded by advertising. When Arthur Hudson fell upon hard times, he sold the station to Columbia Records who were flying high during the jazz boom of the 1920s and saw radio airplay as a good way to promote their artists. This period in history was referred to as the 'Roaring 20s' as the American economy accelerated on the back of rising wages and cheap credit. It was therefore the perfect storm for the Madmen of Madison Avenue who, in search of brand differentiation, began experimenting with the idea of endorsement-style advertising such as casting Hollywood actresses to add a touch of class to the promotion of beauty products.

The Madmen took to radio like an extra shot in their evening cocktail with hundreds of new stations funded by advertising. They then became hungry for live sports content after the 1927 heavyweight title fight between Joe Dempsey and Gene Tunney delivered a jaw-dropping audience of 50 million listeners. Back in the UK that same year, England v Wales become the UK's first live outside sports broadcast, with Lieutenant Colonel 'Teddy' Wakelam behind the BBC microphone and delivering a very different style of commentary to Martin Tyler: 'Well, the first half has been about as exciting as anyone could wish for. They're off again and changing over Jones is taking it and he's kicking to the left. Wales are defending the south end now. And Harding's throwing it in. A fairly long one. England have it, I think its Tucker, he's down on the ground, England have heeled, out to Warton, Laird, Corbett, Lock, out to Gibbs, Gibbs is going down the line, he's got past Andrews and he's up to the 25, he kicks across, the English pack are up. The return ball's there, well-done sir.'

The Growth of Television

The first successful transmission of a television picture occurred three years after the launch of BBC radio and is credited to Scotsman John Logie Baird. However, for many years there was little excitement about this new medium since radio had established itself as the nation's link to the outside world during the war years, with families regularly gathering around the wireless to hear the reassuring voice of the King and Prime Minister Winston Churchill. When the war was over, Brits continued to be unenthusiastic about television. The hardware was expensive to buy and, unlike in America, there was no cheap credit available to help pay for it. The TV licence was also double that of the radio licence, which was money most didn't have to spare. In the words of the author Martin Kelner, 'The BBC seemed in no hurry either to persuade people to alter their viewing habits. The general attitude within the BBC, seems to have been that television could kindly sit in the corner and behave itself, we were quite happy with the wireless, thank you very much. Television was considered an irrelevance in the post-war world of rubble and rationing. Radio, after all, had helped win the war, not just through the BBC's broadcasts to embattled Europe, but by raising spirits at home.'

In the United States it was, however, a totally different picture with interest in TV growing fast as both NBC and CBS expanded their capabilities and were joined by a third network calling itself the American Broadcasting Company (ABC). The Madmen were therefore starting to get excited about television, and as Leo Burnett, one of America's post-war advertising gurus commented, 'Television is the strongest drug we've ever had to dish out. Maybe that's why our hands shake a little when we take the cork out of the bottle.'

The Original Hipsters

Anyone who has studied the history of advertising will be familiar with the name Bill Bernbach, who along with Burnett and David Ogilvy introduced a new level of sophistication to brand marketing by encouraging advertisers to appreciate the importance of image, personality and the power of compelling narrative: three of the key ingredients that lie at the heart of the modern sports marketing industry. Burnett subsequently became notorious for his imaginary creations like the Marlboro Man and Tony the Tiger, while Ogilvy's mantra was that every campaign had to have a 'big idea' behind it, such as the copy he wrote for Rolls-Royce to describe its smooth ride: 'At 60 miles an hour, the loudest noise in this new Rolls Royce comes from the electric clock.'

Bill Bernbach was, however, a very different kind of ad-man to Burnett and Ogilvy and, after having served his time on Madison Avenue, felt Burnett's myopic focus on USP, and Ogilvy's formulaic approach of headline, strong image, swish copy, logo, was creating boring advertising. He therefore felt a creative revolution was needed and in 1949 started one of his own with a group of revolutionaries calling themselves Doyle Dane Bernbach (DDB): a band of New York hipsters who unveiled the following chest-thumping launch manifesto: 'If you stand for something, you will always find some people for you and some against you. If you stand for nothing, you will find nobody against you, and nobody for you.'

They therefore wrote ads for Polaroid that had no text. Well, pictures were what the product was about, right? And 'We try harder' was the understated positioning they developed for Avis, who wanted to place customer service at the heart of their brand proposition. Then there was their work for Volkswagen, which *Ad Age Magazine* once voted as the best campaign of all time. An unknown German car company trying to sell cars to Americans ten years after the end of the war – not a straightforward brief, as Bob Levenson, the creator of VW's 'think small' campaign, explains: 'It was a pretty audacious thing for a car company to call its own car a lemon. It's still audacious to run a picture of your product with a headline suggesting something is wrong with it. But it was such an arresting combination, and when you read the ad, you found out the car was a lemon because it had a scratch on the glove compartment and was rejected just because of that. The last line was, 'We pluck the lemons, and you get the plums.'

The Founding Fathers

In the early days of American football, the big college football matchups attracted crowds of more than 30,000 fans who loved the pageantry and tradition of these great rivalries. However, the pro league version of the game (which changed its name to the National Football League in 1922) was far less popular than the college game, with the matches regarded by many as boring low-scoring brawls. There was, however, one NFL team who were starting to attract a loyal following and which was owned by Tim Mara, a successful event promoter in New York. This was an exciting time in Manhattan with Babe Ruth hitting home runs for fun at the Yankee Stadium, Broadway shows selling out fast and prize fighting now legalised at Madison Square Garden. Mara was therefore often in the middle of promoting such events. He had no intention of owning a pro football franchise, until he had a chance encounter with Joe Carr, the first president of the NFL who in 1925 persuaded him to pay $500 for the franchise to create a team in New York. Here's how his grandson, John, describes this chance moment in time: 'Thus were born the New York Giants, owned by a man who barely knew football's basic rules. He just thought, I'm a promoter … in New York … this is sports … it can work.'

The other NFL team drawing decent crowds was owned by George Halas, son of Czech parents who understood the game far better than Mara since he had played pro football himself. Following retirement, Halas had been approached by the starch makers Staley AE Manufacturing to set up a new franchise in their hometown of Decatur. They were fans of Halas, keen to give the community something to get excited about, and so he was told he could recruit whoever he wanted with the offer of a job at Staley, good pay, and with two hours off every day for the team to practise on company time.

In their first year the team did OK, although covering costs through ticket sales alone in such a small town proved to be tough going, with Halas struggling to attract more than 2,000 fans to his home games. This lost Staley $16k in the first year, which was not something the company could afford to continue funding. To keep the project alive, their owners subsequently offered to gift Halas the franchise and pay him $5k if he relocated it to Chicago and played one final season in the name of Staley. After that he could call the team whatever he wanted.

In the autumn of 1921, Chicago Staley subsequently played their first competitive game at Cubs Park in front of 8,000 fans and in 1922 changed their name to the Chicago

Bears. Tim Mara and George Halas thus became two of the founding fathers of America's regional sports franchise: a business model invented to attract investors by guaranteeing them each a ring-fenced geographic territory they could call their own.

As the populations of New York and Chicago continued to grow, Cubs Park and the Polo Grounds developed into popular places for city folk to visit on their day off and by 1930 both teams were selling enough tickets to make a modest profit. However, things weren't going so well for the other eight NFL franchises who played in smaller American cities and following the Wall Street Crash in 1929 were finding it hard to break even. The smallest team, with a stadium capacity of 10,000, were the Green Bay Packers, who were formed by the Indiana Packing Company in Wisconsin and found it especially difficult to compete. As did Art Rooney, who founded the Pittsburgh Pirates and said this about life as a first-generation NFL team owner: 'In those days, nobody got wealthy in sports; you got two thrills. One came Sunday, trying to win the game. The next came Monday, trying to make the payroll.' Neither the Pirates nor the Packers could therefore match the wages of the Giants and the Bears, and in 1933 Rooney proposed to his fellow owners the idea of a 'player draft', which was an attempt to neutralise the wealthiest teams by giving first pick of the top rookie talent graduating from America's colleges to the weakest teams.

In the land of the free, a professional sports league run by some of the most competitive men you could put in the same room together therefore voted to level the playing field. Further innovations followed, such as splitting the eight teams into east and west divisions and playing an end-of-season championship decider between the divisional winners. A third less high-profile but equally momentous decision was agreed in 1947, which we shall soon discover went on to transform the business model of American sports franchises, as the ten owners voted to allow each other to sell the television rights to their home games.

Video Killed the Radio Star

The NFL teams had spent years experimenting with radio, but by 1946 were still only generating a combined total of $250k from selling their broadcast rights. Nice to have, but small change when Tim Mara was now making $200k per match from selling tickets to games at the Polo Grounds. With only one million American families owning a television, the NFL owners therefore couldn't figure out how this new medium with its blurry black and white images could improve the economics of their business. However, Halas was more optimistic. He'd seen how sports fans had taken to watching baseball and boxing on TV and, having just won the championship, wanted to find out if TV could do for the Bears what radio had done for the Cubs back in the 1920s. He therefore sold the rights to his 1946 home games to a local Chicago cable TV station for $900 per game. The other owners watched on with interest, convinced his fans would stay at home to watch the game rather than buy a ticket – and they were proved right too, with attendances at Wrigley Field falling by nine per cent.

The following year, Dan Reeves controversially relocated his team from Cleveland to Los Angeles as the Rams became the NFL's first west-coast franchise. He knew he had his work cut out building interest in the franchise from this standing start and so decided to throw the net far and wide by televising all his home games. However, having seen what had happened to the Bears, Reeves protected his bottom line by insisting on a clause in the TV deal whereby sponsors of the telecasts would have to reimburse him if ticket sales fell below a certain threshold. It proved to be a smart move, since despite the Rams winning their division that year, the gate at the Coliseum ended well below the agreed threshold with Reeves eventually billing the sponsors for $200k to make up the shortfall.

The strategic issue facing sport was therefore clear: as Leo Burnett had previously said, TV was a 'powerful drug'. So powerful in fact that it led to a significant drop in attendance if games were shown live. The question on everyone's lips was therefore how could leagues and teams unlock the obvious potential of television, without suffering the collateral damage of a significant drop in matchday revenue?

#3 COAST-TO-COAST CABLE
(San Francisco, September 1951)

A potential solution to the TV dilemma presented itself in the autumn of 1951 when AT&T announced the launch of their Transcontinental Coaxial Cable, a technological breakthrough making it possible to send broadcast signals right across the United States. The technique had previously been used to enable rural homes to pick up broadcast signals by linking TV towers and connecting homes via short-run cable. Each household then paid a monthly subscription to a local 'cable provider' for the services they wanted to buy. However, connecting homes in Texas is one thing, but linking Los Angeles to New York via cable was a total game-changer for the NFL since it allowed each franchise to black out the signal to homes close to their stadium to avoid the drop in attendance the Bears experienced.

By 1954, with AT&T willing to rent out coaxial time and 25 million American homes now owning a television set, commissioner Bert Bell knew it was time for the NFL to test the potential of this rapidly growing medium. He thus proposed a deal to the teams for CBS to televise 15 network games and then added a second contract with the fledgling Du Mont channel to broadcast the NFL season-opener, a few local derbies and the Championship Final. The revenue teams received from these games was tiny, but the much bigger news was that they were delivering strong ratings for CBS, and what made this even more remarkable was that the games were being played during the notoriously tricky Sunday afternoon slot. The CBS schedulers were therefore starting to get really excited. After years of experimenting with comedy, cartoons and films, had they finally found the killer programming they'd been looking for to fill the Sunday graveyard slot?

A business model therefore started to emerge whereby the networks could justify increasing the rights fees they paid to the teams due to the extra advertising and sponsorship they were selling, while local cable companies would contribute additional revenue to the TV pot by covering the home games of the team based within their territory. All Bell needed now was a lightning-rod moment and he didn't have that long to wait.

'The few who were in the Yankee stadium on that long excitement-filled afternoon will never forget it' – Chris Schenkel, NBC

The 1958 NFL Championship decider kicked off at 3pm on 28 December and would forever be remembered as the day the NFL announced its intention to knock baseball off its perch as America's favourite sport – somewhat ironically making the announcement on the hallowed turf made famous by Babe Ruth and Joe di Maggio.

The final that year was contested by the Baltimore Colts and New York Giants and at half-time nothing out of the ordinary had happened, with the Colts leading the championship favourites 14-3. The Giants fought back, but Baltimore doggedly hung on to the lead until the final play of the game, when Steve Myhra kicked a field goal to tie the score.

The NFL subsequently found itself in uncharted waters since a draw had never happened before in the Championship game and most of the 30 million watching at home therefore had no clue what should happen next. Neither did the players, with some even shaking hands thinking the title would be shared. The good news, though, was that Walter Smith had thought about this eventuality and buried deep in his rules for American football was guidance that in the event of a draw the game had to enter 'sudden-death overtime' with the next team to score declared the winner. Here's NBC's Chris Schenkel calling the winning play:

'They're down and about a yard and a half to go ... the Colts at the line of scrimmage ... flanker to the right ... the ends are tight. Unitas takes and gives it to Ameche ... the ball game is over. The Colts of the professional football league are champions of the world.'

The Colts had won with a six-yard pushover that ended a game later credited with igniting America's love affair with the NFL. Commissioner Bell, Halas, Mara, Reeves and Rooney had spent 30 years of their lives building up pro football through the Great Depression, a world war and countless setbacks but despite these challenges had always understood the importance of putting on a good show which, as Eisenberg explains, was precisely what the NFL served up on that freezing cold evening in New York City.

'The five of them had worked together and encouraged one another for several decades even as their teams competed ferociously on the field. They had made poor choices but many more good ones. With their determination to co-operate, their relentless, often unfounded optimism, and their skill as both football men and businessmen, they had built out of nothing something that was substantial and profitable, something millions now cared about.'

As our journey through the history of sport continues, we'll come to appreciate the significance of this moment in time as the value of NFL broadcast rights reached $1bn in 1990. By 1998 that figure had doubled; it reached $3bn in 2006, and today the rights generate a whopping $10bn a year. The ability to control and distribute content – via cable – was therefore a catalyst for this success since it presented teams with the controllable platform they needed to unlock the economic upside of television. The launch of coast-to-coast connectivity and the spark of the 'Greatest Game' were therefore two of the most pivotal moments in the history of American sports marketing and proved Leo Burnett right when he said television was a powerful drug. The trick now, for the class of 1958, was to get the dosage right – especially with the hallucinogenic version of colour TV on its way.

#4 THE MATTHEWS CUP FINAL

(London, 2 May 1953)

The English may well have invented the game of football, but they were less than enthusiastic about sharing it with the rest of the world. The four home nations did eventually agree to join FIFA when it was established in 1904 but resigned a few months after the First World War was over, when the Allies' enemies were allowed to remain as members. The four FAs then re-joined in 1924, but swiftly left again when FIFA insisted that international players should be paid for the wages they lost out on when playing for their country, which as we now know was a red line in British sport. England, Scotland, Wales and Northern Ireland therefore boycotted the first six FIFA World Cups.

Despite this superior attitude, as post-war Europe tried to right itself, Britain's perceived invincibility on the world stage was fading fast. India had won its independence in 1959 and four years later there was the humiliation of Suez. The nation's decline in sport was evident too after Team GB returned from the 1952 Helsinki Olympics with a single gold medal.

The following year the England football team lost 6-3 to Hungary, which was their first-ever loss to a foreign side at Wembley, and the Ferenc Puskás-inspired team proved it was no fluke either when they thrashed England 7-1 in the return fixture in Budapest. America had created a successful college system, the East European nations were investing heavily in state-sponsored sports, yet Britain continued to champion the ideals of amateurism. The University of Birmingham was subsequently commissioned by the government to review what was going wrong and the authors of the report didn't hold back, with the following damning criticism: 'In a world which regards success in sport as an index of national vitality and national prestige and in a world which contains so many governments which are "professionals" in the organisation of sport, the British Government remain amateur.'

The Wizard of the Dribble

Despite the nation's sporting decline, one Englishman continued to excite everybody: a dazzling winger from Stoke called Stanley Matthews, whose father was a professional boxer and had instilled in him a lifelong commitment to fitness. Matthews was 14 years old when he signed for his hometown club on wages of £1 a week, and 18 years later he joined Blackpool for a record transfer fee of £11,500 and a bottle of whisky. During an extraordinary career, Matthews won 54 caps for England and played in both the 1948 and 1951 cup finals, but was on the losing side both times.

An FA Cup winner's medal was therefore the one thing missing from this man's impressive CV and that became the narrative that gripped the nation in 1953 when Blackpool once again made it to Wembley. By now, TV penetration in the UK had limped up to 20 per cent but, with this match billed as the most significant sporting moment for years, an estimated ten million people crowded around any TV they could find to watch.

For 70 minutes the game didn't go to plan, with Bolton taking a 3-1 lead, until the superior fitness and technique of Matthews kicked in, with a match-winning performance. Following a last-gasp winner, BBC commentator, Kenneth Wolstenholme thus calmly told the millions watching at home, 'There's the man Matthews, at long last he's done it.'

On the international stage, West Germany dominated world football in the early 50s with their revolutionary lightweight boots with interchangeable studs individually made by the Adidas founder Adolf Dassler, who even travelled on the team bus to tell the German coach which studs each player should wear. When they heard about this innovation, the Manchester bootmaker CWS offered to make Matthews a similar pair and these were the boots he wore that day at Wembley, with his signature cleverly embossed on both feet. Following the fairytale of the cup win, these boots became every boy's dream birthday present with sales exceeding 500,000 units and earning Stan sixpence per pair.

Stanley Matthews is regarded by none other than Pelé as one of the greatest footballers of all time. He is the only player to have been knighted while still playing professional football and the first winner of the European Footballer of the Year award. However, this is a book about the marketing of sport and so he joins our Hall of Fame for signalling a new optimism in Britain, with the Matthews Cup Final and Queen Elizabeth's coronation a month later at Westminster Abbey proving the catalyst that turbo-charged British interest in television.

- - - - -

#5 THE TV BOYCOTT OF THE MELBOURNE OLYMPICS
(22 November 1956)

In 1954, the Tories passed their highly anticipated Television Act and, after nearly 30 years, the BBC monopoly finally came to an end with news of the launch of a second national network. It was to be called Independent Television (ITV) and would consist of 15 separate regional franchises which would each be privately owned and all funded by advertising. One of the first licences was awarded to London Weekend Television (LWT) to allow them to broadcast exclusively in the London area from Friday evening to the end of transmission on Sunday. Associated-Rediffusion (AR) was awarded the London weekday licence, Granada Television secured the north-west, and Associated Television were chosen in the Midlands, with the other regions of the UK having to make do with BBC1 until more nationwide transmitters were installed. These three regions subsequently went on air on 22 September 1955 with the following corny commercial from Unilever the first to be transmitted: 'The tingling fresh toothpaste that does your gums good too. It's tingling fresh. It's fresh as ice. It's Gibbs SR toothpaste.' The BBC, meanwhile, kept calm and carried on as if nothing much had changed and continued also to dismiss the idea of paying for sports rights. After all, they saw themselves as journalists and, since print media didn't pay to report on sports events, they saw no reason why they should be treated any differently.

The following year Melbourne was hosting the Olympics for the first time and their organising committee (MOC) saw it as a prime opportunity to showcase the attraction of

Australia to the world. Their big media idea was therefore to produce an official feature-length film which would be released in cinemas once the Games were over. However, they were also interested in generating worldwide news coverage whilst the Games were taking place and were therefore delighted when ITV offered them £25k for the rights. The new kids on the block then demonstrated their commercial nous by signing a deal with TV manufacturer Westinghouse to produce a daily round-up show, which they planned to distribute in the United States to help drive the sales of the TV sets they manufactured.

When the BBC and US networks found out about the deal, they were furious and repeated their mantra that sport was news and so every broadcaster around the world should be given nine minutes of free content every day, like the cinema newsreels supplied for such newsworthy events. They also leaned on the IOC to pressurise the MOC to cancel the deal, but Avery Brundage had no interest in getting involved in the spat since he was of the view that the Olympics had survived without TV for 60 years and so it was up to the organisers what they chose to do with their broadcast rights. For their part, Melbourne didn't want a news blackout – just to make sure there were no spoilers for the official film – so they offered broadcasters three minutes of daily highlights, which was quickly rejected, resulting in the BBC, Canadian, US and European news agencies all collectively refusing to cover the Games.

Looking back in time, while the Melbourne Olympics obviously suffered from minimal international news coverage, the dispute proved to be a spectacular own goal by this cohort of broadcasters since it established a crucial precedent for how sports rights would be awarded in the future. Michael Payne was the marketing director of the IOC for many years and summarises the significance of this moment in time as follows: 'An important milestone had been passed – sports, and Olympic sports in particular, would no longer be free. It is interesting to reflect what the status of the global sports scene would be if the IOC and the Melbourne organisers had backed down and accepted that broadcasters should receive the same access rights as their colleagues in the print media.'

Even though the British public had been starved of coverage of the Melbourne Olympics, they generally approved of ITV and the skirmish also gave the BBC a much-needed kick up the backside, which they responded to by launching a new Saturday afternoon sports show called *Grandstand*. They also made sure they didn't get ambushed so easily again by locking down the other events they didn't want to lose on long-term contracts, including the Grand National and the Boat Race in the spring, the FA Cup and Rugby League Challenge Cup Finals in May, Ascot in June, the Wimbledon fortnight and Test cricket across the summer.

ITV was OK with this, since the regional nature of their network meant it was tough getting network agreement to schedule live sports and they also had no intention of starting a bidding war with the BBC for sports rights, since most of their advertisers at this time were targeting female audiences and so their sales teams were calling for soaps and quiz shows rather than the jeopardy of sports coverage. With English teams entering the European Cup in 1958 and the home nations now entering the World Cup, ITV did, however, turn its attention to football in 1960 by signing a deal with the Football League to show 26 live games from the 1960/61 season. The first match they televised was billed as a rerun of the 1953 FA Cup Final, which they figured would be a banker game, although unusually for him the now 44-year-old Stanley Matthews was out injured and, when word spread, Blackpool's stadium was half empty. ITV's relationship with the Football League then deteriorated over the following weeks when the top clubs started to worry about the negative impact live TV might have on their matchday attendance. ITV were sympathetic and therefore agreed to only show the second half of their games but even that didn't reassure some of the top clubs, with the deal collapsing after Arsenal and Tottenham refused to let ITV film at either Highbury or White Hart Lane.

PART THREE
You Say You Want a Revolution?

'This is my generation. This is my generation, baby' – The Who

---

The Swinging 60s

Bobby Moore. The Beatles. Mary Quant

THE 60s were a pioneering time for mankind, with a moon landing and the first non-stop circumnavigation of the planet by Robin Knox Johnston. It was also a scary time, with talk of atomic bombs, the Vietnam War and growing civil unrest in America following the assassinations of John F. Kennedy and Martin Luther King. During all this turmoil, as historian Timothy Garton Ash observes in *Homelands*, young people started to detach themselves from the values and behaviours of their parents: 'The force behind it was a new and numerous generation; the baby-boomers, erupting on the public stage, making their voices, tastes, desires, and ideals heard, in a sweeping, anti-authoritarian *prises de parole*. The young were seizing the microphone.'

In 1967, this spirit of revolution spilled over into the world of sport when Muhammad Ali refused the Vietnam draft and was stripped of his world championship belts and threatened with jail time. However, Ali's force of nature made him impossible to silence as he himself grabbed the mic and told the media, 'Why should they ask me to put on a uniform and go 10,000 miles from home and drop bombs and bullets on brown people in Vietnam while so-called Negro people in Louisville are treated like dogs?' In the words of Marc Bolan, a cheerleader for this generation, 'You can't fool the children of the revolution.'

One year later, Mexico City then took centre stage as the satellites enabled the 1968 Olympics to become the first Games shown live on TV, with black American sprinters Tommie Smith and John Carlos both qualifying for the 200m final. In an explosive race, Smith won gold to become the first sprinter to run the event in under 20 seconds, with his team-mate claiming the bronze medal. At the medal ceremony, the two men mounted the podium barefoot and with their heads bowed they raised black-gloved fists in support of the Black Power Movement when the Stars and Stripes was hoisted above the Estadio Olímpico. The controversy then intensified further during Smith's post-race interview, when ABC's Howard Cosell asked, 'Are you proud to be an American?' to which he replied, 'I'm proud to be a black American.'

This was the final straw for IOC president Avery Brundage, who ordered his countrymen out of the athletes' village and even tried to confiscate their medals. After the dust had settled, Smith was then asked why he'd carried out this protest. 'We were concerned about the lack of black assistant coaches. About how Muhammad Ali was stripped of his title. About the lack of access to good housing and our kids not being able to attend the top colleges.'

> *'Like it or not, we live in interesting times. They are times of danger and uncertainty; but they are also the most creative of any time in the history of mankind'* – Robert Kennedy

The other protest gathering momentum in the 1960s was the fight between sportsmen and women for fair compensation. The first serious challenge to the British sports authorities took place in 1961 when English footballers – led by Fulham striker and players' union chairman Jimmy Hill – began a campaign to scrap the £20 weekly salary cap. Once again, with very public messaging, Hill told the clubs they were not taking the players' request seriously enough and that they would strike the following Saturday unless changes were made. Even Stanley Matthews offered his solidarity: 'I've done well out of the game,' he said, 'but could I ignore the injustice to my colleagues? Loyalty to the players won. My hand went up.'

With three days to go, Hill was summoned to the Ministry of Labour to negotiate with Football League chairman Alan Hardaker, who backed down quickly when he realised this was no bluff, and the strike was subsequently called off, with Hill's team-mate Johnny Haynes the first to benefit when he was handed an £80-a-week pay rise to keep him at the club.

The foot on the brake of professionalising was, therefore, that the people running the show used the notion of amateurism to maintain the status quo: golfers and tennis players had to scratch a living earning exhibition money, and anyone wanting to play top-flight rugby, cricket or baseball needed to get a normal job to help pay the bills. Even Tom Finney, one of England's greatest-ever footballers, carried on working as a plumber while playing for Bolton Wanderers. With no sponsors to satisfy and clubs wary about television coverage, the lack of money in sport was therefore not considered a problem by sport's first administrators, with veteran journalist David Miller summing up the attitude of the IOC president like this: 'Brundage had many misunderstandings, evident in his repetitive speeches that the amateur played only for recreation and fun, the professional only for entertainment. That amateur sport was for the participants and professional sport for the spectators; sport that was not amateur was not sport at all; amateurs gave, professionals only took ... it was more obvious than ever that he had overstayed his time.'

'Suspicious Minds'

Brundage may well have had the power to throw Smith and Carlos out of the athletes' village but one thing he couldn't control was a 'boot war' that had broken out in Germany between brothers Adolf and Rudolf Dassler, who before the war worked together in the family shoemaking business in Herzogenaurach, a small Bavarian village near Nuremberg. During the war, Rudolf served as an SS officer, while Adolf remained at the factory and switched production to making 6,000 pairs of boots a month for the

German army. When the war was over, the two brothers fell out spectacularly following difficult questioning by the war crimes committee. Once both men were cleared, there was therefore no way they could work together and so they agreed to split the business, with Adolf, (or 'Adi' as he now liked to be known) calling his company Adidas and remaining in the main Herzogenaurach factory, while Rudolf took over the smaller factory on the opposite side of the Aurach river and called his company Puma. Their 60 staff were given the choice of where they wanted to work.

One of the key features of the Adidas product was that their boots had reinforced leather stitched on the side for added protection of the foot. This was made out of three thin strips of leather cut from the same hide as the rest of the shoe. One day, a test boot was made using white leather strips, which the shoemaker took to his boss and commented how distinctive it made them look. Adi agreed and realised that it could help differentiate Adidas from all the other black boots on the market and so, in 1948, his lawyer registered a trademark described as a logo that was '*die Marke mit den drei Streifen en*' – the brand with three stripes.

The sibling rivalry quickly intensified and my favourite story of how competitive it all became is told by Barbara Smit in her excellent book *Pitch Invasion,* which charts the history of these two companies and involves England centre-half Jack Charlton, who was getting so annoyed by all the hassle he was getting from the sales reps that he threatened to wear Puma on one foot and Adidas on the other. On the eve of the 1966 World Cup Final, England captain Bobby Moore therefore stepped in to take control of the situation and told the Adidas rep his players would all wear his boots if they were each paid £1,000 in cash. This was serious money in 1966, representing a few months' wages and double the bonus the FA had promised the players if they won the World Cup. However, even Moore couldn't control his right-back Ray Wilson, and goalkeeper Gordon Banks, who secretly continued negotiating with the Puma rep back at the England hotel. He was doubtless feeling pretty nervous about what he was going to say to his boss when he returned to Herzogenaurach and in desperation therefore agreed to pay both players £2,000 if they wore Puma in the final, which explains why, if you carefully watch old footage from Wembley, you'll see 20 English and West German players wearing the three-stripes of Adidas, and these two fellas running around with leaping cat boots on their feet and Cheshire cat-sized smiles on their faces.

The governing bodies of world sport couldn't decide what to do about this boot war. It was getting embarrassing and intensified at the 1960 Rome Olympics when it got out that German 100m gold medallist Armin Harry had been paid by Rudolf Dassler to run in Puma spikes. A young Phil Knight, the soon-to-be founder of Nike, described what he saw: 'The world's two biggest athletic shoe companies – run by two German brothers who despised each other – had chased each other like keystone cops around the Olympic village, jockeying for athletes. Huge sums of cash, often stuffed into running shoes or manila envelopes, were passed around.'

Two years later, Pelé also signed with Puma and famously knelt down to tie his laces before the kick-off of Brazil's first group match at the 1970 World Cup. This was the first final shown in colour and someone savvy at Puma had figured that with Pelé the star attraction, the TV director would instruct his cameraman to zoom in for the money shot. And there it was. Adolf's son, Horst, was furious when he heard about the Pelé deal, since a few months earlier he had thought he'd agreed a 'Pelé-pact' with cousin Armin, who had recently taken over running Puma's day-to-day business from his father. Both men knew a bidding war for the Brazilian would get out of hand, and in an unusual accord they therefore agreed neither of them would chase his signature. However, the chance to sign football royalty (and get one over his cousin) was obviously too tempting for Armin, who secretly made the Brazilian a record four-year, $120k per annum offer to promote the Puma brand.

Four years later, the Adidas team thought they had their revenge when their home World Cup Final in Munich was to be contested by two Adidas-sponsored teams: West Germany, captained by 'Kaiser' Franz Beckenbauer, and the 'total football' team from the Netherlands featuring sport's hottest new superstar, Johan Cruyff. The Germans won that final 2-1 with a winner from Gerd Müller, but if you watch the game back on YouTube you'll notice Cruyff's #14 shirt only carries two stripes, since he too had a personal agreement to promote Puma. This conflict between club, country and individual players has existed for years, with David Beckham signed to Adidas, yet wearing Umbro when playing for England and Nike when playing for United. However, Cruyff was far more maverick than Beckham ever was, so when he played for the Netherlands he taped over one of the stripes on his arms.

The walls of amateurism were therefore shaking as savvy athletes shopped themselves between Puma and Adidas on the football pitch, and Converse and Adidas on the basketball court, and Cruyff became so attached to the two stripes that when he retired from playing football, he launched a clothing brand and made his iconic #14 shirt the centrepiece of the range. It was, of course, orange and had two stripes on each arm, as Cruyff blustered, 'Two stripes belong to me, especially in combination with the number 14. They're part of my identity, and that doesn't belong to Adidas, but to me.' Or, as his lawyer might have said if he spoke German, *'Die Marke mit zwei Streifen.'*

#6 COLLECTIVE BARGAINING OF TV RIGHTS

(New York, 30 September 1961)

There were big boots to fill when NFL commissioner Bell unexpectedly passed away in 1960, with 33-year-old executive Peter Rozelle the surprise choice to replace him. He was Dan Reeves' general manager at the LA Rams and hadn't made it on to the owners' shortlist, but was well liked, and so when none of the other candidates could secure enough support, he was regarded as a strong 'compromise candidate'.

Bell had come up with the original TV rights trading model, which allowed each team to sell their own home games providing they blocked the TV signal within a 75-mile radius of their stadium. This concept was first introduced in 1947 following the Rams' poor attendance figures we spoke of earlier and drew an immediate challenge from the US Justice Department who argued it amounted to restraint of trade, which was dismissed by Judge Allan K. Grim, with the exception of live radio broadcasts, which he ruled couldn't be blocked the same way.

The decision was referred to as the 'Grim decision' and was especially grim for fans without a ticket to the game and who lived inside the 75-mile exclusion zone. It was, however, a decisive ruling for the NFL and delivered the dual benefit of increasing exposure for the teams when they played away and protecting the gate when they played at home. And it worked too, with matchday attendance rising from an average of 23,000 per game in 1950 to reach 44,000 by the end of the decade. Rozelle therefore had no issue with Bell's strategy and had seen for himself when working at the Rams the negative impact of uncontrolled TV coverage. However, what he was concerned about was that if teams continued to sell their games independently then they would undersell themselves to the networks.

CBS, for example, had nine NFL teams under contract, while NBC showed one game a week featuring either the Colts or the Steelers. The Browns, meanwhile, had gone rogue by launching their own TV channel and were negotiating carriage deals with cable operators outside their franchise area. This move had naturally infuriated CBS, since their games often went head-to-head with the Browns' coverage and so Rozelle was told they would cut their support of the sport unless he protected their rights. A further frustration for Rozelle was that the decentralised nature of the current model led to an imbalance in the way revenue was shared, which he didn't feel was in keeping with the ethos of trying to ensure a level playing field. The Giants, for example, generated $175k a year from their CBS deal, while the Packers earned $100k less, and so what he wanted was a league-wide mandate to negotiate with the networks on their behalf – leaving them free to decide what to do about local cable.

'The Times They Are a Changing'

Watching all this was Lamar Hunt, the 28-year-old son of Haroldson Lafayette Hunt. A self-made oil billionaire, *Fortune Magazine* once described him as the wealthiest man in the world. Through his family trust fund, Hunt Jnr could therefore buy pretty much anything he wanted – except, of course, a pro football team, since the NFL owner cartel tightly controlled the awarding of new franchises. He therefore tried relentlessly to persuade one of the 12 owners to sell to him and also lobbied Bell, and then Rozelle, to grant him an expansion franchise for his home town of Dallas. Both proved unsuccessful. However, Hunt wasn't someone who gave up that easily and so he concluded that if the NFL wouldn't let him join their league, then he'd start a new one and invite other wealthy Americans to join in. On 4 August 1959, the 'American Football League' (AFL) subsequently kicked off with the New York Titans, Boston Patriots, Buffalo Bills and Houston Oilers making up the Eastern Division, and the Los Angeles Chargers, Denver Broncos, Oakland Raiders and Lamar's own team, the Dallas Texans, forming the Western League.

The NFL owners had seen it all before and fully expected this new league to fold as quickly as it arrived. After all, plenty of young pretenders had tried to gatecrash their party over the past 40 years and none of them had made it work. However, this cohort were different. They were incredibly well-funded, looking to introduce pro football to new geographic audiences and even willing to pay top dollar in the draft to outbid the NFL teams.

Peter Rozelle then looked on enviously when Hunt announced an $85m TV deal with ABC and achieved precisely what he himself had wanted to put in place, and so he argued persuasively to his ownership group that they needed to expand the league to 21 teams to stop any more new owners joining their rival, and that he wanted their mandate to run a competitive rights auction to secure a similar league-wide TV deal for the NFL.

This was groundbreaking stuff; the NBA had introduced collective bargaining a few years earlier, but the model allowed their franchises to keep the revenue they individually generated from selling their home games. MLB, meanwhile, was a free-for-all with wide variation over how each club traded their individual TV rights. However, this cohort of NFL owners continued to believe having a competitive league was crucial to their commercial success, and as Wellington Mara, son of Tim, put it, 'Individually we were making more money off television, little as it was, than anybody else. After all, we were the only game in New York. But what he [Rozelle] was saying was that it was good for the league, and Jack [his brother] and I always felt we had to consider that because the league was more important than any team. Without the league, what did we have? If other franchises were in trouble, then so were we. This was our philosophy, no matter what.'

Getting the support of the owners was one thing, but Rozelle now had to convince the politicians it was a good idea since it remained illegal under US competition law for sports franchises to block-negotiate their broadcast rights. He therefore successfully lobbied senators for anti-trust exemption as the Sports Broadcasting Act of 1961 lifted the ban. Here's how sports historian, Michael MacCambridge, explains the difference it made: 'The business model that emerged through the 50s, 60s and 70s viewed the leagues' teams not as a number of restaurants vying for supremacy on a single street, but instead a chain of restaurants, with every franchise across the country competing among themselves to be the best, but each dependent on the survival of the whole to truly prosper.'

The big reward Rozelle had promised his owners then duly arrived at the start of the 1962 NFL season when he called a press conference to announce news of the NFL's first-ever league-wide TV contract: a two-year deal with CBS worth $9m, which he persuaded the teams to divide equally, and so the tiny Green Bay Packers received exactly the same share as the mighty New York Giants. Two years later, with the CBS deal up for renewal, Rozelle then launched his next move, which was to conduct sport's first competitive TV rights auction that elicited sealed bids from all three networks. This was a tense time in America, with people deeply suspicious of one another as Cold War tensions grew and the media was full of stories about corporate espionage. CBS subsequently retained the contract, but only after Rozelle trebled the price to $28.2m, with rumours swirling around the sports media that a mole inside ABC had tipped CBS off that they were submitting a bid of $26m. The age of the dark art of media rights negotiations had begun.

As for Lamar Hunt and the AFL? Well, they didn't fold in the way Bert Bell and his owner group predicted and continued to be a thorn in the backside of the NFL owners for a further seven years, forcing up player salaries, often winning out in the draft and splitting the fan base in New York and Los Angeles, where there were now two pro football teams to support.

As player salaries rocketed, the NFL was thus confronted by its greatest-ever 'either/or moment' and, on 4 April 1966, Tex Schramm, the president of the Dallas Cowboys, swallowed his pride and told Hunt he and his cohort of owners were open to a merger which would allow all eight AFL teams to join the NFL.

In the autumn of 1970, Rozelle subsequently took on the role as commissioner of the enlarged NFL, with *American Century* summarising his contribution to the sport like this: 'There is no one more important to the development of the NFL in the era of television than Pete Rozelle. For 29 years, 1960–1989, Rozelle ruled atop the league as commissioner and by the end of his tenure, had become the most powerful man in sports.' His genius was to appreciate the serendipity that exists between sport and television and that creating competitive tension is crucial to drive up the value of rights.

In 1963, he then launched NFL Properties, which was a new division responsible for selling league-wide sponsorship and official merchandise, and set up an in-house content division called NFL Films, which was briefed to generate incremental revenue from non-live programming. It was a bold move with skilled filmmakers hired to produce and distribute content of cinematic quality to keep audiences on the hook outside of gametime.

As part of Rozelle's growth strategy, he changed the name of the Championship to the Superbowl, which established a day in January that has grown into the most crucial day in the US advertising industry calendar, and which in 2024 attracted a US audience of 120 million. He didn't duck the complex issues either, fighting racism, which used to be a big problem within certain NFL ownership groups, and hiring ex-FBI agents to keep players away from the gambling syndicates, which was another problem he'd inherited from the Bell era.

So, Peter Rozelle claims one of the top spots in my sports marketing Hall of Fame for inventing the business model which not only transformed the NFL into the most profitable property in world sport, but for providing a blueprint for other sports to follow. It wasn't of course all down to him, since on his watch he benefited from the allure of the New York Giants, the romance of the Packers and running a sport that the Madmen and their clients grew to love. Even the legendary sports commissioner David Stern, who ran the NBA for 30 years, doffs his cap to Rozelle with the following words of humility: 'He taught us how to use television and how to get the most out of sponsors. NFL Properties led the way for NBA Properties, and both of us led the way for the other sports.'

- - - - -

#7 MARK McCORMACK AND IMG

(Chicago, January 1960)

Someone who would have been keeping a close eye on what was happening in pro football was Mark McCormack. A qualified lawyer and good circuit golfer but not good enough – in his opinion – to make a living from the game, the more he looked at how the marketing of sport was evolving, the more he felt golf was being undervalued and that the top golfers were getting short-changed by both promoters and products who exploited their image rights. He therefore couldn't understand why his peers didn't use agents to negotiate on their behalf and decided to set up a dedicated golf representation business called the International Management Group (IMG) to help maximise their career earnings.

After signing a few good tour players, McCormack then approached the best golfer of the day, whose wife handled his commercial affairs and knew very well he was becoming the star attraction on the golfing circuit. Mrs Palmer told McCormack if he wanted to represent her husband's commercial interests then he would have to drop all his other clients and focus purely on building his career. It was a big call, but he figured ten per cent of Arnold Palmer's career earnings could potentially dwarf those of his other clients put together and within months it became obvious he'd made the right choice, when his client won the 1960 Masters and went on to dominate the majors for the next decade. This is how author Matthew Futterman describes this game-changer of a decision for the sports marketing industry: 'The extraction of Arnold Palmer from Wilson, and Palmer's ability to take control of his name, his value and everything associated with it would stand as the template for every deal McCormack would try to make for every iconic athlete and property for the rest of his career.'

In 1965, McCormack visited England to attend the Open Championship at Royal Birkdale and while in the UK visited Wimbledon. Like the rest of us, he fell in love with its traditions and pitched Herman David, president of the All-England Club (AELTC), the idea of producing a highlights film which IMG would sell to broadcasters outside of the UK. The conversation was well outside David's comfort zone, but McCormack persisted and three years later a deal was agreed that kick-started an enduring 50-year relationship. In the first year of their partnership, AELTC made $70k profit from IMG's commercial efforts. However, as their activities expanded, turnover eventually reached $13m by 1988 and today, through selling a mix of television rights, sponsorship, tickets, merchandise, VIP hospitality and official score data, the Wimbledon fortnight generates pre-tax profits north of $50m.

The IMG/Wimbledon partnership coincided with tennis taking its first step into the 'open' era, which allowed professional tour players to play in championships like Wimbledon and the Davis Cup. McCormack therefore moved fast and signed the 1968 Wimbledon champions Rod Laver and Margaret Court as new IMG clients, and soon hundreds of other sportsmen and women, including Jackie Stewart, Chris Evert and Lee Trevino, followed them on to the agency's books. Following his success in golf and tennis, McCormack then launched an innovative licensing business and a golf apparel division, which was followed by youth academies and the creation of TWI, his TV production and distribution business.

Sports Illustrated magazine once described Mark McCormack as the 'most powerful man in sport' and it's hard to disagree, when we reflect on the dominant position IMG established under his leadership. He therefore joins our All Stars for being the first entrepreneur to come up with the idea of a marketing agency dedicated to promoting sports events and sporting talent.

Ad Agencies Discover the Power of TV

In the 1960s, with the cultural revolution led by Twiggy, Mary Quant and The Beatles transforming the lifestyle values of young people in Britain, it was only a matter of time before the 'DDB effect' hit the London advertising scene, with young people like John Hegarty (the founder of the creative agency Bartle Bogle Hegarty) deeply inspired by their work. 'What [Doyle Dane Bernbach] did was create an entire generation who wanted to work in advertising. Before us, advertising people still secretly yearned to be artists or novelists. But we wanted to be part of that whole

60s revolution in music, fashion, and design – and we felt we could do that through advertising.' Excited by what was happening in England, the US advertising giants opened London offices, although none of them – not even DDB – made their mark on British popular culture like Collet Dickinson Pearce (CDP): a band of creative people who opened their doors in 1960, and became one of London's first agencies to get their heads around the storytelling power of TV advertising and produced some of the most memorable advertising of all-time:

'Happiness is a cigar called Hamlet'
'Fiat cars, hand-built by robots'
'Hovis, as good for you today as it's always been'
... and a glass of Cinzano spilled over an unimpressed Joan Collins.

All four of these iconic campaigns were created by CDP and will make Boomers smile, while everyone else will be familiar with an enduring line CDP copywriter Terry Lovelock came up with at 3am in his Marrakech hotel room: 'Heineken refreshes the parts other beers cannot reach'. The creative talent that came out of this brilliant agency was truly extraordinary, with another copywriter called Charles Saatchi eventually starting another famous agency with his brother Maurice, along with Peter Mayle who wrote the best-seller *A Year in Provence*. Frank Lowe was their account man and founded both the award-winning agency Lowe Howard Spink and the sports marketing group Octagon, while David Putnam, who directed *Chariots of Fire*, worked in the agency's production department alongside Alan Parker, who made *Mississippi Burning*, and Ridley Scott of *Bladerunner* fame. This was therefore the generation of British Madmen and Madwomen who taught UK plc that brand marketing sells: an 'aha!' moment which fuelled a 40-year bull run for the advertising business and generated the millions of advertising dollars and pounds that would fund the imminent explosion in the value of sports rights. Yeah, the 60s were an important decade, baby.

PART FOUR
Shamateurism

'It's just second nature, it's what we've been shown, we're living by your rules, that's all we know'–
Joy Division

The 1970s

Pelé. Billie Jean. Cruyff

THE WORLD was a challenging place to live in the 1970s as President Nixon continued America's unpopular war in Vietnam and tensions rose in the Middle East. Ted Heath had to try to deal as best he could with the consequences of all this turbulence, including surging oil prices, high inflation and countless strikes. However, with one million people out of work, his Conservative government lost the 1974 General Election to Labour, who inherited a nation bristling with tension, and the mood of young people was perfectly captured by someone in the crowd at one of the first Sex Pistols concerts in Manchester who growled, 'There was a lot of trouble at gigs at the time, and we didn't particularly shy away from that. We quite liked it. We liked the edginess and that atmosphere and the potential for trouble. We came from football backgrounds.' Wherever you went, people seemed angry, with the cheerleaders being a band called Sham 69 who howled, 'I'm trying to be someone in life. We're the people you don't wanna know. We come from places you don't wanna go.'

With the growing profile of the Olympic Games, the IOC found itself an easy target for angry protesters too and events turned seriously ugly at the Munich Games in 1972 when eight masked gunmen scaled the wall of the Olympic village, kidnapped 11 Israeli athletes and demanded the release of 200 Palestinian prisoners from Israeli jails. This was followed by a shootout at Munich airport which led to the death of five terrorists and all but one of the athletes. The next Olympics were held in Montreal and were memorable for the 'perfect tens' of Romanian gymnast Nadia Comaneci and the seven gold medals American swimmer Mark Spitz won in the pool. However, away from the sporting action, the Montreal Organising Committee found itself at the centre of another political storm when 27 African nations walked out of the athletes' village on the eve of the opening ceremony. This was a period in history when the world of sport was isolating South Africa to try to force its government to renounce apartheid. The protesting nations were therefore furious after Avery Brundage refused to ban New Zealand, despite the fact their rugby team had participated in a tour of South Africa.

The rollercoaster of a decade for Brundage then came to an end in 1979 with 60 nations caving in to pressure from President Jimmy Carter to boycott the next Games in Moscow after the Soviet Union invaded Afghanistan ten months before the opening ceremony.

'Look Sharp, Be Sharp'

One man who would have found the whole shamateurism debate bizarre was Roone Arledge, a New York television executive who started his career at NBC and by 1958 had worked his way up to the position of head of sports at their rival, ABC. What he was liking, however, was that the relationship between broadcasters and advertisers was developing into a deeply symbiotic one with live sport delivering the scale and audience profile advertisers wanted to reach. They were therefore increasingly open to committing advertising dollars in advance to ensure they secured a guaranteed share of premium sports inventory, which in turn gave the networks confidence to bid for sports rights and was the reason CBS were able to bid so high for the new NFL contract, since they had Ford Motor Company dollars in their back pocket. These deals became known by media buyers as 'upfronts' with Gillette one of NBC's biggest supporters through their commitment to *The Gillette Cavalcade of Sport* – an umbrella brand NBC created for them to present their sponsored content. A crucial part of the package was Friday night boxing, which was often broadcast from Madison Square Garden and during its run featured legendary fighters such as Rocky Marciano and Sugar Ray Robinson. The show therefore became an institution across the United States for over 15 years with its 'Look Sharp, Be Sharp' theme tune a favourite march for college bands to play.

However, by 1958 NBC were tiring of boxing and getting concerned about the rumours of rigged fights and illegal betting and so they informed Gillette they were going to drop it from their Friday night schedule and replace it with other sports. At the time ABC had a tiny portfolio of sports rights and, as Arledge explains in his memoir, this was a significant decision for NBC and one that not only proved to be a pivotal one for his network, but a gamechanger for the future of sports broadcasting in America. 'NBC thought boxing had run its course, which prompted Gillette to conclude that NBC and Gillette had run their course. Gillette was bringing all its business to ABC, which not only meant the fights [they sponsored *Friday Fight Night* on NBC], but enough additional advertising dollars to go after a whole sports schedule.'

One year later, Gillette stunned the NBC sales department by switching $8m of their annual spend on sports advertising across to ABC. It was a budget equivalent to $100m today and gave Arledge the war-chest he needed to secure an impressive portfolio of new sports contracts. Next on his hit list was college football, which he signed in 1960, followed a few years later by luring the NBA away from CBS. Then he created an innovative new magazine show called *ABC Wide World of Sports*, which showcased new sports to American audiences, such as the Le Mans 24-hour race and cliff-diving from Acapulco. It was a fresh format that had never been tried before and became a huge hit for ABC and was soon generating ad sales of $150k per minute. NBC walking away from boxing subsequently woke a sleeping giant as Arledge used Gillette's support to make an audacious offer of $6.5m to cover the Mexico City Olympic Games and then made sure of holding on to these rights by doubling the rights fee for Munich and giving the Montreal Organising Committee a 24-hour, take-it-or-leave-it offer of $25m to maintain ABC's status as the home of the Olympic Games for another four years.

#8 'WELCOME TO MONDAY NIGHT FOOTBALL ON ABC'

(New York, 20 September 1971)

In 1970 Arledge made his boldest move yet and one which would revolutionise the future presentation of live sport on TV, when he paid Peter Rozelle $8.5m for the right to broadcast the NFL on Monday nights. He'd seeded the idea himself with Rozelle two years earlier and so was furious when the commissioner gave first option on the new package to NBC and CBS, but the good news for Roone was that both networks passed on the opportunity since neither had managed to get live sport to rate in primetime. Arledge, however, had other ideas and told his colleagues he was going to 'put the showbiz into sports' and they enthusiastically bought into his vision and allocated the show a five-hour slot and generous production budget.

By way of background, during the 70s, pro football coverage on TV was shot with a single camera on the 50-yard line and another behind each goal. This was a legacy of how scared sports authorities were that watching sport on TV could excite fans more than the real thing. As a former commissioner of MLB once famously said during the early days of television, 'The view a fan gets at home should not be any better than that of the fan in the worst seat in the ballpark.'

Part of the Arledge plan was therefore to change that attitude by doubling the number of cameras in the stadium with one cameraman permanently trained on the faces of the players and fans in the stands to capture the emotion of the game. To fill the five-hour slot, he also hired ex-pros who were tasked with explaining what was happening on the pitch, and introduced production enhancements such as slow-motion replays, which had rarely been used before in live sports. Here's Roone's poetic description for his new baby, which he christened *Monday Night Football* (*MNF*): 'Football as entertainment. Football at night under the lights, helmets gleaming, uniforms dazzling while shots from blimps overhead made the whole stadium resemble a jewelled oasis floating in the darkness.'

The first *MNF* broadcast aired on 20 September 1970 with the Cleveland Browns taking on the New York Jets at the Municipal Stadium. It was sponsored by Ford, presented by Howard Cosell, and ABCs rivals had no clue what was about to hit them: namely a power format that was soon pulling in audiences of 30 million and record ad revenue. If the 'Greatest Game' lit the fire for the popularity of the NFL, then *Monday Night Football* unleashed a flame-thrower on it, with *Variety Magazine* commenting that theatre attendance on Monday nights was, 'in a real nosedive as a result of ABC's pro football'.

ABC's success at securing the top sports contracts was therefore down to the strong relationships Roone Arledge established with sport's top decision-makers and dangling irresistible cheques in front of them to avoid a rights auction. In the lead-up to the Moscow Games, NBC subsequently wised up to his strategy and deployed John Le Carré-style tactics to land the US broadcast rights from the Soviet Organising Committee. Roone was furious, but his anger quickly dissipated when news broke of the broadcast ban from the White House and, to ensure he didn't get outmanoeuvred for Los Angeles, he made a record $225m offer to the cash-hungry OC to lock in their rights. ABC Sports were on a roll, and Arledge wasn't finished either, as he offered Rozelle $600m to retain the *Monday Night Football* slot for a further five years. CBS and NBC were seriously rattled; losing the Olympics was bad enough but no way would they get marginalised in pro football too, and so they responded with equally aggressive bids of $700m to hold on to their cherished Sunday afternoon slots.

In one contract cycle, the annual value of NFL broadcast rights therefore increased from $162m to $420m and, following the success of *MNF*, the networks realised that if sport could rate well in primetime, then the value of the programming on a cost-per-hour basis was cheaper than other genres of original content. With new studio formats, time-outs, and the introduction of pundits, there was also the opportunity to stretch out the coverage of a single game to five hours, which meant the Superbowl could squeeze in 50 minutes of advertising. Here's Arledge explaining the maths for his Munich Olympics bid and paying a compliment to his pal, agent and negotiator Barry Frank along the way: 'We simply had to figure out a way of pushing past the $10-million barrier [that NBC had bid], and it was Barry Frank who devised it: expand coverage to 67 hours, and for two-plus weeks take over all of primetime, where the largest loot was to be mined. Sell about 500 commercial minutes at an average cost of $48k each, and total revenue would be just shy of $24 million – enough to cover the cost of rights, facilities and production, with a healthy profit left over.'

So, there we have it. The calculation of how free-to-air broadcasters valued sports rights back in the day and explained by the rainmaker who fired the gun on hyper rights inflation.

- - - - -

#9 BERNIE ECCLESTONE BUYS BRABHAM

(Chessington, June 1971)

One of the few people to have been omnipresent throughout the history of modern sports marketing is Bernie Ecclestone, whose story began in the 1960s after building up a successful second-hand car business. By 1971, he'd made enough money to pay Jack Brabham £120k to buy his famous F1 team, which bought him a seat at motorsport's top table and would eventually make him one of the wealthiest men in Britain.

At the time, the sport was loosely organised under a voluntary trade body called the Formula One Constructors' Association (FOCA), which was made up of representation from the other team owners of that era, including Frank Williams, Colin Chapman and Ken Tyrrell. Following attendance at a few of these meetings, Ecclestone soon realised none of these men had much interest in the business of motorsport. All they really wanted was to enjoy the thrill of racing and so were happy enough to individually agree an appearance fee with promoters. Sensing an opportunity, Ecclestone therefore offered to make their lives easier and to negotiate central deals on their behalf – in exchange for a modest two per cent commission.

The story of how this moment in time led to Ecclestone assuming management control of F1 is told brilliantly by Tom Bowers in his book *No Angel, The Secret Life of Bernie Ecclestone*, with the spoiler alert that he quickly discovered race promoters could afford to pay a far higher share of their profits to the teams. The following year, Bernie therefore offered to personally guarantee his on-track rivals a fixed fee to race in an agreed number of Grands Prix, plus a concrete commitment to reduce their transportation costs if they agreed to travel together and let him negotiate a central logistics deal. And all he wanted in exchange was a written mandate to act on their behalf and commission of four per cent for his trouble.

He was taking a huge personal risk, with no guarantee of making money, but this man was a gambler at heart and the prize on offer was too irresistible not to give it a go. Here's Bowers' take on this pivotal moment in the history of Formula One (F1): 'No one demurred. Unanimously, the team owners expressed their acceptance of his offer. No one would question whether Ecclestone was pocketing additional commission on the transport costs or whether he expected an additional payment for himself from each circuit. Shedding the burden of negotiating 15 separate race fees in the 1973 season and the transportation of cars and people around the world at cheaper rates was a double relief. They could focus on racing, winning and enjoying themselves.'

As the circuits begrudgingly negotiated with Ecclestone, he skilfully played them off against one another, pushing for higher and higher rights fees with the rate card to host a Grand Prix reaching $300k by 1975. He had no hesitation, either, in punishing those who refused to meet the asking price, with the Canadian Grand Prix dropped from the race calendar that year after refusing to pay up and returning a year later with their chequebook wide open. With televising sport in its infancy outside of the United States, Ecclestone also decided to insert another new clause into his venue contracts which granted all the television rights to FOCA. Another genius move that would deliver a significant financial dividend in a few years' time.

- - - - -

#10 THE WOMEN'S PRO TENNIS BREAKAWAY TOUR

(San Francisco, 6 January, 1971)

There are a few sportspeople who can justifiably claim genuine 'greatness', with Johan Cruyff and Serena Williams both on my list. One or two others like Tiger Woods and Usain Bolt also single-handedly changed the economics of their sport, while Tommie Smith and Megan Rapinoe used the platform sport gave them to campaign for societal change, and Jimmy Hill and Ed Moses fought hard to get a better deal for their peers.

Then there's Billie Jean King (BJK). A woman who stands on the shoulders of greatness and can justifiably lay claim to all four of these extraordinary achievements: the world's best female tennis player, an influential activist, innovator, tireless campaigner for societal change and creator of the tenth of our most significant moments in this story.

'All I'm askin' in return honey is a little r.e.s.p.e.c.t'

Billie Jean was born in 1943 in Long Beach, California and her father was a firefighter. There was therefore little privilege growing up in her home and, as she recounts in her autobiography, she needed to do odd jobs around the neighbourhood to earn the money to pay for her first tennis racket. As her passion for tennis grew, she became frustrated at the unfairness of male tennis players receiving college scholarships while the top female players had to pay for their own coaching. In 1967 after she won the treble of the singles, doubles and mixed doubles at Wimbledon, she won a £45 gift voucher and talks about how she was forced to accept what she refers to in her book as the 'green handshake', which were under-the-counter appearance fees paid by promoters: 'Tennis association officials were behaving like feudal overlords. They told us where to play, when, and what not to say. They maintained power by keeping the amateur players dependent on the crumbs they rationed out.'

Wimbledon was the first significant tournament to recognise change was needed and, following BJK's victories, Herman David described amateurism as a 'living lie' and announced that the following Wimbledon Championship would become the first Grand Slam to allow amateurs and professionals to compete side by side.

This was a good start, but the top female players were frustrated that so few events were still being organised for them and remained angry about the condescending attitude they felt was shown to them by the male-run tennis authorities and the disparity in the quantum of prize money they received. Billie Jean therefore fired the gun on a four-year campaign for equality at a press conference during the 1970 US Open, when she announced she was being joined by eight of the other top female players in forming a breakaway women's pro-tour.

This was the same year that tobacco advertising had been banned on TV in America and companies like Philip Morris were therefore on the lookout for alternative ways to promote their products. The 'liberated' women of the 70s were also the primary target market for their Virginia Slims brand and so they felt its proposition of 'you've come a long way baby' was a perfect fit with the values of a rebel women's tennis tour.

With $500k of sponsorship in the bank, this group of women subsequently quit the USLTA tour, and held their first event in San Francisco on 6 January 1971. The first prize was $2k, with the rebels unveiling their (then) bold manifesto, 'To make sure that any girl in the world, if she's good enough, would have a place to compete; that women and girl athletes would finally be appreciated for their accomplishments, not just their looks; and that we'd be able to make a living.'

It doesn't sound like too much to ask, does it.

The relationship between the Virginia Slims Tour and the US tennis authorities was a challenging one and Billie Jean proved to be a combative spokesperson who had no intention of backing down. The dispute, therefore, rumbled on for two more years until the 1973 US Open put everyone out of their misery by announcing they would be introducing equal prize money. The following year, the rebel tour was therefore organised under the auspices of the newly created Women's Tennis Association (WTA), and formally sanctioned by the USLTA.

However, for Billie Jean, the battle was far from over and she continued her crusade for equality by accepting a provocative challenge from ex-pro Bobby Riggs, to try and beat him over the best of three sets. This was a time in American history when women were fighting back against years of sex discrimination, with US lawmakers having just passed the landmark Title IX legislation which ruled that, 'No person in the United States shall, on the basis of sex, be excluded from participation in, be denied the benefits of, or be subjected to discrimination under any education program or activity receiving Federal financial assistance.'

Riggs had, however, clearly not read the small print of Title IX and proceeded to wind BJK up with his chauvinist pre-match commentary. ABC also stoked the controversy by calling the game *The Battle of the Sexes* and in typical Roone Arledge fashion hyped the event as something that was way bigger than a made-for-TV exhibition game. With 30,000 packed inside the Houston Astrodome, and a further 90 million watching at home, Billie Jean subsequently delighted millions of women by defeating Riggs 6-4, 6-3, 6-3 to claim the winner-takes-all prize of $110k. As she explains in terms relevant to that moment in time, 'People were divided over who was going to win, and they were arguing it out at their kitchen tables, around the vending machines at work, inside beauty salons and corner bars. Countless wagers were made. Husbands promised their wives to take over the ironing for a week if I won; bosses vowed to make the coffee for their secretaries.'

Mexican Stand-off in SW19

It wasn't just in women's tennis where anger was building between sports leaders and their players, with Arnold Palmer and Jack Nicklaus tired of being bossed about by the all-powerful PGA of America and so forming a similar player-led breakaway tour. Meanwhile, the top male tennis players were annoyed about being excluded from amateur-only events and copied the golfers by creating the Association of Tour Professionals (ATP), a trade body designed to give them a unified voice against the International Lawn Tennis Federation (ILTF).

As we're starting to establish by now, many of sport's most decisive moments are caused by sudden flash-points that have been years in the making, and one of the most pivotal in tennis history occurred in 1973 when Yugoslav player Niki Pilic received a letter from the All-England Club that banned him from playing at Wimbledon that summer. The reason they gave was that the ILTF had informed them Pilic had contravened their rules for participation in Grand Slams by refusing to play for his country in an earlier Davis Cup match.

Pilic, however, saw the situation very differently and tried to explain that he left the tie early after having helped Yugoslavia to an unassailable 3-1 lead, and since the final game was a dead rubber (and he wasn't paid to play Davis Cup), he argued he was within his rights to leave. His fellow ATP members were furious when they heard about the ban, which was yet another example of the tennis authorities throwing their weight around. They therefore borrowed from the Jimmy Hill playbook and threatened a boycott unless Pilic was reinstated.

Both sides fully expected the other to back down but when no resolution had been reached on the day of the men's singles draw, the players felt there was only one solution left open to them: the nuclear one, as 80 players, which included the top 12 seeds and defending champion Stan Smith, all walked out of Wimbledon. As Pilic opined to the *New York Times*, 'They could do whatever they wanted. We had no control over the sport. We had to do something.' AELTC, therefore scrambled around to make up the numbers with the official records stating that the 1973 Championship was won by Jan Kodes, who was the original #15 seed but chose not to boycott.

Once the Wimbledon chalk-dust had settled, both sides realised an unpleasant line had been crossed: rules in sport are important, but fans pay to watch the top stars and so even the most dogmatic members of the ILTF knew something had to give to solve this embarrassing breakdown in relations. In the following weeks the players and the ILTF therefore worked through a series of rule and format changes to give the players more freedom to choose where they played. They were also offered seats on the board of a newly created Tennis Council, and there was a review of the quantum of prize money on offer and how it was distributed. In the following era of Borg, Connors and McEnroe, men's tennis went on to enjoy its finest decade and so the significance of this Mexican stand-off in SW18 was therefore profound and is neatly summarised by Matthew Futterman like this: 'With a set schedule and a clear understanding of who would be playing when, CBS and NBC would commit to long-term broadcasting deals. Almost overnight, tennis had completely changed. It's always dangerous to connect a single event with a larger, macro phenomenon. But the boom that tennis experienced once the players won their freedom and recognition as the most important people in the sport is unlike anything any other sport experienced during the past 50 years.'

- - - - -

#11 NEW FIFA PRESIDENT
(Berlin, June 1974)

Horst Dassler was fascinated by the family business and aged 21 was asked by his father to fly to the 1956 Melbourne Olympics and persuade as many of the top athletes as he could to wear the three stripes of Adidas. His strategy involved hanging out in the athletes' village with a bag of shoes and handing them out to medal prospects, which seemed to work, since 70 medals were won by athletes wearing Adidas spikes at the next Olympics.

Eventually, however, Horst started to tire of this approach and wondered whether a better way to build the brand's high-performance credentials would be to get close to the suits who ran the international federations. After all, it was they who set the rules, so being inside their tent seemed like a much better strategy than chasing these messy boot deals with individual athletes. Over the next few years, he therefore recruited a network of Adidas ambassadors to build relationships within football and Olympic sports to act as his eyes and ears.

In June 1974, the World Cup was due to take place in Germany, and during the tournament there was to be a vote to decide who would become the next president of FIFA. The incumbent was an Englishman, Sir Stanley Rous, who had held the role since 1961 and done a good job dealing with the complexity of a fast-growing sport. Dassler already had a relationship with Rous, and it therefore suited him to have a European football president he knew, so his football ambassadors were instructed to campaign for the incumbent president.

The alternative candidate was João Havelange, a successful businessman from Rio who had previously led the Brazilian Sports Confederation before mounting a campaign to replace Rous. Havelange stood with a popular manifesto of increasing the number of teams participating in the World Cup from 16 to 24 with the pledge that most of these new places would go to non-European nations. In addition, he said he would organise a Junior World Championships, fund stadium construction in less wealthy countries and deal with the political issue the African nations felt Rous had ducked – to ban South Africa from FIFA. Havelange lobbied the national FAs tirelessly and treated the FIFA election like a US presidential campaign and always with his secret weapon by his side: Edson Arantes do Nascimento, or Pelé to his friends. Soon the Dassler network was reporting strong support for Havelange and that crucially he had secured the support of the African Confederation.

On the eve of the vote, Horst, therefore asked for an impromptu meeting with the heir apparent and told him he was willing to switch allegiance. It was support that proved crucial too, since in the end the vote went two rounds before the Brazilian eventually defeated Rous by 16 out of a possible 200 votes. An understanding was then struck between the two men that would go on to transform the commercial fortunes of FIFA and establish a symbiotic relationship which Barbara Smit summarises like this: 'Havelange would hold the door wide open for Dassler in international football, provided the German helped him to garner the funds that he needed to make good his costly election promises.'

- - - - -

#12 FREE AGENCY

(New York, 13 December 1975)

Legend has it that the first competitive game of baseball was played in New York in 1840, which 30 years later led to the creation of MLB. The eight founding team owners had no problem paying their players to play – that was until some of them started threatening to join other teams unless they were paid more money. Hence the introduction of the Reserve Clause which allowed owners to list five of their players that were off-limits from poaching. And by 1880 the number of players covered by the clause had grown to cover the top ten players, and a league-wide salary cap of $2,500 had been introduced.

The players hated the way their livelihood was being controlled, especially since the popularity of baseball was booming through the extra capacity created by the construction of much bigger ballparks like Fenway Park. However, this additional revenue didn't trickle down to the players and by the 1950s the average MLB salary had increased to only $13k pa. The economic reality, therefore, was that only the very best players like Mickey Mantle could earn a living from the game and everyone else had to take a second job or risk getting released or traded to another team if they complained.

In 1965, when ABC tabled a record $5.7m offer to commissioner Bowie Khun to broadcast 'the game of the week', the players saw the writing on the wall and decided it was time to hire someone to help them fight for their share of this TV money. The cosy owner cartel of the past 70 years was about to become decidedly less cosy.

Marvin Miller was born in the Bronx and developed his career as a dedicated union man after cutting his teeth at the mighty US Steelworkers' Union. He was therefore an unusual choice to lead a small union representing 500 baseball players. His tenure didn't start well either, when the owners decided to end their funding of the players' union. In the past, recognising their players had legitimate expenses to cover, they had gifted them the $150k rights fees they received from televising the All-Star game. However, the arrival of Miller signalled new battles ahead which they had no intention of funding.

The new man was not deterred by the rough welcome and simply responded with a plan to replace this lost money, and his first move was to secure $60k in sponsorship from Coca-Cola to allow them to show pictures of MLB players on their bottle caps. Next, he swung his bat at Topps, who were paying players $125 to print their image on collectible trading cards, which were hugely popular back in the day, with the reps spinning it to players that it was a great honour to be selected. Miller was not so gullible and succeeded in doubling the fee to $250 and negotiating an eight per cent royalty on the retail value of these cards, which was shared through the player pool.

Both were good wins, but the win Miller wanted more than anything else was to abolish the Reserve Clause, which he saw as restraint of trade and if scrapped would enable his members to act as free agents and thereby create an open market for their services.

There had been numerous challenges to the clause over the years, but the blockage was always a legal precedent first established in 1922 by Supreme Court Justice Oliver Wendell Holmes, who ruled that baseball's principal role in society was to 'give exhibitions of baseball which are purely state affairs'. This basically meant playing pro baseball was exempt from federal anti-trust law. Miller therefore needed to find a player who was either brave enough (or daft enough), to work with him to get this ruling overturned in the courts.

He had to wait until 1974, and then along came Jim 'Catfish' Hunter. The son of a farmer from North Carolina who had pitched Oakland Athletic (The As) to three consecutive World Series victories, Hunter was happy in San Francisco, doing well on a salary of $100k, and having the greatest season of his career. With his contract up for renewal, his lawyer, Charlton Cherry, therefore called a routine contract renewal meeting with team owner Charlie Finlay, with the main request that a proportion of his client's future salary could be deferred for two years and invested into an annuity. When he retired, Hunter would then cash in the insurance policy and save himself a big chunk of tax. It was a smart tax-planning idea that was all above board with the IRS and not without precedent. Finlay initially agreed to this request, but then unexpectedly changed his mind and then refused to budge. Hunter's lawyer was furious, complained to Marvin Miller, and so presented the union boss with the perfect test case.

In the weeks leading up to the court hearing, the other MLB owners pleaded with Finlay to back down since they knew the consequences for all of them if he lost. However, for reasons known only to himself, he doggedly refused, and on 13 December 1975 the case convened in front of a mild-mannered jurist called Peter Seitz. He was no fan of baseball but listened carefully to the evidence that was put in front of him and then wasted very little time making his ruling and uttering a few words which would have seismic consequences for the future economics of baseball: 'Mr. Hunter's contract for service to be performed during the 1975 season no longer binds him and he is a free agent.'

The irony of the Seitz ruling was that the very thing the Reserve Clause was created to stop then immediately happened, when Cherry fired the starting gun on a bidding auction for Hunter's signature. Well, it's not every year you get to sign the pitcher of the year, with a win-ratio of 81 per cent and earned run average of 2.49. If Finley hadn't been so stubborn, and the other team owners had stuck to the spirit of their non-poaching agreement, then who knows how this situation would have played out. However, a feeding frenzy immediately broke out with eight teams despatching their top negotiators to North Carolina to try and secure Hunter's signature, with the Yankees owner eventually tabling a knock-out five-year/$3.35m offer that was 15 times higher than anyone else was being paid in the MLB. In 1976, Hunter pitched the Yankees to their first World Series victory in 15 years and then two years later his arm gave out.

The significance of the Hunter v Finlay case was therefore deeply profound for American sports since it handed Miller the all-important precedent he'd been seeking and was soon followed by a second high-profile case on behalf of Andy Messersmith. He was the star pitcher of the LA Dodgers, and this next ruling went on to establish the Collective Bargaining Agreement, which set a transparent revenue-sharing formula between players and the owners.

#13 THE GODDESS OF VICTORY
(Portland, Oregon, 1975)

Stan Smith didn't win another career Grand Slam after the player walk-out at Wimbledon. However, after his victory in 1973, Dassler was keen to ramp up his brand's tennis credentials in the US and Smith was the obvious player to choose, since he was both American and the reigning Wimbledon champion. When the two men signed this partnership, neither of them, however, could have predicted the extraordinary success the 'Stan Smith' shoe would go on to have, as it emerged as uber-cool footwear for the likes of David Bowie and the Beastie Boys to wear. Since its launch the brand has sold 50 million pairs and two of my daughters have owned a pair, although neither had any clue who this man was when I asked why they chose them:

'Because they were very "in" and my first pair of designer trainers. I thought the Stans were understated [they're plain white] but also branded,' said Georgie. 'Oh, is it Stan, I thought it was Sam,' replied Annie.

Around the same time as this tennis shoe was hitting the shops, another shoe designed by US track and field coach Bob Bowerman was proving popular with hard-core runners in the United States. It was produced by Blue Ribband Sports who were based in California and had been created in 1964 by Stanford graduate Phil Knight.

Within a few years, Knight was turning over $5m and ready to jazz up the name of his company. Following a series of random internal brainstorms, his staff came up with the name Nike – the goddess of victory – which was the best of the bunch, and so Knight paid an art student $50 to come up with a logo. Her name was Carolyn Davidson, and after various iterations she created a squiggle motif to convey the feeling of running motion, telling Knight it was called the 'swoosh'. Knight liked his new logo and was excited about the growth potential for his company, and so as soon as he received a payment from his customers, he placed another big order with his Japanese manufacturers for more product. The problem Nike had, therefore, wasn't selling enough shoes, but managing cash flow. The story of how close this behaviour came to putting Nike out of business is described vividly in the book *Shoe Dog*, which is Knight's account of the early years of his company, in which he shares an incident that fits perfectly with the narrative of this book.

It was 1975 and Nike had a growing reputation in America, with the sale of its products doubling each year. However, as a result of its intense ambition, the company often exceeded its overdraft limit and so eventually the Bank of California (BOC) lost their patience and told Knight they were closing his account. And with its patchy trading history, no other bank was seemingly interested in taking Nike on.

Knight had, however, established a strong relationship with the account manager at his Japanese trading guarantor who was called Tadayuki Ito and believed Nike had the potential to grow into a $20m account for his company. After carefully studying the books, Ito therefore persuaded his bosses to settle the outstanding BOC debt and underwrite a new banking facility. This is how Knight describes this lifesaver of a moment for his company as he walked out of his old bank after having just told the manager where to go: 'When we were all outside the bank, I bowed to Ito. I wanted to kiss him, but I only bowed. "Thank you," I said to Ito. "You will never be sorry that you defended us like that."'

Nike kicked on to become one of the key protagonists of this story and anyone who invested $1k in Blue Ribband stock in the 1970s today holds stock in Nike Inc worth $800k. We therefore must give an appreciative nod to Tadayuki Ito for believing in Knight. Without him, there would probably have been a very different outcome to the fortunes of the company, and who knows, maybe also the story of sports marketing with no Air Jordan to talk about later and perhaps no Tiger, Sampras or Venus as we know them today.

Let's spare a thought too for Carolyn Davidson, since the Nike brand and her swoosh logo now carry a global brand equity value of $26bn and was recently voted by the brand gurus of Interbrand as the 11th most-loved brand in the world. Although maybe let's not feel too bad for her, since after graduating from Portland State she freelanced for Knight who was unable to afford to pay her the daily rate she wanted and so gave her a few stock options to make up the shortfall. These she eventually sold for a cool $1m.

Sports Marketing 1.0 – 'hello, we're over here'

The idea of sponsorship has been around for years with Roman gladiators putting the names of wealthy benefactors on the side of their chariots, and if you watch old footage of the 1924 Paris Olympics you'll notice billboards for Coca-Cola. However, the growth of the modern sports sponsorship industry has always been directly linked to the evolution of broadcast media, with cricket one of the first to embrace TV, in the 1960s, as it attempted to figure out how to stem the decline in attendance at county games. In keeping with a key theme of this book, the answer then presented itself quite by chance when the neighbouring counties of Nottinghamshire, Leicestershire and Derbyshire found themselves with a few spare days on their hands between fixtures and so decided to play a series of one-day games, over 50 overs per side.

One-day cricket caught on quickly and eventually led to the creation of a new one-day knockout cup competition. At the time, a 20-something British PR executive called Patrick Nally was making a name for himself brokering some of the early sports sponsorship deals and his business partner was Peter West, who was presenter of the BBC's cricket coverage. He therefore knew how to get things done inside the inner sanctums of English cricket and the BBC, and so when Nally recruited Gillette as potential sponsor of this new competition, West worked his magic to ensure the deal wasn't blocked under the BBC Charter (which banned advertising within BBC programming). The success of West and Nally also coincided with the UK government banning cigarette advertising on TV, and like in the US, tobacco companies were again looking for new ways to promote their brands. In 1973, Gillette was therefore outbid by Benson & Hedges to secure sponsorship of this competition, and they were joined four years later by rival brand, John Player, title sponsoring a new one-day Sunday League.

Gurus of marketing say the first step towards building strong brand equity is to ensure as many people as possible in your target audience know you exist. Brand awareness, as it's known, is therefore a key metric used to measure the success of marketing campaigns. It's also something sports sponsorship delivers on brilliantly, since unlike TV advertising, sponsor branding is closely woven into the editorial of sport through logo exposure on a shirt, car, or stadium perimeter. With most sports events on the BBC at this time, brands were therefore increasingly able to reach big audiences and without being interrupted by advertising.

Next in line for a sponsor makeover was Test cricket and a five-year/£1m deal with little-known insurer Cornhill, to sponsor England's home Test matches, with West again working his magic at Lords and Television Centre by smoothing the way to allowing a bright yellow Cornhill logo to appear in the outfield. It was therefore impossible to escape Cornhill's presence at Test match grounds, and within five years their brand awareness had increased from two per cent to 20 per cent, which made them the second-most recalled insurer in the UK. It was now official. Sports sponsorship worked, and here was the high-profile case study to prove it.

#14 THE OFFICIAL PARTNER
(Argentina, 1978)

Horst Dassler and Patrick Nally were introduced in 1974 and hit it off straightaway. What could be better than combining Nally's marketing nous with the political clout Dassler had established for himself within world sport? They therefore decided to form an alliance to help the newly elected Havelange secure the money he needed to fulfil his election promises.

Within a few months, Dassler was in discussion with executives from Coca-Cola and pitched them the idea of becoming FIFA's first global sponsor, which was well received, and Nally and the newly appointed FIFA marketing manager, Sepp Blatter, flew to Atlanta to pitch Coke's global board – returning with a three-year/$1.2m commitment to support the president's plan to accelerate the growth of football in developing countries. With this success under their belts, Dassler and Nally set their sights on the next World Cup, which was being held in Argentina in 1978, and formalised their alliance by creating a new joint venture sponsorship sales company which they called SMPI.

If you watch old footage from the 1974 World Cup, you'll notice perimeter boards advertising brands such as Martini and Coke. However, this inventory had not been sold by FIFA, but directly by the local organising committee and their host venues. The SMPI approach was therefore revolutionary, since their idea was to target advertisers with a much more sophisticated sell and to act as FIFA's broker with companies who were keen to associate themselves with the World Cup. To show Havelange and the organisers in Buenos Aires how serious they were, Dassler and Nally also placed a tempting cash guarantee on the table in exchange for being granted the exclusive right to sell advertising at the 1978 host venues. However, in addition to controlling the perimeter advertising, they also wanted to include in their marketing packages the right to offer brands an association with the FIFA World Cup trademark and its mascot.

As Nally contemplated how to market these rights, he concluded competitive tension was going to be key to driving demand and that brands would pay a strategic premium for exclusivity. He therefore came up with the idea of 'category exclusivity', which meant that only one brand from each product category would be allowed to associate itself with the World Cup. It was a breakthrough idea that worked brilliantly too with Gillette, Coca-Cola, Phillips, KLM and Canon all signing up to become the official razor, soft drink, TV, airline and camera partner of the 1978 FIFA World Cup.

The work of SMPI caught the eye of several other sports keen to understand how they too could create marketing packages for their own events, with Nally subsequently hired by the IAAF to create a blueprint for their first World Championship, and by the ILTF to market the Davis Cup. They also found the money Chris Brasher needed to launch the first London Marathon and then made their biggest bet yet with a $10m minimum cash guarantee to FIFA to grant them the rights to market the 1982 World Cup with the partners from Argentina joined by newbies Seiko, Fuji and Camel as official partners.

The money was crucial to enable Havelange to fulfil his election promises and foundational to the Havelange legacy of increasing FIFA's sponsorship and media revenue from almost nothing when he took over in 1974, to reach $1.7bn by the time he hung up his boots 24 years later. Meanwhile, West Nally went on to become the training ground for the first cohort of sports marketers – people like Jochen Lenz, who went on to launch the UEFA Champions League; Michael Payne, who played such a pivotal role turning around the commercial fortunes of the IOC; and Karen Earl, who set up her much-admired sponsorship agency. As for the legacy of Patrick Nally, well, his idea of the official partner has proved an enduring one and is one of the reasons the sponsorship industry now generates $100bn a year. He therefore fully deserves his slot on our All-Stars team.

- - - - -

#15 THE SUPERSTATION
(Atlanta, 1976)

The investment in cable infrastructure and regional television accelerated rapidly across the United States during the 1960s and soon the industry's leaders realised live sport was crucial content to help them win and retain new subscribers. Cablevision subsequently agreed to buy the exclusive rights from the owners of Madison Square Garden to show the home games of the New York Knicks, while Ted Turner, the owner of WTCG, which served Atlanta, went a step further by acquiring his local baseball franchise the Atlanta Braves. In 1975 he was paying $500k a year for the rights to show their games and evidently figured a smart hedge against paying inflationary rights fees would be to simply own the franchise.

The Braves finished last in the National League West during Turner's first three years of ownership, but his strategy was right out of a Harvard textbook for how to execute vertical integration: Own the team. Own the content. Own the distribution channel. Own the customer. When Turner signed players, he therefore looked upon them as 'a programming cost', which must have pleased Marvin Miller no end after he offered Al Hrabosky $2.2m to pitch for the Braves. Here's author John Helyer's amusing description of the charismatic appeal of this player: 'Al Hrabosky was the made-for-TV relief pitcher. He wore a menacing Fu Manchu moustache. He stood behind the mound between hitters, facing the center-field camera and visibly psyched himself up for his next opponent. Then he'd whirl and purposefully stalk back up the mound. He was a great act and an OK reliever, and he was known as the "Mad Hungarian".'

If I was going to sit next to one man at the Rainmakers Hall of Fame dinner then I'd like it to be Ted Turner because I think his story is fascinating. He was a highly ambitious man who inherited his father's Atlanta billboard business at the age of 27 and diversified the company into local radio. With the advent of satellite delivery and his ownership of a baseball franchise, the Braves, he then expanded the footprint of Turner Communications further into TV.

His founding station was called the 'Superstation', which launched on 17 December 1976 and became one of the first to connect to cable operators via satellite, uploading the signal from his studio in Atlanta and bouncing it off the RCA transponder into millions of homes in the Midwest. To fund the venture, Turner charged cable companies a carriage fee of 15 cents per subscriber per month, and soon vast areas of rural America without a local TV station or baseball team to support had become committed fans of the Braves.

However, it wasn't in the MLB owner manual to allow pro baseball games to get beamed into rival franchise areas. The other team owners were therefore furious with Turner and told Bowie Khun to suspend him from league meetings and to lobby Congress to get this station banned. Khun subsequently argued that the Superstation was devaluing the broadcast rights of the other team owners, while Turner counter-argued that he was simply offering consumers choice and trying to compete with the monopolistic behaviour of the American sports franchise system. 'I asked legislators to imagine a world where the heads of Ford, GM and Chrysler sat down and the Ford guy says, "I get everything east of the Mississippi. General Motors, you get west of the Mississippi and Chrysler you can have the state of Michigan." 'In the end, Congress sided with Turner. Satellites were revolutionising all walks of life in the late 70s and so why, they ruled, should broadcasting be protected from such innovation? Within a few years, the channel was generating $177m from 20 million committed subscribers attracted by the Superstation's diet of old movies, sitcoms and, of course, hours and hours of coverage of the Atlanta Braves.

After the gloom and political tension of the early 1970s, the decade therefore ended with a buoyant US TV advertising market which was providing the money needed by CBS, ABC and NBC to pay decent rights fees to the top sports. The NFL teams were also now earning more money from selling their TV rights than they were from selling matchday tickets and so having figured out how network TV and cable channels could co-exist, America's top sports properties were getting excited about the future. The economy was booming, competition was driving up demand, and the TV networks were flush with advertisers. The 80s therefore looked 'Made for TV'.

PART FIVE
Made for TV

'81, 82, 83, 84 ... New Gold Dream'
— Simple Minds

The 1980s

Liverpool FC. LA 1984. Maradona

ON 4 JUNE 1984, Columbia Records released Bruce Springsteen's seminal album, *Born in the USA,* which was the perfect anthem to announce the birth of a new global entertainment business. In January of that year, Steve Jobs and Chiat Day rewrote the rules of advertising and turned the Superbowl into the most lucrative media-buy on the planet. Two months later in a small gym in Utah, two young men lit a fire underneath the sport of basketball as Phil Knight rewrote the playbook for how brands and athletes worked together. In the summer, Peter Ueberroth showed everyone how to make money from hosting an Olympic Games, and on an ongoing basis, Roone Arledge continued to scare the living daylights out of NBC and CBS with bids of $225m for the Summer Olympics, $600m for the NFL and $309m for the 1988 Calgary Winter Olympics. When we look back at the game-changing moments that have taken place in the modern sports marketing business it's therefore striking how many of them took place during the four game-changing years of 1981, 82, 83 and 84, which were fuelled by television's newfound love affair with sport, a burgeoning advertising market and the myopic ambition of a small group of determined people.

The 80s was also a period of great change in Britain, when the ripped jeans of punk rock were replaced by the frilly shirts of the New Romantics and young people became glued to MTV and freed by the Sony Walkman. Change was also in the political air with the radical pro market economics of Margaret Thatcher, who cut taxes, sold off the nationalised industries and encouraged us to buy our own home. If you lived in London and the south your feeling of wealth was therefore greatly enhanced and went up a further notch in 1986 following deregulation of the financial services industry which created thousands of new jobs in the City. A moment in time the media branded 'the Big Bang' and delivered the most prolonged period of economic growth Britain had seen since the end of the Second World War.

Thatcher was also fixated on making Britain's labour market more competitive, and one of her other key objectives was to reform the unions and create a more flexible labour market, a policy which proved disastrous for millions of skilled workers as an intense period of de-industrialisation ripped through the once proud communities we heard so much about earlier. Hundreds of thousands of jobs were subsequently lost in the shipyards of the Clyde, the coal mines of South Wales and the steel industry of Sheffield, with all three industries seen as collateral damage on the path to making Britain PLC more competitive.

UB40 sang about the soaring unemployment in Britain but 'I am the one in ten' was too much to accept for Britain's miners and led to a bitter strike and months of pitched battles with the police. As the daughter of one miner reflected 40 years later, 'The pit was life, it was everything. We might not have had much money, but we were honest folk. Love and safety and security: 1984 to 1985 removed all of that.'

Societal anger also spilled over into the world of football in 1985 with turf wars breaking out up and down the country and mob football back in fashion, when Sunderland fans clashed with Chelsea supporters at Stamford Bridge and a serious riot broke out at Kenilworth Road between supporters of Millwall and Luton. English football's own *annus horribilis* then continued a few months later with the horror of the Bradford fire at the Valley Parade stadium which killed 56 spectators, and a further 39 people died following crowd trouble between supporters of Liverpool and Juventus at the 1985 European Cup Final.

Unfortunately, Margaret Thatcher had no interest in trying to understand football fandom and was taken aback when FA secretary Ted Croker told her this wasn't a football problem but a much broader societal issue her government had inflicted on football. Good for you, Ted, but, as ever, the 'Iron Lady' wasn't for turning and looked upon football hooliganism as a law-and-order problem that would only get solved through heavier policing, national identity cards and a ban on alcohol at grounds.

Who are Accrington Stanley?

Despite this undercurrent of societal tension, a decade of economic growth proved to be good news for the TV advertising industry with more and more agencies proposing television advertising to their clients and the size of the worldwide TV market reaching £110bn by the end of the decade. As one media buyer once said to me, 'You lot hand us a bucket and we simply chuck money into it,' and it was true; owning a TV franchise at this time was a licence to print money. In the cosy UK TV monopoly of the late 80s, life was therefore very uncomplicated, and the process would go something like this: a creative agency like Saatchi would sell their client a 'big TV idea' and if their media buyers could drag themselves out of the Carpenters Arms they would tell them how, where and when to run the campaign. Once the budget was approved, these buyers then called us and we'd haggle for a few days over what share of their campaign budget we were getting and once that was agreed the campaign was booked into gigantic computers taking up the entire desk. For the next four weeks we'd then have a daily arm-wrestle over the quality of the programming on the schedule and once the campaign was over we'd go out for lunch on expenses to celebrate a job well done. It was a ritual that was great fun and life-changing for me when I took the Vitbe bread media buyer, Alison Lister, out for lunch in Soho, as a few years later she became my wife.

However, the toxic environment surrounding British sport meant it lagged well behind the television industry in its commercialisation and by 1985 the UK sponsorship industry was worth only £200m, with ad agencies showing very little interest in getting involved other than casting the likes of Ian Botham in Shredded Wheat commercials or getting Frank Bruno to promote HP sauce with a cheesy endline which definitely didn't flow from the silky pen of David Ogilvy: 'Only one sauce can give all Frank's favourite foods the necessary punch.' One ad which did, however, make people smile was for the National Dairy Council, with Accrington Stanley FC put on the map in a famous commercial featuring two young Liverpool fans who were talking to each other about the benefits of drinking milk: 'When I grow up he [Ian Rush] says if I drink enough milk I'll be good enough to play for Accrington Stanley,' says the first boy. 'Accrington Stanley? Who are they?' answers the second boy in a thick Scouse accent.

Given the poor image of football and their cosy duopoly, the BBC and ITV therefore managed to get away with paying modest rights fees to the clubs who could have really benefited from their support at this time, since they faced fierce economic headwinds linked to the rising cost of policing and trying to maintain their crumbling stadia. With unemployment within football's northern heartlands running at 15 per cent, many loyal fans also couldn't afford to go to the game and others like my dad and I were put off by all the aggro. Matchday attendance during the 1984/5 season therefore fell sharply to 17 million for the first time since records began, which was 40 per cent lower than the heady days of the early 70s when Liverpool, Leeds and Derby ruled supreme. The FA and Football League knew they had to do something to ease the financial pressure on the clubs and so lifted some of the restrictions that were holding them back: to encourage more commercial people into the game they therefore allowed club directors to be paid a salary; to encourage new investors the profit distribution cap was raised to 15 per cent; and, to generate more revenue, clubs were allowed to carry sponsor branding on the front of their team shirts, with Liverpool the first big club to sign a commercial partnership in 1979 as they unveiled Hitachi as their first sponsor before switching to Crown Paints in 1982. Two years later, Arsenal began their 17-year relationship with JVC and Manchester United landed a record £500k deal with Sharp. Meanwhile, the Football League also embraced brands with the League Cup changing its name to the Milk Cup in a three-year deal worth £6m and Canon paying £10m to become the first title sponsor of the Football League.

These sums are of course tiny in comparison with today's shirt deals, but 40 years ago when clubs were fighting for their financial lives, they made a significant difference when we consider that Liverpool only generated £2.4m from their title-winning season of 1979/80. Here's what chairman John Smith had to say after announcing the deal with Hitachi to disgruntled Liverpool fans: 'The days are gone when a club like ours could control their destiny on the money coming through the turnstiles. It is absolutely essential to generate income from other sources. We have agreed to this deal to help safeguard the long-term financial interest of the club.'

- - - - -

#16 THE LAUNCH OF ESPN

(Connecticut, 9 September 1979)

Someone who had been observing the activities of the Superstation with great interest was Bill Rasmussen – the ex-head of communications of the New England Whalers – who was looking to raise money to launch America's first dedicated sports channel. As he explained to *Forbes Magazine* in 1979, he found it a tough sell: 'I got a $9,000 advance on my credit card, Scott [his son] put in some money, my family put in some money, and we started looking for investors. I remember going in to visit Taft Broadcasting, and the head of Taft figuratively patting me on the back and saying not only would our idea not work, but cable was going to be gone in a few years as well.' Eventually, Rasmussen secured funding from the John Paul Getty investment arm and called his station the Entertainment and Sports Programming Network (ESPN). Like Ted Turner and HBO, he also reserved satellite time with RCA but went much further in his commitment to produce content by booking an entire 24-hour transponder.

On 9 September 1979 ESPN went live from its (nearly finished) production centre in Bristol, Connecticut with Scott providing the following rallying cry in a pre-launch interview with *Sports Illustrated*: 'What we're creating here is a network for sports junkies. This is not programming for soft-core sports fans who like to watch the NFL game and then switch to the news. This is a network for people who like to watch a college football game, then a wrestling match, gymnastics meet, and a soccer game, followed by an hour-long talk show on sports.'

Rasmussen hired Chet Simmons from ABC as his president with the brief to figure out how to fill up 24 hours of programming. Simmons found the early days tough going, since he was handed a limited budget to buy sports rights and so his producers became skilled at squeezing out the pips from any opportunity that came their way. In 1980, for example, they broadcast the first ever live NFL-draft, showed early rounds from the US Open and random softball and Aussie Rules games on tape delay. Their flagship deal was with the National Collegiate Athletic Association (NCAA) to cover 15 college sports. Here's Rasmussen explaining his pitch to Walter Byers, then executive director at the NCAA: 'NBC had the national TV contract back then but only aired the Final Four and some regional tournament games, a handful of contests in all. I told Mr. Byers, "We want to do every single game you haven't committed to the [major] networks." He said, "Every single one?" I said "yes" and he said, "Do you mean to tell me that if Lamar Tech plays Weber State in some regional first-round game, you'd put that on the air?'" And the answer, of course, was 'yes' since it filled up two hours of airtime.

ESPN earned its stripes during those early years and by 1982 the cable companies had grown to really like the channel, since it was proving popular with their hard-core sports fans. They were therefore happy to include it in their program bundle and to sell ESPN inventory to advertisers, with the first big deal with Budweiser who allocated $1.4m of their $400m annual media budget to ESPN. It worked, too, since they re-signed the following year with a much-increased commitment. This is what Michael Roarty, Bud's director of marketing had to say about their early support of the channel: 'We gave them $1 million that first year. And if we hadn't, they'd have gone under. I believed the beer drinker was a sports lover. The next year we gave them $5 million. I think it turned out to be the best investment we've ever made.'

Despite this welcome deal, Rasmussen and his team were still losing $1.5m a month, and while Getty Ventures continued to support the business, they'd lost confidence in Bill and Scott. In 1983, Bill Grimes was subsequently hired from CBS to turn the company around and quickly realised the business couldn't be sustained by advertising. He therefore visited the top cable companies and asked them to pay him a distribution fee to carry the channel. At the time, there was precedent for this with premium channels like HBO and the Superstation, but not for a random sports channel with no significant rights. However, one of the lessons we're learning about rainmakers is that they think differently to the rest of us, and many, like a guy I used to work with at Channel Four, use the art of the deadline to get what they want. His name was Matt

Shreeve ('Shreevy') and he used to give media buyers 30 seconds to say yes or no to a deal if he felt the negotiation had stalled. He'd then hum the theme tune to our popular quiz show *Countdown,* and if they hadn't made up their minds within the allotted 30 seconds the deal was off. 'I mean it,' he used to say after 15 seconds, and word soon got out that he did, after he packed up his bag when time was up. 'C'mon , we're off,' he would say, and we'd trot off behind him, trying not to laugh. Grimes didn't go that far, but he did tell the Cablevision boss that unless he agreed to pay up then his customers would no longer be able to watch ESPN the following Monday.

Charles Dolan was one of America's most successful cable operators and unused to the experience of being hustled by a start-up sports channel. However, he obviously concluded he didn't want to risk losing some of his most loyal subscribers over a few cents he could easily pass on to his customers and so eventually agreed to pay Grimes ten cents per subscriber – per month. It was less than the 15 Turner was getting, but still a game-changer for ESPN.

When Getty Oil was bought by Texaco, they sold ESPN for $227m to their long-term admirers ABC, and three years later, the station had a crucial rainmaking moment when it broadcast the 1987 America's Cup from Western Australia. We mentioned in Chapter One the rich history of this event, which was first raced for in 1885 but, despite many challenges, no one had managed to wrestle the trophy away from the NYYC until Aussie skipper John Bertrand won it in 1983. That traumatised members of the NYYC, who turned their backs on losing skipper Dennis Conner, while he was equally determined to redeem himself and launched a rival campaign with the San Diego Yacht Club. This therefore became the compelling narrative that made insomniacs of millions of Americans and attracted a slew of new premium advertisers to ESPN.

The success of the America's Cup coverage and the strong relationship Grimes had built up with Peter Rozelle then led to the station's first significant rights contract: a three-year/$50m deal granting ESPN rights to four pre-season NFL games, eight Sunday evening matches, the Pro Bowl and hours of shoulder programming produced by NFL Films that the networks couldn't find space to air. Their producers then packaged it all up as *Sunday Night Football* and by the end of the first year of televising the NFL, it had become the first cable channel to achieve 50 per cent penetration of US households.

#17 NEW IOC PRESIDENT
(Moscow, August 1980)

After the horror of Munich, financial meltdown at Montreal and the Moscow boycott, the IOC entered the 1980s in real trouble. The backing of corporate America had always been crucial to the economic health of the Olympic Games, with the IOC banking on their 30 per cent share of the TV money raised from the Moscow Games. The news that the White House was banning NBC from covering Moscow therefore dealt a near-fatal blow to the organisation, leaving them with $200k of cash in the bank and only $2m of assets to use as future collateral.

The long-term economic prospects for the Games weren't helped either by the spiralling cost of staging the event after Montreal incurred $1bn of financial overruns from hosting the 1976 Games. Lake Placid and Los Angeles were therefore sole bidders to host the 1980 Winter and 1984 Summer Games. Michael Payne describes the dire situation the IOC found itself in like this: 'At the start of the 1980s, the situation looked bleak. Given the political boycotts and unappealing commercial proposition, it was little wonder that the IOC was having great difficulty finding any city willing to stage the Games. The risks were simply too great.'

Horst Dassler had discovered in football that building relationships at the highest echelons of the sport was indeed a far more effective marketing strategy for his company than negotiating messy boot deals. He was aware too that elections were being held during the Moscow Games to find the next president of the IOC, and so offered to advise his preferred candidate over how developing a global marketing strategy for the Olympics could help him win votes, like it had for João Havelange.

Juan Antonio Samaranch was a far less abrasive character than his predecessor and supportive of embracing the Olympic Games as a commercial marketing platform. He'd also lived in Moscow since 1977 while serving as Spain's foreign ambassador to the Soviet Union, and so was the ideal choice to succeed Lord Killanin, who was happy to retire to Ireland after presiding over the rollercoaster of the past eight years. Dassler was confident the Games offered brands a strong commercial platform and struck up a good relationship with Samaranch as the two men set to work developing a plan to secure the financial viability of the Olympics through corporate sponsorship. However, unlike the 1978 World Cup, which had largely been sold on the exposure brands would get on TV, a red line for Samaranch and his colleagues was offering venue branding. He wanted 'clean venues', and so it was crucial to secure approval from as many of the individual national Olympic committees (NOCs) as possible to include their domestic marketing rights in the worldwide packages Dassler wanted to sell.

At the time, there were 167 NOCs, and many were suspicious of the IOC's motives for this marketing plan following the legacy of mistrust that Samaranch had inherited. Another significant challenge was to interest corporate America, as he knew the United States had to be one of the nations that opted in. And they were already successfully exploiting the five rings. Unlike most of the other inexperienced NOCs, the chairman of the United States Olympic Committee (USOC) was also a highly skilled negotiator after having served under President Ford as treasury secretary; William E. Simon therefore made it perfectly clear to Samaranch that he had no intention of handing over his marketing rights unless he was made a significant offer. In the end, 154 NOCs were tempted by the cash commitments and Simon was also eventually persuaded by a generous revenue share offer from the IOC, that journalist Mihir Bose summarises like this in his book *The Spirit of the Game*: 'The original IOC formula for distributing the marketing money was that half should go to the city hosting the Games. The other half was meant to be split 80 per cent to the national Olympic committees and 20 per cent for the IOC. The USOC insisted it could not be treated like other national Olympic committees and secured half the amount intended for all the world Olympic committees put together. As George Orwell wrote in *Animal Farm*, "All animals are equal. But some animals are more equal than others."'

The second important part of the Samaranch plan was to make the Olympic calendar of events more appealing for would-be host nations by introducing the idea of 'demonstration sports'. They included tennis, which was riding high in the era of Borg and McEnroe, and golf with Americans Jack Nicklaus, Tom Watson and Lee Trevino dominating the majors. Samaranch, therefore, announced the IOC would allow future hosts to nominate several sports that would resonate strongly with home fans and that the Summer and Winter Olympics should be held alternately, every two years, rather than in the same calendar year. Not only would this relieve the organisational burden on the IOC, but the US networks welcomed the idea too, since holding two Olympics in one year saturated the North American ad market. Here's what Payne had to say about the Samaranch plan: 'The Olympic movement had a choice: to continue its amateurish and peripheral way into extinction or to re-invent its organisation and outlook for the modern age. It chose the latter.'

#18 THE CONCORDE AGREEMENT
(Paris, 19 January 1981)

In 1981, there were two big sticking points for Bernie Ecclestone to agree with the equally dogmatic head of the governing body for motorsport (FIA) over the future direction of travel for F1. The first, was to decide which organisation had the authority to sanction the annual race calendar and to monetise the rights, while the second related to who should take the lead on setting the technical rules for the sport. The team principals were frustrated by the increasingly acrimonious stand-off between Bernie and Jean-Marie Balestre and became especially concerned when he threatened the FIA with a breakaway World Championship. To end the brinkmanship, Enzo Ferrari and John Hogan of Philip Morris (who sponsored both Ferrari and McLaren) were thus despatched to Paris on behalf of the FOCA to broker an accord. The deal was named after the street upon which it was signed, with the Concorde Agreement handing authority for technical rule-setting to the FIA, and the commercial rights to FOCA. Ecclestone was delighted and wasted no time inserting a new clause in his circuit contracts that assigned television rights for every race to the FOCA.

We shall come to see how valuable these rights have become, so this seems an extraordinary thing for the promoters to have agreed to, although we must remember that in the early 80s most broadcasters had very little interest in showing live F1 races. Not only did they fill up two to three hours of valuable weekend airtime, but race start times were haphazard due to the global nature of the F1 race calendar, and the numerous crashes that took place in this era which resulted in long periods of inactivity while tracks were cleared of debris. The sport was, however, entering a golden era of rivalry between Nikki Lauda, Mario Andretti and Alain Prost, and so Bernie approached the European Broadcast Union (EBU) in search of a Europe-wide TV deal.

The EBU was a trade body of the leading European state broadcasters such as ITV and RTL, who had started bidding collectively for global events to share the cost of production and satellite bookings. To the delight of Ecclestone the response from them was an enthusiastic one with 30 stations (including the BBC) willing to make a commitment to televise the 15 races scheduled for 1984. Sure, the rights fee was a modest $3m, but the broadcasters were prepared to work together to cover the cost of production, which meant team sponsors were going to benefit from 30 hours of global brand exposure and a tenfold increase in media value.

If you watch old footage from the 1960s, you'll notice random branding for oil and tyre companies around the racetrack, and a few retro brands like Cinzano and Martini buying into the lifestyle values of F1. However, with this new global platform, Bernie wanted the presentation of the sport to look far slicker, with a warning shot occurring in 1985 when the BBC refused to broadcast what they considered to be poor-quality pictures from Spa. He therefore decided to take a leaf out of the NFL playbook and bring TV production in-house, along with limiting the number of trackside advertisers to only six brands to clean up what he believed looked on TV like logo soup. He was also furious when the Williams team turned up at Silverstone with a double-decker bus to house their entourage and decided he wanted to turn race weekends into a premium VIP experience like at Ascot and Wimbledon. With a further tweak to circuit contracts, these rights –

along with trackside advertising – were novated to a new division called All Sport Management with the 'Paddock Pass' quickly emerging as one of the most sought-after VIP invitations in the sporting calendar.

'Money for nothing'

By 1995, estimates were therefore that through a combination of circuit fees, TV money, trackside advertising and hospitality packages, Ecclestone was clearing $300m from his share of the commercial activities of FOCA, with the only cloud on the horizon being that the original Concorde Agreement was soon to expire. To consolidate his grip on the sport he therefore needed a new one signed, and had been working the corridors of power in world motorsport to make sure his nemesis Balestre wouldn't get in the way. The outcome of this lobbying was that his good friend Max Mosley was appointed the new president and so a new deal was agreed upon without the commotion of the first. Mosley was then asked if he would permit the transfer of the new FOCA/FIA contracts (incorporating all the commercial rights and agreements relating to F1) into a new holding company called FOCA Administration Limited, which was controlled by Ecclestone and his family trust.

The coup was complete: from humble origins selling second-hand Ford Capris on the streets of London, to one of the wealthiest people in Britain. Here's Bowers' summary of how he pulled it off: 'Formula One's development into a global business owed everything to two events; Ecclestone had soundly beaten Balestre [in 1981] and, second, he had halted fragmentation of the sport, whereby each country presented a different spectacle. His new financial model in Europe and Australia compelled circuit owners to accept his standards and pay for everything, and, critically, receive no income except from the entry tickets. "I would have taken the entry ticket money too if they'd let me," said Ecclestone.'

#19 THE CREATION OF ISL
(Lucerne, October 1982)

By 1982, Dassler had mysteriously fallen out with Patrick Nally, liquidated SMPI, and set up a new company called International Sport & Leisure (ISL), which had the backing of Dentsu – Japan's largest ad agency. Their sports business was led by Hayashi Takashi, who had been getting increasingly concerned about how their major competitor, Hakuhodu, was winning new business by pitching sponsorship ideas to Japanese companies. Takashi met Dassler after brokering a deal for Fuji to become the official film partner of Spain '82, and subsequently told colleagues he believed a partnership with the boss of Adidas was the best way for Dentsu to develop into a serious player in the burgeoning world of sports marketing.

This new partnership propelled Dassler into the big time. Not only did he now have a pipeline of ambitious brands to tap into, but he could use the Dentsu credit card to make bolder guarantees to secure the mandates he wanted to sell the big properties. Their media-buying expertise also enabled ISL to enter the world of broadcast rights, as Takashi devised an innovative business model which mirrored the strategy Dentsu used in the 1960s to take control of the Japanese primetime ad market. This involved buying rights from sports properties in the name of Dentsu and broking them on to clients. These payments became known as 'minimum guarantees' and became highly attractive to cash-strapped international sports federations after ISL raised 200 million Swiss francs from broking sponsorship packages for the 1986 World Cup to Coke, Gillette, Fuji, Canon and Toshiba. At this time

Japanese electronics companies were also at the cutting edge of broadcast technology which the ISL team realised was valuable collateral to help broker smaller deals. They therefore created what became known as 'official suppliers' and took commission on the value of the product they bartered such as free Seiko timing equipment or JVC screens in exchange for smaller marketing packages with an equivalent value.

Samaranch was duly elected IOC president in Moscow and proposed to his colleagues that ISL be appointed to develop a marketing plan for Seoul '88, which became known as 'the Olympic Partner' strategy (TOP), and leaned on ISL's learnings from selling the previous two World Cups. Although with unbranded venues they proved to be a much harder sell, since deal values couldn't be justified against brand exposure metrics alone. With a rate card of $11m per partner, the ISL team knew they therefore had to develop a much more sophisticated sell.

At Montreal, for example, it had been a free-for-all over who could associate themselves with the Games, with more than 40 sponsors paying an average rights fee of $50k. Moscow, meanwhile, issued 7,000 licences to manufacture official product, and even Lake Placid with the burgeoning North American ad market to tap up, could only generate $26m in cash. ISL, thus went to market with the opportunity for brands to benefit through an exclusive association with the positive image of the Olympic Games. Michael Payne summarises their strategy as follows: 'The basic marketing concept ... was to bundle all rights together – the IOC, the Winter Olympics, the Summer Olympic Games and over 160 National Olympic Committees – into a single four-year exclusive marketing package, offering companies one-stop shopping for their global Olympic involvement.'

In the end, nine companies pledged $96m, which included the IOC's regular supporters of Coca-Cola and Kodak, joined by new partners such as Brother and Panasonic, who were recruited through the Dentsu network. This is how Carole A. Pressley, senior vice-president for marketing at FedEx, summarised the attractiveness of the new proposition for her brand: 'We have chosen to help all teams and all participants, rather than one particular team, in one particular sport, from one particular country. TOP has enabled us to do so.' The trusty lever of category exclusivity worked its magic again too, with another founding partner, Visa, unable to pass up the opportunity to poke fun at Amex for missing out, with their agency coming up with the brutal line, 'Bring your Visa card, because the Olympics don't take American Express'. Through their tie-up with Dassler, Dentsu, therefore, became the first big ad agency group to enter the sports marketing business. Their shareholding in ISL enabled them to carve out the rights they wanted for their clients, while benefiting also through shareholder dividends: 'double bubble' as it affectionately became known in the sports industry.

Despite the untimely death of Horst Dassler at the age of 53, ISL went on to establish itself as a significant power-broker in the sports industry by making multi-million-dollar cash guarantees to sell rights to the World Cup, the World Athletics Championships, and the ATP Tour. We shall come to see the financial bubble this created, but despite their eventual demise there's no denying the game-changing role this company played in developing the modern sports marketing industry.

- - - - -

#20 THE END OF AMATEURISM
(Baden Baden, 3 September 1982)

With the increased exposure sport was now getting on television, a few media-friendly athletes started to do well from personal endorsement deals. Chris Evert, with the carefully manicured 'girl next door' image IMG cultivated for her, and the flashy smile of Kevin Keegan proving alluring to brands. However, most sportsmen and women still needed to earn a living through other means to put food on the table, as the notion of the amateur athlete became an idea well past its sell-by date. It was an ethos which was also proving impossible for sports leaders to police, as top track stars like double Olympic champion Lasse Viren, and 400m world record holder Edwin Moses made it clear to promoters that they expected to be paid to race. The going rate was around $2,500, which meant their event only had to sell 500 extra tickets to cover the outlay of one top athlete – a no-brainer when it could get promoted with the X-factor of an Olympic champion on the start line. Few, therefore, had a problem paying appearance fees and some even actively hired 'fixers' to recruit athletes and hand over the brown paper bags in stadium car parks. A change in mindset was therefore badly needed – especially in athletics, where anxiety levels were rising with rumour of the top runners plotting a breakaway league. Well, the golfers, tennis pros and cricketers had done it – so why not the blue-ribband sport of the Olympics? As well as this threat, IAAF president Adriaan Paulen was worried that the uncomfortable drama surrounding Munich and Moscow had the potential to kill off the Olympic Games. He therefore hired SMPI to come up with a blueprint for his own World Championships.

'Shamateurism: playing a sport while officially being an amateur' –
The Oxford English Dictionary

A potential solution was presented in 1981 by a group of athletes led by Moses, who came up with the idea of the Athlete Trust Fund (ATF). This they suggested was a kind of savings account within which athletes would deposit their appearance money, prize money and endorsement deals until they retired. During their career, the athlete's own national federations would then approve the drawdown of legitimate day-to-day expenses and any excess would be cashed out when the athlete retired. This was exactly what Paulen and Samaranch had been looking for: a modern plan that acknowledged athletes should be allowed to earn a living from their sport but still keeping the spirit of amateurism alive. The ATF was therefore approved at the 1982 IOC Congress with Samaranch encouraging all the other international federations to adopt a similar approach. By the late 1980s, most of the top sports had become comfortable with the workings of the ATF, and the IOC had also relaxed their ruling for participation in the Olympics by allowing professional footballers, golfers, tennis players, and even NBA All-Stars to compete at the Games. Samaranch therefore figured out something none of his predecessors could work out, which was how to allow athletes to earn a living from playing sport, but continue to respect the values of the Olympic movement. This is how he explained the fine line to journalist David Miller: 'De Coubertin's philosophy existed at the beginning of the century. We are now near the end of the century and must move with the times. Of course, it is possible for Sebastian Coe to make a lot of money. I am happy for him. What makes him Olympian is not the money he earns away from the Olympics, but how he deports himself. He's sporting to his opponents, speaks out for what he believes, and gives time for developing the interests of others.'

#21 CALGARY TV RIGHTS AUCTION
(Lucerne, January 1984)

Brundage and Avery had themselves always played a passive role in TV negotiations and left the organising committees to close deals with broadcasters, on the understanding they would get their 30 per cent cut. However, when Samaranch took charge, he became annoyed when he found out that the IOC were collecting only $33m from the blockbuster $225m contract ABC had signed with the Los Angeles Olympic Committee, after their board deducted $125m of facility and infrastructure costs from the revenue share calculation.

Having seen how the NFL rights auction had played out in New York, Samaranch therefore spotted his opportunity to drive up the value of the next Winter Games in Calgary, which, due to the favourable time zone, he knew would be a much bigger ratings winner in the United States than the previous European venue. He therefore asked for permission from his colleagues to oversee this negotiation and appointed IMG executive Barry Frank as his advisor, a man who had previously worked for Roone Arledge at ABC and so knew all his moves.

The first recommendation Frank made was the unusual one of inviting all three TV networks to Lausanne to participate in a face-to-face auction. To further raise the stakes, he also proposed that the event schedule should run over 16 rather than 14 days – which would build in a further valuable weekend of coverage for advertisers. In addition, he suggested Samaranch should signal an openness towards scheduling the events that were of most interest to US sports fans, like ice-hockey, in primetime, which would further drive the ratings.

After much back-and-forth in the elegant surroundings of the Lausanne Palace Hotel, ABC eventually won the auction with their final offer of $309m, which was five times more than Arledge had paid for the rights to Sarajevo. The bidding went to six rounds with CBS dropping out at $190m, and NBC and ABC tied after round five on $300m. The media industry was agog, and with good reason too, since even though ABC won the auction, they ended up losing $65m on the contract. Arledge was furious with how he'd been played by his old assistant and describes the emotion of that weekend like this: 'Another round. We went to $300m – $19.5m higher than NBC, and in between, Jim [head of rights at ABC] got hold of Barry and started shouting at him, "This is crazy. It has to stop!" "I know", Barry said, "I'm trying."' Samaranch and Frank were not going to receive an invitation to the 1984 ABC summer BBQ, but with this deal his presidency was off to a flying start and despite how unpopular that mad weekend in Lausanne proved to be, it arguably saved the Olympic Games from ruin.

- - - - -

#22 APPLE AND THE 1984 SUPERBOWL

(Tampa, 22 January 1984)

After the NFL and AFL agreed to merge, it took 18 months to codify the details of the union. To excite fans, the committee created to oversee the coming-together met in the summer of 1966 to plan the new season and Lamar Hunt asked about the timing of the Championship game, which he mischievously referred to as 'the Super Bowl'. Until that meeting, there was no such thing, and no one had even been briefed to come up with a new name, but with merger plans moving at speed, and no Bill Bernbach on hand to work his magic, the name stuck after the networks started referring to the final game of the season as 'Super Sunday'.

Fast forward to the 1980s. The golden age for advertising and the decade when advertiser spend tripled as brands discovered the storytelling power of television. What was also interesting about this time was how the globalisation trend was shaping the ad agency business with creative inspiration coming not from Madison Avenue but from British agencies. We talked earlier about the influence of CDP, but who can remember the 60-second extravaganzas created for British Airways by Saatchi & Saatchi? 'The World's favourite airline' – serenaded by the operatic 'Flower Duo' soundtrack helped transform a once-tired state-owned airline into the carrier of choice for the 1980s business traveller. And what about the famous Levi ad created by John Hegarty and his BBH team who had model Nick Kamen stripping down to his undies in a laundrette to the soundtrack of 'I Heard it Through the Grapevine', making jeans cool and Motown hot again with a new generation of fans. Then there was THAT ad in 1984, created for the disciples of Apple by New York start-up Chiat Day as a parody of George Orwell's dystopian novel and aptly called ... *1984*.

> *'On January 24, Apple Computer will introduce Macintosh. And you'll see why 1984 won't be like 1984'.*

If you've not seen this ad then please watch it on YouTube. It's a timeless epic, written by Jay Chiat, directed by Ridley Scott, and championed by Steve Jobs. A commercial that cost millions to produce and yet ran only once in the centre-break of the 1984 Super Bowl and a few times in cinema. The total media budget was therefore less than $1m with the cost of this single spot in the Super Bowl swallowing up half the budget. *Campaign Magazine* is the trade journal for the advertising industry and summarised the impact of *1984* as follows: 'The commercial revolutionised the way high-tech products were promoted, the empowerment they could bring and how they could combat conformity and boost originality. Apple sales topped $150m in the 100 days following the debut of *1984*.'

As a sporting spectacle, Super Bowl XVIII ended up an uneventful 38-9 win for the LA Raiders v the Washington

Redskins. However, the action that day wasn't taking place on the pitch, but in the half-time ad break: a moment in time that propelled the Super Bowl into the most important event in the US advertising calendar and, by 1994, 30 seconds in the Super Bowl, was selling for $1m and had increased to $3.5m by 2012. By 2024 (powered by Taylor Swift) the event attracted an audience of 120 million in the United States and generated an astonishing $600m in ad revenue for Fox Sports as the cost of 30 seconds of advertising soared to $7m. Here's how *Campaign* summarises the legacy of this TV commercial: '1984 established the NFL Super Bowl game not only as an essential sporting fixture, but as the annual showcase for the best TV advertising. Every year on the first Sunday in February, agencies and their clients roll out their most sensational work for more than 90 million TV viewers. And because it's a premium live event, it stubbornly resists ad-skipping technology. On the contrary, great commercials have become part of the reason for tuning in. If you're looking to build brand awareness among American adults aged 35 and under, the Super Bowl is one of the quickest ways of doing it – if not exactly the cheapest.'

- - - - -

#23 THE NBA PLAY-OFF FINALS
(12 June 1984)

By the late 70s, the NBA was suffering from a serious image problem and most of its franchises were losing money. Television ratings were poor, performance-enhancing drugs were a problem and few sponsors wanted to be associated with the game. The sport needed a rainmaker and eventually found one in the shape of David Stern, a 40-year lawyer from Brooklyn who was appointed commissioner in 1984. However, NBA's transformation pre-dates Stern and tracks back to the campus arena of the University of Utah, which was the location for our next gamechanger – the 1979 NCAA college basketball final between Michigan State and Indiana State.

The significance of this game was that it was the first time Larry Bird and Earvin Johnson Junior met each other on a basketball court. Bird was playing for Michigan, while Johnson wore the colours of Indiana, who came out on top that day with a match-winning performance – but the real winner was the NBA, since the game attracted a TV audience of over 50 million and ignited a 12-year rivalry that would push the sport into the major league of US sports.

Larry Bird was 23, white, shy and from a small town in Indiana called French Lick. He played rough and tough and had no interest in being popular on or off the court. Meanwhile, Earvin 'Magic' Johnson, was black, confident and from an early age dreamt of nothing other than playing in the NBA: they were therefore opposites caught in the headlights of a nation trying to deal with the far-reaching problems of racial tension and inequality.

Despite their different backgrounds, these two men did, however, have two things in common. The first was that they were 6ft 9in tall and so were often unplayable on a basketball court. And second, they were both drafted after the 1979 NCAA final, with Bird joining the Boston Celtics and Johnson signed by the LA Lakers. Neither team had won the NBA Championship for years, but that all changed after Bird and Johnson joined their ranks, with the Lakers winning/finishing runner-up in eight of the ten NBA finals held in the 1980s, and the Celtics winning three and losing two. The high-water mark for the Bird v Magic rivalry happened in the final game of the 1984 play-off final, which the Celtics won 109-102 and attracted the largest-ever NBA audience. It was an 'aha' moment for Stern, who had been shown that player rivalries held the key, and so briefed his producers to ramp up the Bird v

Johnson narrative and look out for other interesting duels to amplify within the other NBA franchises.

David Stern passed away in 2020 having dedicated 30 years of his life to developing the NBA brand. His legacy was to turn a sport which had completely lost its way into one that in 2016 signed $24bn of TV deals, and multi-million sponsorships with Google, PepsiCo and Louis Vuitton, an unthinkable scenario in 1984 when CBS were sole bidder for the rights and willing to pay only $23m to televise ten games (most of which were also aired on tape delay to avoid clashing with *Dallas* and *The Dukes of Hazard).* The secret to this sport's extraordinary turnaround was therefore learning to control the narrative, viewing the NBA as a soap opera which began in October and concluded with the drama of the April play-offs, with the story told through the star power of the NBA's top players. The West Coast fans had the glamour of Magic Johnson to get excited about; East Coast fans loved their local hero, Larry Bird, and New Yorkers headed to Madison Square Garden to watch Hall of Famer Patrick Ewing.

Along with the NFL, the NBA was therefore one of the first sports properties to set out to build a brand with values and personality in the way a marketing-led company like P&G would understand. Stern was ruthless, too, with his broadcast partners, moving the television contract to NBC when he felt CBS weren't giving the NBA enough love, and switching to ESPN when NBC ran out of money. He also recognised that recruiting new fans was crucial to keep the sport relevant to young people and insisted that his broadcast partners also produced 'shoulder programming,' targeting new audiences. NBC therefore ran NBA promotions in primetime and scheduled Saturday morning shows to interest youngsters. Stern also developed a myopic focus on the TV product by making sure he had the final say on choice of producer and pundit selection, which delivered its finest moment at Michael Jordan's last dance and the 1998 NBA final when everything came together with a Super Bowl-sized TV audience of 72 million.

On Stern's watch, the NBA also managed to keep out of the tortuous labour disputes that so troubled the NFL and MLB by agreeing a transparent revenue-sharing formula between owners and their players. Meanwhile, a salary cap prevented team costs from spiralling out of control with a fixed 53 per cent of total league revenue going to payroll. We should also give an appreciative nod to Juan Antonio Samaranch who gave the sport of basketball a massive shot in the arm by allowing NBA players to participate at the 1992 Barcelona Olympics. The Dream Team of Michael Jordan, Johnson, Bird, Ewing and Scottie Pippen not only captured the nation's hearts, but catapulted the profile of the NBA on to the global stage.

- - - - -

#24 THE LOS ANGELES OLYMPICS
(28 July–12 August 1984)

The idea of centralised marketing for the Olympic Games had to wait until Seoul in 1988. However, one man who couldn't wait that long was Peter Ueberroth, who had been appointed CEO of the Los Angeles Organising Committee. Like Rozelle and Stern, Ueberroth was another surprise choice since he had little experience of sports administration after a career spent building America's second-largest travel agency. However, the Organising Committee were not looking for a political figurehead or ex-sportsperson to run the show, but someone who knew how to raise money, since their commitment to the taxpayers of California was that the $500m budget needed to stage the Olympic Games in 1984 would be entirely funded by the private sector.

The good news for the new CEO was that corporate America was starting to get excited about the first Summer

Olympics to be held in North America since 1960 and so Ueberroth encouraged his sales team to pitch hard. When Kodak dragged their feet, he therefore had no hesitation contacting Takahashi and telling him the film category was his if he could persuade Fuji to come up with $7m in the next 72 hours. Dassler must have then loved every second of what unfolded as the might of Dentsu swung into gear to underwrite the deal on behalf of their client and Takahashi set to work convincing Fuji this was their golden opportunity to grow market share in the United States. Ueberroth also took a leaf out of the Rozelle school of negotiating by running an auction between Coca-Cola and Pepsi for the coveted official soft drink category, which Coke won with a bid of $12.6m. And he created new assets to sell, such as the Olympic torch relay that ran from New York to Los Angeles, which helped secure AT&T as the official telecommunications partner. At the final count, Ueberroth's team had therefore raised a record $123m of sponsorship from a portfolio of 35 companies, which was six times more than Lake Placid had generated from marketing their Winter Olympics two years earlier.

The political backdrop to the sales cycle wasn't easy either, since following the Team USA boycott of Moscow it was only a matter of time before the Soviet Union retaliated, and while Ueberroth worked hard to try and persuade the Soviets to participate, they played along with him for a while before announcing their withdrawal along with several other Eastern European countries on the first day of his torch relay. However, there was good news too when the People's Republic of China announced they were sending a team to the Olympic Games for the first time since 1956 after having withdrawn from Melbourne when the IOC decided to recognise Taiwanese athletes.

After all the drama it therefore came as a relief when the Olympic cauldron was finally lit inside the stadium and 84 pianists played tunes on 84 pianos and a 750-piece college band marched across the in-field of the Los Angeles Memorial Coliseum while an 11,000-strong choir sang 'Thriller', by Michael Jackson, who in 1984 was the hottest pop star on the planet. President Ronald Reagan then declared the Games open – although it should really have been Ronald McDonald with all the commercial razzamatazz going on inside the stadium.

Anyone who has ever watched the coverage of the Olympics in the United States will know the regular unfurling of the Stars and Stripes is all that really matters to the American TV audience, and so it was in LA after Team USA topped the medal table and delivered the highest US Olympic audience of all time. With such impressive viewing figures – plus the strength of the TV ad market – Roone's judgment to break the bank was therefore vindicated as ABC generated $435m in revenue from advertisers and turned a profit on the contract of $75m.

'Ambush I'm in disguise. Ambush takes you by surprise'

With Nike sales riding high on the back of the 80s jogging craze, and with his cash flow now under control, Phil Knight identified an Olympics in his own backyard as the perfect moment to announce the brand to a global audience. Like Steve Jobs, he also turned his back on the usual suspects from Madison Avenue and hired a local Californian start-up agency called Wieden + Kennedy (W+K) to shake things up. The two founders, Dan Wieden and David Kennedy, knew securing official rights wouldn't play well with Knight, so they came up with the idea of telling the Nike story via association with a small group of Team USA athletes who they believed personified the values of his brand. The millions of dollars saved from not buying rights would then get spent driving awareness of Nike through disruptive PR and high-profile advertising. It was a strategy that became known in the advertising business as 'ambush marketing' and which debuted in Los Angeles after Nike signed sprinter Carl Lewis and middle-distance runners Mary Decker and Alberto Salazar as 'brand ambassadors'.

With talent secured, W+K produced a stylish 60-second TV spot featuring Lewis, Decker and Salazar looking unbeatable against the backdrop of 'I Love LA' sung by Randy Newman. The city was also plastered with giant billboards featuring similar images and, to make friends with journalists, Knight threw wild beach parties, with the media glad to escape the stiff cocktail parties organised by Ueberroth and Samaranch.

The strategy worked brilliantly and invented a new approach to marketing sportswear which Nike deployed at all future World Cups and Olympic Games. At the 1996 Atlanta Games they then debuted 'Just Do It', with IOC executives shouting the exact opposite back at them as their lawyers tried in vain to protect their official sportswear partner, Reebok, from ambush. It had modest impact, though, with Nike billboards barking back at them, 'If you're not here to win then you're a tourist', and a bandit pop-up Nike town was built on the outskirts of the city. As for attention-grabbing PR, well, few stunts have ever been bettered than that pair of gold Nike spikes Michael Johnson wore in Atlanta as he tore down the home straight to win the 200m in a world record time of 19.32 seconds.

The Los Angeles Games was therefore a pivotal moment for the Olympic movement as it became the first Olympic Games to make a profit: delivering a net surplus to the city of $215m and record revenue of $718m, which was achieved following the securing of that massive TV rights contract, raising record sponsorship and generating ticket sales of eight million. Peter Ueberroth was subsequently lauded on the front cover of *Time Magazine* as, 'The man who saved the Olympics' and was even tipped to run for president. However, the MLB brotherhood courted him relentlessly, and so once the Games ended, he accepted their offer to take over from Bowie Khun as the new commissioner of pro baseball.

'Hello. Is it me you're looking for?'

When Peter Ueberroth started work at MLB in the autumn of 1984, he couldn't believe how such successful businessmen could so easily lose the plot when negotiating player contracts, especially during the bunfights that regularly broke out when a top free-agency player became available. As Ted Turner remarked, 'For some major league owners, these were just a hobby. After being successful in other fields, owning a team satisfied their egos and gave them publicity.' The big problem was that this cohort of owners didn't like to lose and, with player wages skyrocketing, Ueberroth didn't hold back at one of his first owners' meetings, when he told them to stop paying their players so much money.

His next move was to dust off his Olympic black book and hit up corporate America for league-wide sponsorship deals, with blue-chip brands including IBM, Coke and Equitable Life all coming on board. As was so often the case with this man, his timing was perfect too, since the strategy coincided with a national beer war that had broken out between Budweiser and Miller Lite. The two brands were fighting with each other to secure the best advertising slots, to associate themselves with the top teams and to secure pouring rights at America's top ballparks. One industry estimate was that in 1984 the Bud brand subsequently poured 70 per cent of its $400m annual advertising budget into sports, and that 65 per cent of this was spent in and around baseball. Author John Helyer summarises the battle like this: 'By the 1980s, beer was the mother's milk of baseball. Its [Bud's] war with Miller was also a huge factor in driving up the value of baseball's broadcast rights.

TV could pay big for baseball rights, knowing Anheuser Busch and Miller would pay big to advertise. Baseball was summer; summer was beer; and beer was huge money.'

In addition to sponsorship dollars, Ueberroth also eyed the lucrative licensing revenue on offer from player trading cards. After the introduction of collective bargaining, these rights passed from the players' union to MLB Properties and were soon generating an astonishing $450m per season. Finally – and inevitably – he called his pals at the TV networks and whipped them up into a bidding frenzy for the next round of MLB broadcast rights, an auction that generated licence fees north of $1bn with Arledge agreeing to pay $575m over the next six years and NBC pitching in with a further $550m. Peter Ueberroth was therefore the man with the Midas touch when it came to the marketing of sport. One of our top rainmakers whose success came from viewing the Olympics and pro baseball as pure play business propositions. He subsequently devised his own version of the official partner concept to extract millions of dollars out of corporate America, drove through collective bargaining to maximise the value of media rights, and was one of the first to figure out how to generate substantial league-wide revenue from merchandise and licensing. As Sade sang in 1984, he was a smooth operator from LA to Chicago.

- - - - -

#25 MICHAEL JORDAN AND NIKE
(Chicago, 26 October 1984)

With his running business doing well, Phil Knight turned his attention to basketball and the dominance Converse and Adidas had established in the NBA. His strategy was to pay college coaches to push Nike footwear and sign rookie players in the draft – neither of which was working very well. The growth market for sneakers was young urban Americans who were excited by the hip-hop look of MC

Hammer and DJ Jazzy, who were regularly appearing on MTV wearing these rival products. As the new kids on court, Knight was therefore pushing his colleagues to come up with ideas that could break the cultural stranglehold these two brands had over the sport. Rob Strasser and Sonny Vaccaro, who ran marketing for the Nike basketball division, responded with a radical recommendation – to spend the entire $500k budget that Knight had given them for recruiting players in the 1984 draft on one player: 21-year-old Michael Jordan, who had just been drafted by the Chicago Bulls.

Strasser had heard Jordan's parents were on the lookout for a shoe deal for their son and that his agent was in advanced negotiations with Adidas, which was the shoe Jordan had always worn at college. Converse were also courting him, although they already had Bird, Magic and Dr J (Julius Erving) in their stable, so Jordan would need to be content being #4 on their roster. Not how he pictured himself then or has ever since. However, having never worn Nike shoes in his life, Jordan had no interest in visiting the Nike Campus in Portland, Oregon – but in those days he did what his mum Deloris told him to do. When the family arrived, Strasser subsequently rolled out the Nike red carpet and started to explain their plan, which was to make him the face of their basketball business. As the presentation continued, Strasser then played his trump card, which was that if Jordan signed with Nike, then they would produce a signature shoe called the Air Jordan, which would be designed in the colours of the Chicago Bulls, with a stunning prototype unveiled in the meeting. Finally, Knight agreed to do something he'd never done before with any other athlete in any other sport, which was to pay him a royalty on every pair of shoes carrying his name. It was an unprecedented move and proved to be the deal clincher too, since not even Converse had agreed to that for the Bird & Magic show.

There were, however, strict rules in place in the NBA at this time which insisted that all players had to wear white trainers. The red and black trim of the Air Jordan therefore didn't fit at all with David Stern's brand playbook and he told Knight he would fine Michael $5,000 every time he walked on to the court wearing them. This was music to Knight's ears. Sneakers were part of the hip-hop uniform since they too were anti-establishment and banned from places like the workplace and schools. Jordan was subsequently told to carry on wearing his shoes and that Nike would pay any fines thrown at him, as W+K stoked up the controversy with the following ad: 'On September 15, Nike created a revolutionary new basketball shoe. On October 18, the NBA threw them out of the game.' The camera pans towards Jordan, who looks down at his Air Jordans as the ad signs off with the killer end line 'Fortunately, the NBA can't stop you from wearing them … Air Jordans from Nike.' Swoosh. This shoe had just become way bigger than footwear.

'I used to want to be like Michael Jordan. Figure I would make the NBA and make me a fortune' – Schoolboy Q

The Nike sales team were excited by the potential of Air Jordan and projected retail sales of $3 million over the four-year term of the initial Jordan contract – a forecast that in the end proved a little light, as the brand connected with young people in a unique way, with sales reaching an astonishing $162m in the first year alone. The reward for Jordan was therefore a new deal guaranteeing him $18m over the next seven years, plus five per cent royalties on the future sale of all Jordan-branded footwear. The global brand ambassador was born.

Looking to build on this success, a year later the W+K creative team of Bill Davenport and Jim Riswold went to the movies to watch a Spike Lee film. It was called *She's Gotta Have It*, which was an edgy romantic comedy set in Brooklyn: a low-budget affair shot in black and white that centred on sexual freedom amongst black Americans. Lee starred in the film as the fictional character, Mars Blackman, and as the two men left the cinema they chatted excitedly about how brilliant they thought it had been and an idea started to form in their heads for the next Air Jordan commercial. The following morning, they plucked up the courage to ring Lee and pitch him the idea of starring alongside Jordan in the advert as Mars Blackman. He was a committed Nicks fan, but like everyone, loved Jordan, and the two men ended up producing an iconic film with the following genius voiceover written by Riswold:

'Yo, Mike, what makes you the best player in the universe? Is it the vicious dunks?' – Mars
'No Mars' – Jordan
'Is it the haircut?' – Mars
'No Mars' – Jordan
'Is it the shoes?' – Mars
'Nah' – Jordan
'Is it the extra-large shorts?' – Mars
'No Mars' – Jordan
'Is it the short socks?' – Mars
'No Mars' – Jordan
'Then it's gotta be the shoes.'

This unlikely combo had just created the next game-changer for the Air Jordan brand. One that would reinvent how brands worked with athletes: creating pop culture-styled advertising that zoned in on the human side of sportsmen and women. Lee's spot was political, challenging of American history, street-smart and featuring the hottest actor money could buy – Michael Jordan. With these weapons on your feet, not only did you play great ball, but you were also sticking two fingers up to the establishment – and all for $65. Here's Justin Timberlake explaining the importance of the product to a cohort of young people growing up in the 1990s: 'Everybody was like "you gotta get a pair of Jordans". Every year, we would save up, I would cut grass and do chores to earn money and then wait in line at Footlocker.'

Michael Jordan, of course, went on to become a sporting megastar, winning six NBA Championships with the Bulls between 1991 and 1998 and in five of those seasons nominated as the sport's most valuable player. For the marketing of sport, his was also the bravest, most all-in, disruptive athlete ambassador partnership anyone had ever put together. A masterclass from Messrs Knight, Strasser, Wieden and Kennedy on how to make an individual athlete synonymous with a sports brand through the potent combination of promoting an extraordinary athlete in a way that a generation of young people could really identify with.

When Jordan retired from the sport in 2003, the sales of the Air Jordan range had never been stronger, and even now – aged 65 – he remains a cultural icon with the brand still generating an extraordinary $6.6bn of retail sales, which accounts for eight per cent of Nike's global turnover. Here's how none other than Barrack Obama summarised the impact of this man: 'There are great players who don't have an influence beyond their sport and then there are certain sports figures who become a larger cultural force. Michael Jordan helped to create a different way in which people thought about the African American athlete and a different way in which people saw sport as part of the entertainment business.' John McEnroe and Kobie Bryant followed. Then Tiger, Serena, Ronaldo, Biles, Mo and Nadal as the 'boot deal' of the 70s morphed into a life-changing financial event for the world's top athletes. Now, when Nike come knocking, you know you're something special.

PART SIX
Media Fragmentation

'No one told me life was gonna
be this way'

The 1990s

Michael Jordan. Man United. Ayrton Senna

THE WORLD became a giddy place on 9 November 1989 as Europe's borders were thrown open when the Berlin Wall came tumbling down and the Soviet Union started to collapse. One year later, the polarising reign of Margaret Thatcher came to an end too after she was booted out of office by her own party and replaced by John Major, who was himself booted out by the British people in 1997, but not before helping re-boot British Olympic sports.

The nation then fell in love with Tony Blair and his New Labour party who wooed us with talk of Cool Britannia, and with Manchester, walking the walk better than anyone else as United won six league titles and the Hacienda became Mecca to generation rave.

Blair became so enamoured with modern popular culture that he invited the likes of Kate Moss and Noel Gallagher to Number 10 and proudly told us he was a Newcastle United fan as the nation fell back in love with football after the drama of Italia 90 and the creation of the Premier League.

Tony subsequently raved that 'Things can only get better' … and he was right for the economics of sport. They did get better – much better, in fact, as the value of sport's top properties soared following strong demand from pay-TV channels. The fragmenting media world wasn't confined to television either, when British entrepreneur Tim Berners Lee figured out how to connect remote computers together: Intel launched the Pentium processor, Apple unveiled the Mac and by 1999 the sale of home computers had reached 190 million units. We then put up with beeping and screeching and waited patiently for our 56k modems to boot up. Still, we were surfing, and knew this internet thingy was going to change our lives – we just had to figure out how.

#26 THE LAUNCH OF BSKYB
(London, 2 November 1990)

Besides the FA Cup Final, the World Cup, the European Cup Final and a few England internationals, there was very little live football to watch on British television until the 1990s. In fact, there was very little live sport at all – only *Grandstand* on BBC and *World of Sport* on ITV, which filled up Saturday afternoon with endless hours of horse racing, wrestling and rugby league. The most excitement I had growing up was therefore watching ITV's *Big Match* on Sunday afternoon: a programme that showed highlights of one of the previous day's games and forged my love of Crystal Palace with their fancy strip and flamboyant manager.

In 1978, ITV then tried to secure exclusivity for English football highlights, but it caused so much upset that questions were asked in the House of Commons after the tabloids referred to it as the 'snatch of the day'. A friendly concession between ITV and BBC was therefore agreed upon whereby the Football League contract alternated each season before ITV decided to try their luck again at televising ten live games. By the start of the 1985/6 season the relationship between the Football League and broadcasters had, however, reached rock bottom, since the clubs felt their rights were being massively under-valued following a miserly £4.5m joint bid from ITV and BBC.

The season therefore began with a complete TV blackout of the first ten rounds after the offer was rejected, with the clubs convinced the two stations were conspiring to avoid a competitive auction. This feeling then intensified after ITV's head of sport was spotted jumping out of a cab with his opposite number at the BBC on the way to a contract meeting with the Football League. The gentleman's agreement was evidently alive and kicking in 1985 with ITV showing their live games, the BBC showing *Match of the Day* and the two channels happy to go head-to-head on Cup Final day. With little leverage and the need for exposure to satisfy the new shirt sponsors, a deal was eventually agreed for the remainder of the 1985/6 season, although ITV made little concession to the clubs with the offer of £1.3m increasing to £3.1m for the following campaign. The big clubs were furious, longing for competition like American sports had, to give the BBC and ITV a kick up the backside, and were growing increasingly unhappy also with the other league clubs whom they felt sure were holding them back.

'The walls come tumbling down'

My first job out of university involved driving around the Welsh Valleys trying to convince furniture stores, car dealers and even a Greek hairdresser in Cwmbran of the power of television advertising. I was working for HTV, who had the ITV licence for Wales and West, and after ten months managed to escape by getting a transfer to the London office. In 1988 I then joined Thames Television, who now operated the London weekday franchise, and in my first week was told by my new boss to make friends with the formidable Saatchi & Saatchi media buyers. These were the glory years for Saatchi, who spent most of their clients' London TV budget with our rival LWT. My brief, therefore, was to build bridges: 'Go to petty cash, take out £200, and go down to the Carpenters Arms on Friday lunchtime and buy them all drinks ... get them to like you.' Flush with cash, I did as I was told and stood at the bar for over two hours undergoing some kind of weird ritual by responding to regular requests for drinks. The first round was 12 pints of lager, 12 packets of crisps and a Cinzano and lemonade, and it continued from there until I ran out of money.

'How did it go?' my boss asked when I returned to the office.

'They were brutal,' I whined. 'I spent the whole lot, and no one even said thanks.'

'Brilliant,' he replied, 'they like you.'

The TV industry had therefore developed into precisely the type of cosy monopoly that the Thatcher administration was hell-bent on dismantling and in 1990 the Broadcasting Act was passed which declared that, from 1 January 1993, Channel 4 would be required to compete with ITV for advertising. Everyone working in the advertising industry knew the 14 per cent share of their revenue which ITV gave C4 to fund their programming undervalued its commercial inventory. Yes, its audiences were niche – but they were attractive niches, reaching younger and more upscale audiences than ITV, and so were worth paying a price premium to reach. I felt the same way too and so jumped at the chance when approached to head up their business development department.

Not only did this new legislation spin-off Channel 4 as an independent entity, but it also passed two other directives to further stimulate competitiveness in the UK television industry. The first was to create two new national licences: one that would operate a fifth national network and another which would create a morning franchise to compete with BBC Breakfast (and was eventually called TVAM). Both channels – along with ITV and C4 – were to be funded by advertising and all four commercial stations would be free to sell sponsorship of their programmes. In addition, this new legislation announced that British companies were going to be invited to bid for a licence to run three new satellite channels, which was won by a consortium of corporate heavyweights including ITN, Amstrad and Virgin Media who called themselves British Satellite Broadcasting (BSB) and with Rupert Murdoch having already launched Sky TV on the Astra satellite, the two companies were going to slug it out for control of the nascent UK pay-TV market.

People like me working in free-to-air TV sneered at the idea of satellite TV and we put slides in our presentations that showed the millions of people advertisers could reach on terrestrial TV and compared it to the tiny audiences Sky and BSB were attracting. Sky's top show at the time was *The Simpsons*, which just about registered 0.1 per cent of a rating, meaning a few thousand viewers out there watching, as we quipped to amused media buyers, 'It might be cheaper to send people a free sample in the post, or how about creating a spot-the-viewer competition?' If you have no audience, then you have few subscribers and both companies were therefore in a parlous state and suffering losses of over £3m a week, with Sky also nursing a £2bn debt pile. There was only one logical next step, which happened on 2 November when they announced they were merging to create a new company called BSkyB and that Murdoch's right hand – fellow Aussie Sam Chisholm – was taking on the role of CEO.

- - - - -

#27 THE PREMIER LEAGUE
(London, 15 August 1992)

Since 1958, the top tier of English football had been part of a four-tiered Football League pyramid and the modest amount of TV and sponsorship money it generated was therefore shared between 92 clubs. For years, the top clubs had been agitating for change, since they regarded themselves as the stars of the show and saw no reason why they received such a paltry share of the pot. In January 1990, following the recommendations of a government report, this point of view then rapidly moved from one based on fairness to one which was business critical.

The Taylor Report was an inquiry into events that unfolded on 15 April 1989 at Hillsborough Stadium,

Sheffield, which was the venue for the FA Cup semi-final between Liverpool and Nottingham Forest and a day which ended in tragedy after 96 Liverpool fans died following a crush on the terraces. In his report, Lord Justice Taylor framed the terrible events of that day against the backdrop of the poor health of English football at this time: from the poor condition of the grounds many of the top teams played at, to the anti-social behaviour of the hard-core element of its supporter base. Jason Lee played for Nottingham Forest in the mid-80s and described walking out on to a football pitch as, 'walking into a war zone' and Taylor agreed by recommending that within five years all First Division grounds should be made safer and converted to all-seater stadia.

The clubs realised the economic impact this decision was going to have on their future, with the reigning champions Arsenal needing to reduce the capacity of Highbury from 55,000 to 36,000, and while the government would make £200m of funding available, the Football League were told the balance needed to be found by its clubs, with Manchester United estimating it would cost £7m to make Old Trafford compliant. The Taylor Report therefore threatened the very survival of the smallest clubs in the top tier, like AFC Wimbledon and Oldham Athletic, which is why authors Joshua Robinson and Jonathan Clegg believe it was the ultimate catalyst for the creation of the Premier League: 'If they were free to negotiate TV deals on their own – and if they could keep the money for themselves rather than being forced to share it with the lower divisions – this would go a long way towards plugging the new funding gap. English football had been edging towards a breakaway by the biggest clubs for the better part of a decade. Now, in the aftermath of the Taylor Report, they could finally argue it had become a necessity.'

In the autumn of 1990, the chairmen of the (then) 'Big Five' clubs, Manchester United, Arsenal, Everton,

Liverpool and Spurs, arranged to meet Greg Dyke for dinner at LWT's Southbank studio. Despite their suspicions about his agreement with the BBC, Dyke had established a reasonably good relationship with them after agreeing a two-year deal with the Football League worth £22m. The reason for ITV's change of heart had come from rumour that BSB had made a similar bid to make the Football League their flagship sports content.

Dyke was keen to slow the growth of satellite television and therefore persuaded the other ITV regions to support a counterbid and maybe I'm being overly generous to him, but hopefully he had also been listening to us mere mortals in ad sales who were crying out for more male-targeted programming to deliver the audience which the new car, beer and finance advertisers of the 1980s wanted to reach. Dyke subsequently outbid BSB, and from the 1989/90 season onwards, the ITV network aired 21 live games at a cost of £523k per game, which was double the amount they'd previously paid. He also ingratiated himself with the Big Five by guaranteeing each of them £1m out of the £11m pot. After all, he wanted as many of ITV's live games as possible to feature the top clubs, and so that was only fair, wasn't it?

Aside from the future challenges presented by the Taylor Report, the backdrop to this autumn gathering was reasonably upbeat, with English fans starting to fall back in love with football and an audience of 11 million watching on ITV as Arsenal pipped Liverpool to the 1989/90 league title in a dramatic 2-0 away win at Anfield. Meanwhile, England had done well at Italia 90, with 25 million gripped by the heartbreak of Gazza's tears as Bobby Robson's team narrowly lost the semi-final on penalties to the old enemy. Around the dinner table in London that evening were Phil Carter of Everton, David Dein, Martin Edwards, Noel White from Liverpool and Irving Scholar of Tottenham, and this is how Dyke summarises the significance of the occasion: 'When the official history of the Premier League is written, this dinner meeting will surely be seen as the time and the place at which it became a reality.'

The reason he believes this meeting was so decisive was that it was the moment when he broke the news that the next ITV deal couldn't be as one-sided towards them as the last one had been since he'd taken a personal battering from the other clubs when they found out about his cosy side-deal. So acrimonious had the situation become that it led to Carter being asked to resign as chair of the Football League and Dein getting voted off the commercial committee. Dyke continues, 'They very quickly decided that they wanted the First Division clubs to break away from the Football League and set up the Premier League, which would be run by the 22 member clubs in the interests of those clubs. They would sell their own television rights and the proceeds would go to them.'

Manchester United IPO
(10 June 1991, London)

English football clubs have no consistent track record of making money or proving to be a good investment. The past motivation of owners to invest in a team has therefore often simply been the kudos of being involved with something more interesting than the day job. As the Kansas City Mayor Emanuel Cleaver once wryly commented, 'Without the Chiefs and the Royals we'd be Omaha ... Wichita ... Des Moines.' In 1983, Tottenham Hotspur FC therefore became the first club to try their luck raising money on the stock market when Irving Scholar raised £3.8m to help pay off some of the debt he'd racked up following an upgrade of White Hart Lane. However, although the issue was significantly oversubscribed, the shares immediately fell 15 per cent and stayed there for quite some time. As Barclays Bank put it, 'Fans found that, rather than an investment with dividends, they had bought a further emotional share in the club.' For years, the majority of English football clubs therefore remained under the ownership of family trusts with Arsenal FC owned by the Bracewell-Smith and Hill-Wood families for over 50 years and their only dilution occurring in 1983 when they sold 20 per cent of the club to David Dein for £300k. Liverpool FC were owned by the Moores family who owned Littlewoods Pools (one of the biggest employers in the city), and Manchester United by a northern meat trader called Louis Edwards who in 1964 paid £40k for a majority stake. When Edwards died in 1980 his shares passed to his son Martin, and despite losing money in six of the following 12 seasons he remained convinced about United's long-term economic potential and so looked to further increase his father's stake.

By the late 80s Edwards subsequently found himself highly leveraged and needing to raise some money and, after kissing a few frogs, was introduced to Michael Knighton who was a local businessman and rabid United fan. The two men subsequently shook hands on a £20m sale with the prospective new owner so excited that he unexpectedly announced himself at the next home game by running on to the pitch in full replica kit and playing keepy-uppy in front of the Stretford End. This was a strong move, especially since it soon became clear Knighton was unable to raise the money, and so Edwards needed a new plan and took advice from an experienced investment banker as to whether he felt the flotation of United could be successful. His name was Glen Cooper, who was not a fan of football and so offered his unimpassioned view that 'there was a very substantial body of opinion that said football clubs should not be on the stock market; that they were fundamentally not capable of being commercial'. With talk of a breakaway league and English clubs back in Europe, Edwards was, however, more bullish than Cooper and, having failed to find a private investor, told him he was willing to give it a go. In January 1991, Cooper therefore acquired an off-the-shelf company to establish the club's PLC status and placed a valuation on United of £42m, which was based on a multiple of 11 times pre-transfer earnings (which was then the FTSE average for the leisure index). To boost the credibility of management in the eyes of the City he also advised hiring an experienced CFO and a new PLC board, which would be led by the HSBC chairman, Roland Smith; four months later the assets of the club were subsequently reversed into this shell, with the issue limping home after Edwards' broker mopped up the final few shares.

'Time to break free. Nothing can stop us'

Edwards was delighted. Not only could he clear his liabilities and raise the £7m to upgrade Old Trafford, but he still owned 28 per cent of the club and had renewed energy and motivation to help Dein and the other club chairmen get this new league started. The key to a potential breakaway was to get the support of the FA, whose CEO, Graham Kelly, wasn't hostile to the idea since he regarded the move as an opportunity to claw back some of the control the FA had lost to the Football League. He also felt an independent top tier with fewer teams would strengthen the England team, since fewer league games meant England coach Graham Taylor could spend more time with his squad. However, the flaw in the Kelly plan was allowing his chairman Bert Millichip to attend one of the final meetings with the clubs, and he told them it was up to them how many clubs played in their new league. This off-the-cuff remark subsequently meant Kelly failed to get the main concession he was looking for, and was left with the right to approve how many clubs got promoted and relegated and assurance that the new competition would be called the FA Premier League.

Not surprisingly the Football League board were furious when they heard the news of the breakaway and immediately launched legal action, claiming it was unlawful. However, on 31 July 1991, the High Court ruled that since the FA was the governing body of football they were the ones who were best placed to decide its future strategic direction. Ebenezer Morley would have loved it, although holding such good cards I suspect he would have looked to extract far more value from the negotiation than Kelly managed to secure. This is how ex-Tottenham chairman Irving Scholar summarised the importance of Kelly's support in an interview with Mihir Bose a few years later: 'Past attempts at breakaways had resulted in the big clubs being portrayed as villains. This time we were part of the process of an autonomous organisation, dedicated to its own interests, with its own rules, officials and above all money.' Rick Parry agreed, adding, 'The Premier League was the idea of the then Big Five. But if the Big Five had launched the new league, none of the other clubs would have trusted them. It was agreed that the FA would take the lead and incorporate it into its new blueprint for the English game.'

On 23 February 1992, the First Division clubs therefore resigned from the Football League and the FA Premier League was established with the founding clubs of Arsenal, Aston Villa, Chelsea, Coventry City, Crystal Palace, Everton, Leeds United, Luton Town, Liverpool, Manchester City, Manchester United, Norwich City, Nottingham Forest, Notts County, Oldham Athletic, QPR, Sheffield United, Sheffield Wednesday, Southampton, Tottenham, West Ham and Wimbledon (West Ham, Luton and Notts County were relegated in the last season of the old First Division and replaced by Blackburn, Middlesbrough and Ipswich Town).

Two months later, Premier League Limited was incorporated, with 38-year-old Ernst & Young accountant

Rick Parry appointed as its interim CEO, with the brief to set up the governance of the new company through the protocol of the Founder Members Agreement (FMA) that would determine how member clubs made decisions. Once that was done, Parry would then be free to tender the inaugural Premier League TV contract, make recommendations for the governance of the new league and propose how central revenue should be shared between the clubs. As part of his fact-finding mission, Parry travelled to the United States to find out about these mouth-watering TV deals he'd been reading about and, while Stateside, learned about the success of the *Monday Night Football* format, which he decided should be included in his own rights tender. He also took inspiration from how American sports had managed to fairly share revenue and, on his return, called a meeting to propose that 50 per cent of league-wide revenue from broadcast and sponsorship should be split equally between the clubs; 25 per cent of the TV money should be based on the number of times a team were featured in a televised game, and the remainder distributed in relation to the club's final position in the league. Also, to remove decision-making logjams, a two-thirds majority would always be required to decide critical commercial decisions, such as who was awarded the TV contract.

- - - - -

#28 THE PREMIER LEAGUE TV CONTRACT

(Lancaster Gate Hotel, London, 18 May 1992)

The recommendations made by Parry were approved in less than two hours and so he immediately commenced negotiations with ITV, BBC and Sky. The clubs then regrouped in May to decide who they would sign with. The precise happenings at the Lancaster Gate Hotel on 18

May 1992 have been the subject of much speculation over the years, with Liverpool, Arsenal, Manchester United and Everton all said to have supported ITV's offer of £262m. Greg Dyke also thought he had Tottenham onside, that was until Scholar sold the club to Alan Sugar a few months before the vote. He also owned Amstrad, which was a key supplier of satellite dishes to Sky. When he heard about the size of the ITV offer, Sugar ran out of the meeting and was heard shouting the following unlordly words down the phone: 'You've got to blow them out of the ******* water.' It's unclear who exactly Sugar was barking at, but this was not a bidding war Sam Chisholm intended losing, since he'd seen the impact live sports had on driving new subscribers when Sky picked up 100,000 new customers earlier that year after televising the ICC Cricket World Cup from the West Indies. Chisholm therefore woke up his boss in New York to ask for his approval to increase their offer by £50m.

If we return to the FMA, which governed votes like this for Premier League Limited, then the magic number for either Sky or ITV to reach was 14 votes – two-thirds of the clubs. This, if you remember, was a decision none of the clubs paid much attention to a few weeks before, since the Big Five knew if they acted together then they would only ever need one other vote to block decisions they didn't like the look of. However, that was before Sugar went rogue, and so imagine their surprise when the vote fell 14/6 in favour of Sky. Here's what Dyke had to say about the outcome that day: 'Six of the 20 Premier League clubs supported the ITV bid – four of the big five plus Leeds and Aston Villa. Two other clubs abstained. We lost by a single vote, as seven clubs would have been enough to stop BSkyB. We discovered later that Nottingham Forest, whose chairman had promised to vote for us, had actually sent along an office secretary because no one else was available. That vote in favour of BSkyB turned out to be crucial.' It's interesting Dyke reserves his ire for Forest chairman Fred

Reach and his company secretary Paul White, and not the easier target of Alan Sugar. The events of 18 May 1992, are therefore shrouded in 'who said what to whom' andin search of answers Mihir Bose interviewed Sugar a few years later, who finally admitted what everyone wanted to know: 'Yeah yeah yeah, there wouldn't have been a Sky deal without that telephone call.'

Rupert Murdoch once explained News Corp's art of disruption like this: 'Our company has a history of challenging the established, and often stagnant media with new products and services ... You've got to look for a gap where competition in a market has grown lazy and lost contact with the viewers.' When Sam Chisholm persuaded his boss to break the Sky bank in 1991 they did precisely that and subsequently discovered the transformational impact live sport has on the subscription TV business model, as one million homes forked out £5.99 per month to watch Manchester United win their first league title in 26 years. Whomever we point the finger at, this flip-of-a-coin moment therefore changed the face of British television and the broader sports industry forever, not only ensuring BSkyB had a bright future, but waking a sleeping giant that has developed into sport's most successful global franchise. This was a company that at one point was losing £13m a month but was now making an operating profit of £62m on the strength of winning this single sports contract. As Dave Hill, then head of sport at Sky, told the BBC documentary *Fever Pitch*, 'Getting the Premier League became that pot of gold we desperately needed.'

One could argue ITV had it coming after the arrogant way it protected its cartel, with the momentum further swinging away from free-to-air TV a few months later when Sky agreed a £72m/five-year deal with the FA to cover the FA Cup and England's Home Internationals. With ITV left with no premium football rights, we therefore spotted a free-to-air gap and started showing live Serie A matches on Channel 4 which, with the help of Gazza's move to Lazio, were soon attracting an audience of two million on Sunday afternoons. We also exploited the new opportunity granted to us under the Broadcasting Act by selling the broadcast sponsorship rights to our coverage to Peroni, with the bloke who closed the deal as pleased as punch as he was high-fived around the C4 sales floor. That was until Shreevy put him back in his box with one of his classic one-liners, 'Peroni and Italian footy? My mum could've done that deal.'

#29 RUGBY UNION (FINALLY) TURNS PROFESSIONAL
(London, 27 August 1995)

The top rugby union players must have rolled their eyes when they saw the quantum of money pouring into football as the thorny issue of professionalism continued to dog their sport.

The problem was that its loudest voices had never adequately managed to articulate what they even meant by the term 'professionalism,' with the best definition the RFU could come up with quoted by historian Tony Collins as follows: 'Asking, receiving, or receiving a promise, direct or implied, to receive any money consideration whatever, actual or prospective; any employment or advancement; any establishment in business; or any compensation whatever for playing, training, or rendering any service to a club.'

The issue rugby union faced was therefore exactly the same that athletics and tennis were confronted by in the 1970s, which was that its leaders turned a blind eye to their top players getting paid under the counter, as the All Blacks were paid to tour South Africa in 1976, and Welsh players were paid by the Welsh Rugby Union to stop them switching codes. Meanwhile, England captain Will Carling set up a management company to cash in on his rugby career, and emerging rugby nations including Italy and Japan offered big wages to attract overseas stars. However, the big difference between rugby union and other so-called amateur sports was that their leaders were unwilling to try to solve the problem of finding mutually acceptable ways for their players to earn a living from playing the game. To illustrate how out of touch the RFU board had become in 1991, the England squad were told that all the commercial opportunities that came their way had to be approved by a marketing company hired to police the sport. However, this was not a group who were good at being told what to do. We're talking about men like Brian Moore, Paul Ackford and Wade Dooley who had just won the Grand Slam and narrowly lost the 1991 World Cup Final and so for the next four years, as Greg Dyke explains, they could barely conceal their contempt for those who managed the game: 'Never in any sport have I met a bunch of players who so hated the people who ran the game as I found in rugby. It was a straight divide between a bunch of old blokes who loved the "amateur"' nature of rugby and players who trained and played like professionals but didn't get paid. It was a divide both of generation and of class.'

The low point for the sport then happened on 25 February 1991 when the England players asked the press to pay them £5k for post-match interviews following their 25-6 win against Wales at Cardiff Arms Park. In the run-up to the 1995 Rugby World Cup, Carling was then stripped of the England captaincy when he criticised the RFU in a Channel 4 documentary with words which would have horrified his old headmaster at Stowe: 'If the game is run properly as a professional game, you do not need 57 old farts running rugby.'

The French players also joined in the anarchy by refusing to play their 1995 World Cup quarter-final versus the All Blacks unless they were each paid 7,000 francs, but to really understand the absurdity of this era, I will leave it to ex-England and Wasps number eight Lawrence Dallaglio to recount a story from his England debut in 1995 and an encounter he had in the team's hotel reception with England legend Jason Leonard. 'He hauled three bags up to the desk and asked the night porter to ensure his dry-cleaning was delivered to his room before the close of play the next day. Intrigued, I asked the great man what was going on. He informed me that since the game was amateur, the RFU were happy to pick up the laundry and dry-cleaning costs for the players whilst they were resident in the team hotel. With that said, he pulled out a pair of curtains and asked the porter to ensure the red wine stains were seen to ... I couldn't help admiring Jason for his bravado. As it turned out, this was just one of the perks the boys took advantage of to gain some advantage from the amateur system.' In the end, the final nail in the coffin for rugby union's ideological conflict did not, however, come from the size of the Jason Leonard laundry bill, but from its old foe, rugby league and once again Rupert Murdoch and his News Corp colleagues played a starring role

'Living in a land down under. Where women glow and men plunder'

It was 1995, and Sky Sports were flying high in England and Fox Sports had just launched in the United States. Meanwhile, another News Corp company, Fox Australia, were fighting for control of their domestic pay-TV market with Murdoch having identified rugby league as the sport to help them win new subscribers. He therefore made a knockout offer to secure the TV rights to the Australian League (ARL), but this time went further than simply writing a big cheque for the rights and insisted on a total makeover of the sport, with new team names, scheduling kick-off times to maximise the TV audience, introducing innovative on-screen presentation and changing the name of the competition to the Super League.

When the model was duplicated two months later to include the New Zealand Rugby League, the southern hemisphere rugby union nations were terrified, since they knew these deals would inject a massive amount of new funding into domestic rugby league and that unless they responded there would be mass migration of players out of union and into league. These three nations had therefore had enough of standing on the burning platform of rugby's amateur ideology and two days before South Africa's symbolic 1995 World Cup win over New Zealand, stunned the assembled press pack with news that Australia, New Zealand and South Africa had signed a $340m/ten-year agreement with News Corp. This is how South African rugby union president Louis van Aart justified the deal to a packed press conference in Cape Town: 'For some time rugby union has appeared to be threatened by other codes, almost like a wounded impala limping through the bushveld with lions nearby.'

To continue the metaphor, Murdoch and his News Corp team were executing a rolling maul through both codes of rugby and their next move was to propose a five-year/£52m deal to create an English Super League, a condition of which was that the Rugby Football League (RFL) had to move their competition from the winter months to provide Sky with premium content during football's summer break. The size of the offer was once again too tempting for the cash-strapped English clubs to ignore and so the RFL voted to accept the deal, with the new competition scheduled to start the following March, and these historic clubs changing their names like they had in Australia. Wigan, first established in 1863 when its mills were powering the Industrial Revolution, would therefore change its name to the Warriors. Halifax, who won the first Yorkshire Cup in 1876, would start the new season as the Panthers and Leeds would play as the Rhinos. The News Corp coup was almost complete, and rugby union's governing body realised they had no alternative but declare their code an 'open game', with International Rugby Board chairman Vernon Pugh lifting the restrictions on paying players. The shocks then kept on coming when the RFU announced they too had signed with Sky: a five-year deal worth £87.5m, granting News Corp the right to televise England's home Five Nations games.

Oh, what irony. Two days before the centenary of the split between league and union, the RFU, unwavering supporters of the amateur ideology, had finally accepted the inevitable. All that sweat. All those tears. All that free laundry and rude language from Will Carling resolved in the matter of a few months and a few large cheques written by ambitious Aussies.

Rupert Murdoch once said, 'Sport absolutely overpowers film and all other forms of entertainment in drawing viewers to television.' He went on, 'We will be doing in Asia what we intend to do elsewhere in the world – that is, use sports as a battering ram and a lead offering in all our pay television operations.' Over the next ten years, Sky subsequently paid billions of euros for domestic football contracts to launch their brand in Germany and Italy, a trick they also deployed in 1994 when launching Fox Sports in the United States. It wasn't therefore just European football and world rugby which experienced a media rights boom in the late 90s, with Fox, TNT and ESPN all making audacious bids to secure rights to America's top sports properties. ESPN were the most aggressive in the pursuit of premium content and agreed a five-year/$440m deal with MLB to show the *Wednesday Double-Header* and Sunday evening's *Game of the Week*. On 14 January 1998, commissioner Paul Tagliabue called a press conference to announce news which would have seriously impressed the first generation of NFL team owners: an unprecedented eight-year/$9.2bn deal which enabled ABC to hold on to their iconic *Monday Night Football* rights, and their (new) sister company, ESPN, to become sole cable carrier for pro football. This was the most extensive set of TV deals that had ever been signed, with each NFL franchise set to receive $84m a year for the next eight years. Here's the eminently quotable Dave Hill (who by now had left Sky to work on the launch of Fox Sports) explaining how these colossal sums of money could be justified by broadcasters: 'The NFL represents the only firm ground in an increasingly scary swamp. It is the one safe bet, the one thing in the network business that makes sense.'

David Stern saw the writing on the wall and realised the NBA could no longer ignore the pull of cable. Especially when the head of NBC Sports took him for a walk around Central Park and told him they were losing money on their current $1.75bn NBA contract and couldn't renew the deal on the same terms. Michael Jordan had retired, NBC's ratings were down and the dotcom bubble had taken its toll. The following year, Stern, therefore, moved most of the NBA play-off games to cable in a combined $4.6bn/six-year deal with TNT, ESPN and ABC Sports. Travis Vogan wrote a super book called *ESPN, the Making of a Sports Media Empire*, and summarises the new power of ESPN like this: 'Gone are the days when 24-hour sports coverage simply provided a fix for a crazed subculture of sports junkies jonesing for something to watch. ESPN has normalized – and ritualized – practices once considered pathetic symptoms of sports addiction.'

That same year, the most iconic sports franchise in America – the New York Yankees – became the first sports team of the modern era to launch its own dedicated cable network. They called it 'YES' and raised $335m from Goldman Sachs and Providence Equity Partners to fund the venture. Now this was genuinely disruptive. We'd seen Ted Turner buy the Atlanta Braves, but now a sports team had decided to become a media owner themselves, charging fans $2 a month to watch their home games. Not to be outdone, Murdoch joined in the buying spree with a successful $350m bid to buy the Los Angeles Dodgers and a £625m bid to buy Manchester United, which was eventually blocked by the Office of Fair Trading.

Why is Sport so Important to Pay-TV?

The same principle holds true today as it did back in the early days of American cable TV, which is that sports fans can't live without their live sports fix and are willing to pay top dollar, pound and euro to get it – a precedent Ted Turner first proved in the late 70s when he launched his Superstation and, along with HBO, helped construct the win-win relationship that exists between subscription channels and cable operators. 'In addition to telling them how great this service would be for our industry I let them know that the only way we could make it work was to charge a fee of 15 cents per subscriber, per month ($1.80 per year),' Turner said. 'At that point cable was only available to about 10 million homes so even if we were launched in each and every single household, our total cable fee revenue would be $18 million, not enough to cover our annual expenses. We'd try to make up the difference in advertising sales.' The big losers in the hotly contested 90s cable v network TV rights battle were therefore CBS, who may well have been the NFL's home for over 30 years but that counted for nothing after Fox dangled their $1.58bn cheque in front of Peter Rozelle.

These new competitors had deep pockets, hours of scheduling time to fill and a multi-revenue stream business model that enabled them to pay top dollar for sports rights. CBS, meanwhile, had to count on the volatility of advertisers to pay the bills and made one final big bet on sports rights with a wild bid of $1.2bn in the 90s for MLB rights that ended up losing them $500m across the term of the contract.

As for Sky, well their business model differs from linear broadcasters since advertising only represents around 15 per cent of their revenue and differs from ESPN too since they don't rely on cable carriage fees to pay the bills. Their currency is therefore 'Average Revenue Per User' (ARPU), which is the monthly subscription you and I pay to watch their channels, plus the add-on services we might want to buy from them such as broadband, mobile and landline. Since recruiting one million new subscribers in the first season of showing the Premier League, football has also proved to be critical to their success, with evidence of its extraordinary pulling power illustrated by the Setanta case study of 2007, when two Irish entrepreneurs launched a rival pay-TV platform. After securing two of the six Premier League packages on offer, Michael O'Rourke and Leonard Ryan went on to sign up an impressive 700k subscribers, which proved that while people may only spend five-to-ten per cent of their time watching live sport, it's the most valued five-to-ten per cent of their viewing week. However, the viability of their business model and its reliance on football was cruelly exposed three years later when Setanta entered administration after securing only one package of Premier League rights in the next auction, leading to thousands of Setanta subscribers cancelling their monthly direct debit. The second lesson to learn from this case study is, therefore, there's a tipping point in the pay-TV business, which is somewhere between having exclusive rights to 23–46 games of premium football content and explains why Sky and BT Sport were willing to pay up to £9.4m to show 90 minutes of football.

Their producers are thus briefed to eke out every second of value they can from these rights, through covering breaking news stories, showing highlights and extended game analysis, featuring pre-game interviews, magazine programming and by turning transfer deadline day into an epic drama. The life of a football match therefore begins mid-week by establishing the weekend narrative and gets amplified following Friday's press conferences. From then on, it's hyped on a loop with highlights of previous duels and pundit analysis through to game time. There are then 90 minutes of action (hopefully a few goals), followed by in-depth post-game analysis, more interviews, phone-ins, push out the highlights. Rinse and repeat.

> *'We are about change and progress not about protectionism through legislation and cronyism'* – The Murdoch Archipelago.

Following the rugby heist of 1995, Sky wasted no time picking off other BBC sports contracts and BBC director general John Birt seemed happy enough to wave them goodbye as Sky agreed deals with the ECB for England's one-day internationals and secured a slew of golf rights with the PGA Tour, European Tour, US Open and Ryder Cup. As we've heard, the second half of the 1990s was also a good time for ad-funded television, with the UK market now generating £4bn from advertisers, and so money was available in 1997 for ITV to join in the raid by taking over the BBC F1 contract. Even Channel 4 got in on the act by snapping up England's home Test matches, the Cheltenham Festival and rights to cover the Derby. As Dyke wistfully explains, 'The BBC had taken the decision not to compete for many of these sports. John Birt's view was quite logical, that the BBC had limited funds that could be better used in areas like drama and news.' Poor Greg, he was soon to become director general of the BBC and the Murdoch punches kept coming his way.

However, the News Corp smash and grab of England's sporting jewels was a step too far for Britain's politicians, especially after they heard the rumour that Rupert

Murdoch was planning to bid for the worldwide rights to the Olympic Games. John Major's government therefore fast-tracked another Broadcasting Act, which introduced new protections to stop any more of Britain's top events from disappearing behind Sky's paywall. The first group were called the 'A-list', with this legislation demanding the following events were shown live on a free-to-air channels: the World Cups of football and cricket, Wimbledon, the Olympics, the European Football Championships, and the FA Cup and Rugby League Challenge Cup finals.

The 'B-list', meanwhile, could sell their live rights to subscription TV, but only if they also signed deals to show highlights on free-to-air channels. These were the Rugby World Cup, the World Athletics Championships, Test match cricket, Six Nations rugby, the golf Open, the Ryder Cup and the Commonwealth Games. The idea of listed events seriously irritated Murdoch, who saw it as market distortion with author Wendy Gorman Rohn capturing his frustration in a quote from him in her book *The Murdoch Mission*: 'Ever since television first became available, the government has favoured BBC, allowing it to use tax revenues to finance whatever programming the elite thought appropriate to put on air.'

The Globalisation of Marketing

Globalisation was a term first used in 1983 by Professor Theodore Levitt in *The Harvard Review* where he argued that the rapid changes taking place in society and the speed of technological innovation should make companies increasingly confident about selling their products worldwide. He talked also about how capitalism was changing, with the barriers to trade and flow of capital easing, and growing homogeneity of consumer taste making us all like the same things. Another decisive factor driving globalisation was merger mania within the marketing services industry and the formation of what became known as 'holding companies', with the first mover an American-based group calling themselves Interpublic, who owned the McCann Erickson agency and handled the global Coke account. They were quickly followed by WPP, a shell company which was set up in 1985 by the ex-CFO of IMG and Saatchi, Martin Sorrell, who visited the 80s corporate cash machine to buy JWT, Young & Rubicam and Ogilvy. And the same model was replicated a year later when BBDO merged with the rainmakers of DDB to create Omnicom which shortly afterwards added Chiat Day and TBWA to the group. The 1990s was also a time when corporations were looking for enhanced value from their marketing spend and to facilitate this the new role of global marketing director was created to drive efficiencies and consistency across markets. This wasn't an easy job either since most country marketing directors hated being told what to do by these new global people. The international marketing directors were therefore drawn to the holding company model since hiring a single agency drove media and production efficiencies and was also helpful in controlling maverick local marketing directors. It was an idea that resonated especially strongly with American- and Japanese-based companies, who identified sponsoring global sports properties as a powerful platform to help them win the globalisation game.

Sports Marketing 2.0 – 'hello, this is why we're here'

There were a few exceptions in the first wave of sports marketing, such as the clever way Visa and BBDO activated their Olympic rights. But the early sports sponsorship deals were mostly looked upon as cheap media buys with advertisers attracted to the millions of eyeballs their brand would be exposed to on a car, shirt, or around the stadium perimeter. This, however, all started to change when the fragmenting audiences of the 1990s gave birth to another type of marketeer, fighting in much more cluttered markets than the previous cohort, and so started to look upon sports sponsorship as a good platform to place blue water between themselves and their competitors. As audiences began fast-forwarding content on their PVRs, the media planners jumped onboard the sponsorship bus too and recognised that being part of the editorial storytelling was a highly effective way to drive brand awareness.

The 1990s was therefore the decade when sports sponsorship started to develop into a serious strategic marketing platform for global brands.

As more and more money poured into sports sponsorship the media divisions of the holding groups started to get interested. When the average deal values of the 1980s were in the hundreds of thousands, they were happy to let ISL and IMG sell their clients a few perimeter boards. However, the market was now rapidly proliferating, and by the late 90s had developed into a $20bn global business. This was high-margin budget not going through their books and as Mark McCormack smugly told the *Financial Times* in 1991, 'We rent the golf course, take the gate, get the sponsors, do the television, sell the hospitality tents and I commentate on the TV.' It was therefore time to shut the door with Interpublic the first to make a significant move.

We first met their CEO Frank Lowe when he was an account man at CDP in the late 70s and 20 years later he was on a mission to dominate the burgeoning sports marketing scene through buying several independent agencies to create the Octagon agency. In fact, he got so carried away he even bought Brands Hatch. Meanwhile, WPP made a few defensive acquisitions too, such as acquiring the PRISM agency from founder Steve Madincea, whose clients included Ford and Shell who were two of WPP's top global creative and media buying clients. With this new capability, the group could therefore develop the creative proposition for Ford's Champions League campaign through Ogilvy, negotiate the rights with UEFA through their media agency, MindShare, and activate the campaign through PRISM – with all these services neatly packaged into one transparent scope of work which Ford's global procurement department could KPI and audit.

The broking agencies didn't stand a chance and became easy game and were accused of not being strategic, not being creative, having too many conflicts of interest and taking too much commission out of the deals they brokered. The concept of 'double bubble' was also roundly attacked when they found out that some of the brokers were getting paid by the brand to introduce the deal – as well as by the rights holder to find the brand. Nice work if you can get it – and often they did, since some clients were too busy enjoying the VIP hospitality on offer at Lords and Silverstone to appreciate they were having their pocket picked.

From Grassroots to Podium

In 1997, fascinated by the disruption going on in the media business, I left the television world to join one of these holding groups, which was called Tempus Group plc, and one of my responsibilities was to grow their sponsorship business. As media people this meant ad-funded content and broadcast sponsorship; that was until 1998, when we received a brief from one of our planners that would change the course of my own career and the fortunes of a whole sport.

The background was that Commercial Union were merging with another insurance company called General Accident, and their marketing director, Nick Hall, was on the lookout for innovative ideas to help build awareness of the merged company, which they were calling CGU. We ran the numbers to understand what their customers were interested in and discovered athletics delivered an excellent fit. I therefore reached out to Alan Pascoe – the ex-Olympic 400m hurdler – who had recently sold his agency to Frank Lowe and had set up a new one called FastTrack. His founding client was UK Athletics (UKA) who had turned to him for help since the sport was struggling financially and he had therefore helped their CEO, Dave Moorcroft, to negotiate a three-year deal with the BBC.

Despite its problems off track, things were looking good on it with rising stars Dwain Chambers, Paula Radcliffe and Kelly Holmes all predicted to do well at the Sydney Olympics and so we felt the opportunity for CGU to generate brand awareness through 20 hours of exposure on the BBC, plus engage families through a nationwide school programme, was a compelling proposition. We subsequently worked up our own big idea which we called 'from grassroots to podium', and pitched it to Hall, who was one of these new types of brand marketeers we spoke about earlier and quickly spotted where this partnership could take him. After a few tough grillings, he therefore asked us to get a deal done but, given the sport's precarious position, to ensure we built in the necessary financial protections for his company. In our negotiations we thus offered to pay UKA 80 per cent of what they wanted for the title sponsorship rights and another 20 per cent if CGU's brand visibility targets were hit.

Today's sophisticated modern sports marketers are doubtless rolling their eyes at this stone-age story, since linking rights fees to media exposure is now a standard ROI (return on investment) metric. However, back in 1998 we found this wasn't the case at all in an industry that lacked the rigour we were used to as media people. Our approach was, therefore, unusual, and Moorcroft takes credit for agreeing to a deal that was outside of his comfort zone. It proved to be an inspired decision too, which not only paid out in full but led to an enduring 12-year/£100m partnership after CGU merged with Norwich Union and then later rebranded as Aviva.

We were feeling pretty chuffed with ourselves as our reputation started to grow for innovative thinking in sports marketing. However, the stars of the sports marketing 2.0 era were the Vodafone Class of 2000. A business that started out in Newbury selling brick-sized cell phones to small businesses and was rapidly growing into Europe's largest telecommunications company. The global marketing team was led by ex-Coke executive David Wheldon, supported by his sponsorship guru David Pinnington, and was tasked with developing a coherent global identity for Vodafone. With new markets and new products getting added all the time, it needed to be a flexible platform. Sponsorship was subsequently identified as the lead platform to help achieve their objectives and the first deal was signed in 1998 with the England cricket team. This was then followed two years later with a £30m deal to take over from Sharp as the shirt sponsor of Manchester United, and a partnership guaranteed to send any Italian into the 'psycho active high' Matthew Syed spoke of earlier – with Ferrari.

There was, however, no 'hallelujah moment' to the way Team Vodafone associated themselves with sports properties. They were simply looking for their USP – which, as a new company in a fast-growing category wasn't easy to find. The strategy was therefore to place premium partnerships at the heart of Vodafone's global marketing strategy and to benefit by associative halo from the emotional connection millions of sports fans have with these properties. Next, they followed the Nike playbook and amplified these associations through smart activations such as offering customers the chance to win VIP trips to Monza and the chance to play exclusive co-branded Ferrari branded games. And they recruited the star power of David Beckham and Michael Schumacher to feature in their ads, with my favourite spot featuring Becks sending

In 1953 the sale of televisions took off after 10 million people crammed around their neighbours' TVs to watch Stanley Matthews lift the FA Cup for Blackpool at Wembley.

ABC's primetime presentation of Monday Night Football *in 1970 revolutionised the way live sport was shown on television.*

Billie Jean King's expression says it all in this pre-Battle of the Sexes press conference in 1973. She has fought tirelessly her whole life for female equality.

Bernie Ecclestone with his driver Niki Lauda at the US Grand Prix in 1978. His acquisition of the Brabham F1 team handed him a $2bn lottery ticket after he went on to shape and control the fortunes of Formula One.

The 1978 World Cup in Argentina was the first to centrally sell sponsorship packages on a category exclusive basis. The idea proved to be a gamechanger for FIFA and the IOC.

The election of Juan Antonio Samaranch in 1980 as president of the IOC and his openness to embracing the Olympics as a marketing platform saved the Games from financial ruin.

Seb Coe winning gold at the Los Angeles Olympics in 1984. An event which showed cities how to make money from hosting the Games after posting a profit of $215m.

Eric Cantona lifts the inaugural Premier League trophy in 1992. This was the first season shown on Sky and proved crucial to helping Rupert Murdoch open up the UK pay-TV market.

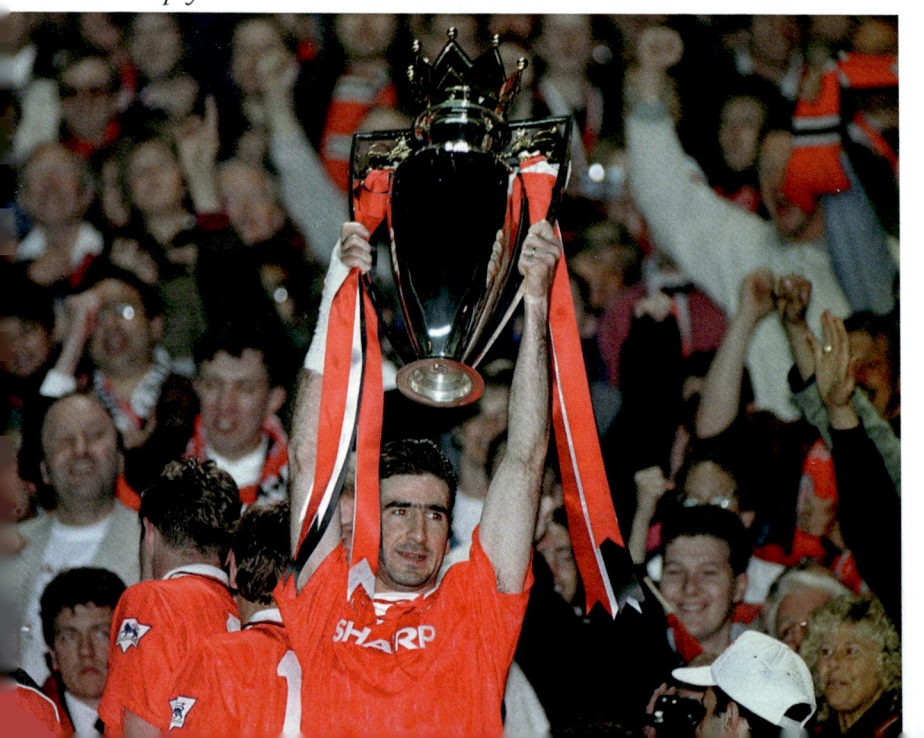

Michael Jordan, Nike and their ad agency Wieden + Kennedy invented the playbook for how brands benefit from the endorsement of sport's top athletes.

Paolo Maldini lifting the European Cup in 1994 for Milan. One of the first to be played under the highly successful Champions League format.

The introduction of T20 in 2003 and the creation of the Indian Premier League five years later transformed the fortunes of cricket.

Brad Pitt starring as Billy Beane in the film Moneyball *became the poster child for the sports data revolution of the noughties.*

In 2005, the Glazer family became the first American investors in English football – a move which has not proved popular with hardcore United fans

Sepp Blatter announcing Qatar as host of the 2022 FIFA World Cup in December 2010. A moment in time which shocked world football and led to a root and branch overhaul of its governance.

The Lionesses on their way to victory in Euro 2022 and smashing through the century-old glass ceiling that has stood in the way of female team sports.

Gary Neville picture messages of his new apartment. He'd just moved to Madrid and was looking fabulous, while poor Gary was sheltering under canvas in rainy old Manchester. The Vodafone Class of 2000 therefore introduced a new wave of thinking to the unsophisticated world of sports marketing. Not just saying, 'Hello we're here,' like the first wave of sponsors did, but speaking from the heart by saying, 'Hello, this is why we're here and hopefully you'll love us a bit more for showing up and sharing your passion.'

- - - - -

#30 THE UEFA CHAMPIONS LEAGUE
(Nyon, September 1992)

A few months after the 1954 World Cup Final a new organisation was established to represent European football, called the Union of European Football Associations (UEFA). Within months, the French newspaper, *L'Équipe* was lobbying them to organise a European Cup, since editor Gabriel Hanot was furious with the *Daily Mail* for proclaiming Wolverhampton Wanderers as 'Club Champions of the World'.

The justification for the showboating by the British media was that as English champions, Wolves had played a series of friendlies and defeated the champions of Russia, Israel, Scotland and even Honvéd, whose team featured six of the Hungarian players that had humiliated England at Wembley. These triumphant headlines therefore resulted in the following repost from *L'Équipe*: 'Before we declare that Wolverhampton are invincible, let them go to Moscow and Budapest. And there are other internationally renowned clubs: Milan and Real Madrid to name but two. A club world championship, or at least a European one – larger, more meaningful, and more prestigious than the Mitropa Cup and more original than a competition for national teams – should be launched.'

In March 1955, at UEFA's first Congress, Hanot and his colleagues were invited to pitch their idea to UEFA delegates and received strong support for a knockout style competition between the domestic league champions of each European nation, played over two legs, with no seedings. Each team would therefore have to beat whatever team came out of the UEFA hat.

Despite the universal enthusiasm from UEFA delegates, there was, however, one national FA who refused to enter a team, since the English felt their clubs had nothing to prove to the rest of Europe and that these extra games would also disrupt their domestic calendar. This dogmatic stance continued on for three years until the manager of Manchester United lobbied the FA to allow his title-winning side of 1957/8 to represent England in the next European Cup.

Eventually, the FA caved in to the force of Matt Busby's pressure, which then presented him with his next challenge: where to play these matches, since they were always played mid-week in the evenings and at the time there were no floodlights at Old Trafford. He therefore approached his noisy neighbours who agreed to rent him Maine Road in exchange for 15 per cent of the gate, which proved to be a profitable move when 43,000 United fans turned up to see their club beat Anderlecht 10-0 in the first round, followed by 75,000 who came through City's turnstiles to watch their next game against Borussia Dortmund. United made it through to the semi-final that year before losing to the legendary Real Madrid team of this era but despite the FA's belief in the superiority of English football it took ten years before the United team, boasting the likes of Best and Charlton, beat Benfica 4-1 at Wembley to become England's first European champions.

This victory was followed by the golden years of 1976–1982 when Liverpool were victorious three times, Forest won the trophy back-to-back and Villa had the biggest day in their 108-year history after beating Bayern Munich 1-0 in the 1982 final. However, the downside to English club dominance in Europe was that the crowd trouble spilled on to the Continent and ended with devastating consequences at the 1985 European Cup Final, when 39 people tragically lost their lives after a wall at the Heysel Stadium collapsed following a fight between rival groups of Liverpool and Juventus supporters. Following the UEFA investigation, English clubs were therefore handed a five-year ban from its competitions and the English FA were left on the sidelines as a sizeable power shift took place.

'We are the Champions my friend'

In 1990, the head of the Swedish FA, Lennart Johansson, was elected as UEFA's new president and was immediately confronted by the powerful owners of clubs like AC Milan and Marseilles agitating for more games between the top clubs and a higher share of the commercial revenue. An argument we first heard in 1888 and which has been repeated pretty much on a loop ever since. UEFA's big idea to placate these clubs was that from the quarter-final stage of the 1991/2 competition, the eight teams left in would be placed into two groups of four and play each other home and away. The two group winners subsequently qualified for the final, with the first played at Wembley and won by Barcelona who beat Sampdoria 1-0 with a wonder strike from Ronald Koeman. The format was a hit with the clubs and broadcasters liked it too, so Johansson announced it would therefore continue under the new name of the 'UEFA Champions League', with the famous jug-eared European Cup remaining as the ultimate prize.

His next priority was to develop a compelling commercial strategy and following bids from various agencies appointed TEAM Marketing (TEAM) to execute the plan. They were a Swiss company run by Jürgen Lenz and Klaus Hempel – disciples of Horst Dassler – who realised the way to win the contract was to make Johansson a firm cash commitment, enabling him to make financial guarantees to the clubs qualifying for the group stages: collective bargaining had arrived in Europe, and its impact would prove to be just as transformational for European football as it had been for the top sports in the United States.

Everything was going well until the clubs read UEFA's matchday playbook which empowered TEAM to manage every aspect of Champions League match nights: from dressing the ground in bespoke branding, to selling VIP hospitality, allocating premium seating, managing TV production and selling venue advertising. The competition would also have its own 'Champions' operatic theme tune which would be played during the TV credits, and before the kick-off of every game. It was, as Craig Thompson, the ex-MD of TEAM explained to *The Athletic*, a highly disruptive plan: 'The majority of the clubs said, "we don't want it", UEFA's executive board said it didn't want it, either, because how can you take the European Cup, where you win or lose, live or die, and put it into a league. Is this an American scam?'

The shock of English champions Arsenal having to hand over the keys to Highbury in the first edition of the new competition (the first English clubs had been allowed to participate in for five years) was, however, made easier for David Dein when he heard the size of the cash guarantee on offer. It was also made perfectly clear that the UEFA playbook was non-negotiable if clubs wanted to participate, as Johansson pointed out the success Lenz and Hempel had had helping to transform the Olympic Games with similarly bold ideas.

Until the UEFA Champions League was created, very little live football was shown mid-week on European television, since Sky had only debuted *Monday Night Football* a few months earlier. UEFA's strategy of selling the

Champions League TV rights was therefore revolutionary with the same live game shown on Wednesday evenings in all participating nations, regardless of whether a 'home' team were playing or not. The matches also always kicked off at 7.30pm GMT with each broadcaster receiving a 45-minute highlights show as part of their rights package, which featured the other three games played that same night. Wednesday evenings could therefore get promoted and scheduled by host broadcasters as highly anticipated 'Champions League nights'.

The format was an instant hit, with ITV picking up the contract in the UK and soon delivering average audiences of seven million when English clubs played, and an incredible 16.5 million tuned in to watch United beat Chelsea in the 2003 final. In a rapidly fragmenting media market these were serious numbers and eased some of the pain for ITV losing the Premier League to Sky. In its first year, the combined sale of broadcast rights was therefore of the order of $75m, which industry observers tell me was ten times higher than the amount of money the clubs raised from selling their European Cup matches independently. By 1997, rights fees had grown to $175m, quadrupled by 2008, hit $1.1bn in 2012 and by 2020 the UEFA Champions League was pulling in an extraordinary $2.6bn per annum from broadcasters, which made it the fifth most valuable sporting property on the planet.

UEFA's sponsorship sales strategy was perfectly timed to appeal to the globalisation trend after TEAM proposed two neat twists to the tried and tested official partner concept. First, they argued that 'less is more' and so limited the number of Champions League partners to four (plus of course Adidas, who had already been signed up as the official supplier of the Champions League match ball). Second, they beefed up the value of these packages by taking advantage of Europe's growing acceptance of broadcast sponsorship and insisting in their negotiations with TV stations that UEFA retained these rights and bundled them up into their own marketing packages. It was a genius move that guaranteed Ford, Amstel, Mastercard and Continental visibility across the geographic footprint of Europe with all four companies signing three-year deals which they renewed over the next four rights cycles, and at ever-increasing rights fees.

In 2005, with more inventory to sell as a result of the increasing number of teams participating in the competition, TEAM persuaded Vodafone to swap their shirt deal with Manchester United for a Champions League package and created enough space also for Sony to come on board with their PlayStation brand. Sponsorship revenue subsequently leaped up to €195m and then doubled again in 2015 when two further slots were added to allow Gazprom and PepsiCo to join the UEFA family. As David Ogilvy might have said in one of his agency's famous IBM campaigns, 'No one ever got fired for buying the Champions League.'

My colleagues and I at WPP and Omnicom have worked with the UEFA Champions League brand for many years, with clients such as Ford, Vodafone, PepsiCo and FedEx, and have watched on admiringly as UEFA built a competition Arsène Wenger once described as 'the third most important trophy' he had to win. By 'win', he also simply meant qualifying to play in it the following year, which he was criticised for at the time since many saw it as a lack of ambition. However, let's not forget that Manchester City were paid £85m for winning the final in 2023, and FC Antwerp received £16m for simply making it through to the group stages. Qualifying for Europe is therefore inked into the business plans of Europe's top clubs and explains why some keep pushing for the perceived 'safety' of a breakaway European Super League.

People often ask me how it is UEFA managed to achieve such extraordinary revenue growth and the key in my view is that they were the first European sports property to truly set out to build a premium sports brand, with others like F1 growing iteratively, and the Premier League and Rugby Super League both shaped by Sky. UEFA benefited too from the flawless go-to-market plan created by TEAM, who cleverly packaged their rights and exploited the steady increase of airtime they had to sell. They also skilfully managed to keep the big five TV markets onside – especially after the very real threat of an Italian-led breakaway in 1999 – with English, Spanish, German, Italian and French teams offered seeded places to smooth their progression through the competition. Finally, the UEFA cash machine whirred a bit faster after games were also scheduled on Tuesday evenings, which opened the door for the pay-TV channels and the big reward arriving in 2015 – a monster £900m deal with BT Sport.

'Go west where the sky is blue'

In 1990, there were only nine states in the eastern half of Europe. However, after the fall of the Berlin Wall and the Velvet Revolution which followed, this expanded to 24 nations and under the Maastricht Treaty they were all eligible to enter UEFA's competitions. As historian Tim Garton Ash amusingly put it in his book *Homelands*, 'A politically interested Snow White who went to sleep on New Year's Day 1989 and woke up on New Year's Day 2007 would have rubbed her eyes in disbelief. Countries such as Estonia, Latvia and Lithuania that did not even exist as sovereign states on most political maps of Europe in 1989, although they had always continued to exist in the hearts and minds of their peoples, were now members of the European Union.' Not only did the creation of the Champions League and the UEFA Cup therefore result in an influx of new money into European football but it also opened the door to a new type of sports marketing agency who were not creative people like we met earlier, seeking big ideas, but TV experts focused on trading broadcast rights.

The catalyst was UEFA's decision to centralise the sale of their games from only the start of the quarter-final stages, which left rights to the earlier rounds in the hands of the individual clubs. This was a well-meaning intention by UEFA to allow clubs to keep revenue from the qualifying rounds but as Europe expanded it ended up creating a casino business with football matches traded like commodities in the City.

The way the business model worked was that generous cash guarantees were made to clubs to allow these brokers to sell any home games they were drawn to play over the next five years; the logic being that if the broker had a portfolio of matches, they were far more likely to draw one of the top clubs in the UEFA draw and, were that to happen, they would be free to sell the game to anyone they wanted to – and at any price. Their secret sauce was that they had excellent contacts with broadcasters around the world who were increasingly hungry for football content. Most of the Eastern European clubs were also playing in their first UEFA competitions and knew very little about the dark arts of trading TV rights – and had no clue either who to speak with to sell the one-off games they might or might not be drawn to play in. It was therefore an attractive option to take a guaranteed annual fee from one of these middlemen, and when the national FAs heard about the magic money, they too got involved by offering to sell their qualifiers for the World Cup and European Championships. The brokers then high-fived each other if one of the smaller nations they had under contract drew either England or Germany and waited for the phone to ring from broadcasters in those countries, who were willing to pay millions for the rights to the match. As Philip Grothe, one of the most successful brokers of this era, told the *Sports-Entrepreneur* podcast, 'You could not go wrong even if you paid premium prices because the market was doubling every two years.'

On the day of one of these UEFA draws, I had lunch in Hamburg, which in the 90s emerged as the media rights trading capital of Europe. My lunch companion had a portfolio of clubs under contract and the draw was taking place in Monaco at 1pm that day and so a few moments later he checked his Blackberry. It was bad news. None of his contracted clubs had drawn a top team and so there would be no big payday for him this time around. However, within minutes his mobile rang, and it was a rival agency who had drawn a top club and knew my lunch companion had excellent broadcast relationships in the 'away' market. He therefore offered to 'sell him the match'. A fee was agreed, a text sent to the broadcasters to let them know he now owned the rights, while an eager assistant back at the office prepared a deal memo. The match was sold before our main course arrived and neither of the clubs (nor UEFA) had any clue what had gone on.

FIFA and UEFA had therefore allowed an unregulated lottery market to form and with football now the hottest ticket in town – and the rapidly inflating sums of money involved – they realised they had to put this genie back in its bottle. Not only was serious money leaking out of the football ecosystem, but it wasn't a good look to have rights to football's top competitions getting hawked about in such a cavalier fashion. It subsequently took a while to unwind the labyrinth of complex long-term contracts between brokers, clubs, federations and broadcasters, but UEFA and FIFA eventually managed to centralise most of their fixtures – but not before a small band of disruptors made some serious money.

Along with the rapid inflation in the value of TV rights, the late 90s and early noughties were also good times for the sports sponsorship business. We've already heard how Vodafone cleverly associated themselves with the lifestyle values of sport – as did technology brands aligning themselves with the high-performance values of F1. But the banks got involved too, with RBS, ABN Amro and HSBC all using high-profile brand partnerships to establish their global banking credentials. However, the biggest growth category was the car industry, with Ford establishing a 20-year relationship with the Champions League, Hyundai signed as FIFA's first official car partner, Mercedes supporting the German national football team, and Vauxhall backing England. It wasn't just football which benefited either, with BMW making a big commitment to golf and Volvo buying the Whitbread Round-the-World Race and rebranding it the Volvo Ocean Race. As sponsorship grew in profile, the one-brand-per-category idea first invented by Patrick Nally was adopted by most sports properties and competitive tension became so fierce in the credit card sector that Mastercard even sued FIFA for $90m in damages after losing their World Cup rights to Visa, claiming it hadn't respected their contracted renewal procedure.

Dotcom Boom

Having worked on the launch of Channel4.com and various interactive TV trials, one of my other responsibilities at my new agency was to develop our digital media capability. This meant I was caught up in the 'dotcom boom': a crazy period between 1995 and 2000, when armies of consultants, marketing people and bankers gave up their successful careers to launch 'internet start-ups'. Excited by the digital gold rush, investors then lined up to throw money at them – with much of it spent on marketing, as the global ad market surged to a value of $280bn.

My own digital team grew from three founding members to a team of 103 in 36 months and at the height of the feeding frenzy we were getting half a dozen new business inquiries a month from these start-ups. Most of them were serious people who began their pitch telling us how they were uniquely placed to disrupt their chosen market. You name it, we heard the pitch, and the great news was that most of them had plenty of venture funding in the bank to spend with us. We therefore swallowed the dotcom playbook, bought table football, a dart board and ordered fresh fruit. We even invented a game of client bingo to keep us amused during new business meetings with the top points scorers being, 'How much does it cost to build a website?' and 'What's search engine optimisation?' If you had a few months of digital experience, like Ollie who appeared in our reception for an interview in 1998, you could name your price in the job market. He was 23 and had been a digital media planner for four months, which qualified him for digital black belt status in those days, although after 20 minutes of random chat we knew Ollie wasn't for us, so I wrapped up the interview early with one final question: 'Do you have any questions for us Ollie?' and indeed he did, as he asked, 'Do I get stock options?' and, 'Can we wear combats in the office?'

'Show me the money'

Someone else who the 90s was good for were America's sportsmen and women, since it wasn't long before all this TV and sponsorship money started to filter down to them. *Forbes Magazine* therefore placed Michael Jordan at the top of their 1994 global sports money league with career earnings of $44m, followed by Mike Tyson on $40m and Wayne Gretzky on $23m. The highest earner in the NFL was Drew Bledsoe the New England Patriots star quarterback who took home $13m, while Cal Ripken Jr of the Baltimore Orioles was the MLB's top earner on $5.6m.

Following their success overturning the Reserve Clause and the influx of wealthy new owners splashing the cash on free agency contracts, one would imagine America's pro baseball players would also have been delighted with their average salaries of $1.1m. However, the world of sport had moved on considerably since the day Marv Miller walked through the door of the MLB Union office, and now every player had a ferocious agent representing their interests. As the fictional character Marcee Tidwell explained to the title character in the film *Jerry Maguire* around this time, 'Now I don't know what you do for your five per cent, but this man, my husband has a whole plan, an image … we majored in marketing, Jerry, and when you put him in a Waterbed Warehouse commercial, excuse me, you are making him common. He is pure gold and you're giving him Waterbed Warehouse when he deserves the big four – shoe, car, clothing-line, soft-drink. The four jewels of the celebrity endorsement dollar.' Word, therefore, soon got out that new owners were pushing for a salary cap, an end to salary arbitration and starting free agency two years earlier, and so in 1995 the baseball mitts came off with the dispute escalating quickly and a bitter strike resulting in the cancellation of the entire 1995 MLB calendar for the first time in its history.

#31 THE RISE OF TEAM GB
(London, 6 January 1997)

The two enduring memories I have of the 1996 Atlanta Olympics are of Michael Johnson and his golden spikes, and the arrival of boxer Vladimir Klitschko on to the world stage. It was, however, a far less memorable time for Great Britain, with Team GB returning home with one gold medal (won by rowers Pinsent and Redgrave) and finishing 36th in the medal table ahead of Belarus, but behind Ethiopia. The brutal tabloid media of the 1990s therefore had a field day, especially when they heard about British divers

Bob Morgan and Tony Ally selling their Team GB kit on the streets of Atlanta to raise some money. After years of underinvestment – with a few one-offs like Sebastian Coe, Steve Redgrave and Linford Christie papering over the cracks – British Olympic sport had hit rock bottom, and while a tsunami of TV money was piling into the top sports, Sky had no interest in becoming its white knight. There was, therefore, only one place left for Britain's National Governing Bodies (NGBs) to turn to for funding.

State funding of sports had been going on for years in China, Australia and Eastern Europe but Britain's NGBs always knew their chance of securing investment during the reign of a sports-disinterested Margaret Thatcher were slim to zero. However, the good news was that her successor, John Major, loved sport and agreed to divert some of the funding from the new National Lottery into a new entity to shake up high-performance coaching in Britain. It was called UK Sport, modelled on the successful Australian Sports Institute, and from 2003 was chaired by Sue Campbell.

One of her first decisions concerned how to distribute this Lottery money and her team therefore came up with a funding formula which they described as one of 'no compromises', which loosely translated meant only athletes with a good chance of winning an Olympic medal would receive funding. It was a controversial approach and probably not one either Pierre de Coubertin or Avery Brundage would have approved of and wasn't popular either with several of the Olympic sports, who felt they were now under the cosh to deliver success. The strategy may not, therefore, have been to the liking of everyone, but it achieved its ultimate goal of improving Britain's sporting performance with Team GB finishing tenth in Sydney with ten gold medals. It also created a new generation of Olympic heroes such as Ben Ainslie and Chris Hoy, who went on to dominate their respective sports of sailing and cycling for years to come. The strategy proved sustainable too as Britain grew into an Olympic superpower, finishing fourth in the Beijing medal table, third in London, second in Rio and fourth in Tokyo.

The decision by John Major to invest in British Olympians is the only one in this book which is genuinely UK-centric. However, I wanted to include it to highlight the positive impact well-targeted government funding can have on driving sporting success. Major often received bad press during his premiership, and his government clearly made mistakes, but when it came to improving British sport, his policies were game-changing and for this reason alone he deserves a place in our sporting Hall of Fame. Seb Coe agrees and here he is summarising the ex-PM's legacy in an interview with *The Guardian* newspaper on the eve of the London Olympics: 'I sat with John Major recently and I said he would quite properly claim all sorts of things from his premiership, but I look back and say that his greatest achievement was to change the face of sport in this country with the National Lottery. The Atlanta to Sydney journey, from 1994 onwards, there is no question in my mind at all that what we started was down to him.'

- - - - -

#32 SALT LAKE CITY SCANDAL
(Lausanne 12 December 1998)

By 1998, the Olympic movement was back on track with the Sydney 2000 quadrennial set to generate $579m from sponsorship and $1.39bn from broadcasters. With big subsidies on offer from the IOC, more and more cities were therefore interested in the kudos of staging the Olympic Games, with prime ministers and presidents now starting to take an active interest.

As a result, bad behaviours started to creep into the bidding process and on 12 December 1998, Marc Hodler, an experienced IOC member, decided to do something about it by staging an impromptu press conference at the IOC headquarters after attending what had been a routine meeting of its members. In those days, a committed rat pack covered these low-key meetings and usually had very little to write about – until this game-changer of a moment, when Hodler dropped a howitzer that threatened the very existence of the IOC and offered up front-page news to a group of journalists who were much more used to filing 200 words towards the back.

The accusation made was that Salt Lake City representatives bidding for the 2002 Winter Olympics had offered 'incentives' to his colleagues to win their votes. These, he alleged, included trips in private jets, scholarships, cash incentives and offers of employment to friends and family. Following an investigation by the IOC, Hodler was proved correct, and a few months later further news broke of Sydney offering athletic scholarships to two African IOC delegates on the eve of the vote to decide who would host the 2000 Summer Games: a vote incidentally which saw Sydney beat Beijing by two votes. Whispers of bribery to influence the outcome of Olympic hosts had been rife for years, but for a veteran IOC member to whistle-blow so publicly shook the IOC to its core. Ken Bullock was one of the trustees of the Salt Lake City Organising Committee and admits they broke the rules, explaining the temptation in the following quote referenced to Michael Payne: 'The Games are an aphrodisiac. If you want something bad enough, you stretch the boundaries.'

Heading into the new millennium, these two scandals therefore presented Juan Antonio Samaranch with the toughest challenge of his 18-year presidency, since both had the potential to destroy the image of the Olympic movement which, for the past ten years, had been sold on the values of fair play and integrity. Samaranch, therefore, knew he needed to act decisively to modernise the governance of the IOC, with an internal investigation resulting in the expulsion of six full IOC members, and a root and branch overhaul of how cities were selected to host the Olympic Games, and how commercial contracts were awarded.

PART SEVEN
Going Global

'Welcome to the new age' – Radioactive

The New Millenium

Usain. Serena. Tiger.

DESPITE WHAT Tony Blair promised us, things didn't get better in the world economy at the start of the new millennium. In fact, they got decidedly worse when the dotcom bubble burst and a global banking crisis led to chaos on the financial markets. Advertising expenditure is highly sensitive to economic shocks like these which, along with ever-fragmenting audiences, subsequently placed significant pressure on the ad-funded networks. The sports sponsorship boom also briefly paused as the distressed banks dumped their sports sponsorship deals and EU legislation finally banned deals with tobacco companies. A few blockbuster companies such as Amazon and eBay were successfully incubated during the dotcom roller-coaster ride, although most of the start-ups burned through millions of dollars on marketing and technology before crashing down to earth as quickly as they arrived.

One of the most high-profile casualties was the merger of Time Warner and America Online (AOL), which was formed back in the 1920s by four brothers Harry, Sam, Albert and Jack Warner, who built up a highly successful theatrical and film business. *Time*, meanwhile, was America's first weekly magazine and the two companies merged in 1990 before being joined six years later by Ted Turner, who merged his own media interests into the group to create one of America's most admired companies. The CEO of Time Warner was Jerry Levine, an old-school media executive who knew the media business inside out having risen through the company's ranks after a successful spell running HBO. In 1998, the company was doing well, with turnover of $26.8bn and benefiting greatly from the growth of cable and the boom in advertising.

However, the mood music on Wall Street at this time was that 'old media was old hat' and investors wanted to know what publicly quoted media stocks like Time Warner planned to do about digital disruption; and anyone unable to come up with a convincing strategy was having their stock seriously marked down. Levine therefore found himself caught in the dotcom headlights and convinced himself that what he needed was a tie-up with an internet service provider (ISP) and began secret talks with the two largest in the United States – Yahoo! and AOL. Within days a deal had been agreed with Steve Case, who had founded AOL in 1981 and had grown the company into the world's biggest ISP with 18 million subscribers. In these crazy days of over-hyped internet stocks, AOL's enterprise value had therefore soared to $125bn, which meant in 1999 it was valued at twice that of Time Warner, despite its turnover being five times lower. Case, therefore, had the balance-sheet leverage to buy Time Warner.

When the merger was announced, the two men eagerly explained the strategic logic of the deal to wide-eyed investors. It was a media first that brought together 'the best of the old with the best of the new' and they talked of 33 per cent top-line growth in their first year together. Case was appointed chairman of the new company and was so excited he put on a tie to celebrate at the press conference. Levine was made CEO and was equally pumped and so decided to take his off for the first time in years. Wall Street loved it and the share price soon soared to $50.

Sadly, though, this joyful honeymoon didn't last long. January 2000, which we now know was the high-water mark of the dotcom era, AOL revenue had also become highly dependent on dotcom advertising, and so when the bubble burst, its advertisers cut marketing spend and the turnover of AOL Time Warner fell off a cliff. As did its share price, which plunged to $9 in less than 30 months. The backlash against Levine from his shareholders was brutal and in May 2002 he was forced to leave the company, with Case following him out the door shortly afterwards, with the duo presiding over what the *Los Angeles Times* described as the 'worst acquisition in merger history'. Post-merger, Ted Turner owned ten per cent of the combined stock of AOL Time Warner and didn't disagree: 'It was clear that if AOL hadn't merged with us, they would be in far worse shape. Instead, prior to the dotcom bubble bursting, they acquired Time Warner with their inflated stock, effectively slowing their own descent while dragging us down with them.' He goes on, 'Over the past two and a half years, my net worth had gone from nearly $10bn to about $2bn.'

'Gold's just around the corner. Breakdown's coming up round the bend'

The world of sport wasn't immune to its share of dotcom horror shows, with Sportal – founded in 1999 by South African entrepreneur Rob Hersov – one of Britain's highest-profile start-ups. His business model was to 'monetise new-media rights' with the company writing sizeable cheques to secure digital rights to a host of top sporting properties and raising £275m from a stellar list of investors including BSkyB, French billionaire Bernard Arnault and Italian Prime Minister Silvio Berlusconi. It was a genius idea, although one that was ten years ahead of its time and the company ran out of money within two years. Another brilliant idea was invented by Australia's triumphant 1983 America's Cup skipper John Bertrand, who believed the future of sports content was immersive and launched a company called Quokka. Bertrand gave us a demo of his technology, which transported us to the virtual summit of Everest and allowed us to sail a virtual America's Cup yacht. It was brilliant tech, and investors thought so too as its share price quickly reached unicorn status. However, with the slow internet speeds of 1999, the reality of digital immersion was some 20 years away and Quokka sadly filed for Chapter 11 bankruptcy two years later.

Back in England, Bernie Ecclestone didn't bother too much about internet hype and was far more occupied with trying to get a new Concorde Agreement signed with the FIA. It proved to be far less stressful than 1981, since his old pal Max Mosley had replaced Ballestre as president of the FIA and was happy to extend the deal for a further 15 years. With the ink barely dry on the contract, Bernie then took advantage of the frothy capital markets and sold half his shares in FOCA Limited to a German pay-TV group for $1.1bn – and they then had to quickly offload them when their debt pile became too high, and it became clear their plans to make F1 a pay-TV proposition was not the golden ticket they'd originally hoped for. Their shares were subsequently bought cheaply by German media group Kirch, although following the stock market crash after 9/11 they too found themselves over-leveraged and their shareholding in F1 was therefore seized as collateral by two German banks.

Other than a few overly ambitious entrepreneurs, the conservative nature of the sports industry insulated most from dotcom meltdown. The one exception was the demise of ISL, whose management had also made poor dotcom investments along with sinking under the weight of the $1.6bn guarantee they'd made to FIFA and agreement to underwrite $1.2bn of guarantees to the ATP Tour. As journalist Mihir Bose commented, 'Such commercial expansion was not only reckless and landed the company in trouble but what was worse was that beneath this was a huge story of bribery and kickbacks, a story that a decade later (2011) has still not fully unravelled. And may never do.' In May 2001, ISL was declared bankrupt by a Swiss court with debts of $450m and became the country's second-biggest corporate failure in history. The IOC had heard the rumours about the troubles ISL were having and had become increasingly worried about their liquidity. They therefore dodged a bullet when they severed ties with the company a few years before their demise. However, FIFA remained loyal to the end and following the collapse of their agency were forced to bring sales in-house.

The big dotcom losers in the world of sport and media were therefore the companies who made bold bets without doing the same due diligence that had served them so well during more sensible times. We've talked already about Time Warner and Kirch, but even ITV lost the plot by believing they could take on Sky with a dedicated 'digital terrestrial' subscription sports channel, which they called *On Digital*, and identified the Football League as their flagship set of rights. To their credit, through cross-promotion of the channel from ITV1, they did win one million subscribers before collapsing in 2002 with debts of £1.25bn.

When the counting stopped, the *Financial Times* estimated that $3tn had been invested in the first digital gold rush and so it's easy to dismiss it as a financial bubble that went spectacularly wrong. One could, however, look at it another way and view it as a period of intense human innovation: the Second Industrial Revolution, delivered electronically, which inspired the next generation of media entrepreneurs who went on to digitise our world and now control 50 per cent of the global advertising market, influence elections and help us decide who to be friends with and where to go on holiday. I'm talking, of course, about Mark Zuckerberg who set up Facebook in 2003, and Sergey Brin and Larry Page, who created Google in their Californian garage one year later. In 2005, just a short drive over the Oakland Bay Bridge, Jack Dorsey then sent out his first tweet, and two years later the iPhone went on sale. This was therefore a truly game-changing 36 months for humanity, that went on to rewire how we communicate with one another and created four companies with a combined enterprise value greater than the GDP of Germany. This is what *Campaign Magazine* had to say about the shifting sands of the 21st-century media landscape:

'Records tumbled: internet spend overtook cinema in 2000, radio in 2004, out-of-home in 2005, magazines in 2006, newspapers in 2009 and television in 2011 … Super-fast broadband, the smartphone and social media accelerated change … US tech giants were exerting a vice-like grip on digital ad growth, despite doubts about online effectiveness. Facebook, which opened a London office in 2007, overtook Channel 4 and Sky to become the UK's third-biggest media owner, behind Google and ITV, in 2017. British media organisations suddenly looked modest in the shadow of Facebook, Apple, Amazon, Netflix and Google, dubbed the FAANGs. Murdoch described it as a "pivotal moment" and sold Sky.'

With the internet and smartphones competing for our attention, live sport thus became 'must-have' content to drive subscription revenue as the NBA and MLB dumped their long-standing linear TV deals in favour of more lucrative contracts with Fox, TNT and ESPN. New channels across Asia and Europe also scrambled to secure the rights to Premier League and UEFA Champions League football as the sports industry caught the globalisation bug.

#33 THE PREMIER LEAGUE GOES GLOBAL

(Kuala Lumpur, 27 July 2003)

In 1931, the English FA took a tough stance on the foreign footballer issue by introducing a rule demanding that Football League players had to have been resident in the United Kingdom for two years before being allowed to play for an English club. In search of our next rainmakers, we therefore head to Brussels, and a meeting of European Community members in February 1978 who announced a new law which outlawed using a player's nationality as a factor determining where in Europe they were allowed to play. The UK had only been granted membership of the EC five years earlier and so this generation of British politicians were keen to show they were committed Europeans and the Football League board were therefore heavily leaned on by Whitehall to lift their ban on overseas players. Within months, Irving Scholar had paid £750k to sign two Argentines to play for Spurs. Ipswich already had a couple of Dutch players on their books, but we'd just been watching Ossie Ardiles and Ricky Villa lift the World Cup on the telly and now they were coming to England to play for a team they couldn't pronounce the name of (which everyone at my school thought was hilarious).

If we fast forward to the end of the 90s, the Premier League clubs were now making decent money from selling their television and sponsorship rights and Rick Parry had signed an improved three-year/£670m deal with BSkyB and sold the overseas TV rights to IMG and Canal+ for a combined total of £98m. He then surprised everyone by announcing he was leaving to join Liverpool FC as their new CEO and that his replacement would be Richard Scudamore, who was the incumbent CEO of the Football League.

When Scudamore started work at Gloucester Place, he reviewed the international TV deal and felt sure the rights were undervalued. To test this theory, he therefore split the rights in the next auction into four geographic packages, which generated offers of £178m from four sports marketing agencies. However, Scudamore felt sure he could still do better and so in 2004 he recommended to his clubs that the league follow the American sports marketing model and bring sales in-house. After all, the Premier League now had the X-factor of Jose Mourinho at Chelsea, global super-stars like Luis Suárez, Ji-Sung Park and Michael Ballack plying their trade in England, and so surely, he argued, the Premier League must be valued as premium content for overseas broadcasters?

'You gotta spread the word around the world'

One of Scudamore's big ideas to support the globalisation of the Premier League brand was to create the bi-annual Premier League Asia Trophy. This was a friendly tournament that every other summer featured three Premier League clubs who were willing to make the trip if there wasn't either a World Cup or Euros taking place. The first competition was held in Malaysia, in the summer of 2003, which Chelsea won in front of 70,000 adoring fans. Similar numbers then showed up to watch games in Bangkok in 2005 and in Hong Kong two years later, which was followed by further sell-outs in Beijing (2009), Hong Kong (2011 and 2013), and for the final Asia Trophy, which was hosted by Singapore in 2015. Manchester United also visited Asia independently in 1999 and 2005 and Liverpool regularly toured Asia from 2010 onward as part of their sponsorship commitment to Standard Chartered Bank, and the response was always the same. Total bedlam.

These tours therefore proved to be marketing gold for Scudamore, who scheduled them to play in territories where there were fiercely contested pay-TV battles going on, with south-east Asia and the Middle East accounting for 40 per cent of his overseas sales during the 2013–16 window. The per capita values of these deals were also extraordinary with Hong Kong's NOW TV stumping up $200m for a three-year contract, which meant 40 per cent of households in the region had to subscribe to the platform to simply cover the cost of Scudamore's invoice. As with the Setanta case study, these numbers quite obviously didn't add up, but if you were a start-up pay-TV platform in Asia and looking for killer content to rapidly acquire new customers and keep your investors happy then nothing did it quite like the Premier League.

On 14 February 2005, Arsenal played Crystal Palace at Highbury in a regular Premier League fixture and Arsène

Wenger's squad included six French players, three Spanish, two Dutch, and players from Germany, Cameroon, the Ivory Coast, Brazil and Switzerland. The historic thing about this game was therefore not the routine 5-1 win for the home team, but that there wasn't a single English player in his squad. The shift in EU labour law goes a long way to explaining how the Premier League managed to transform itself from a league generating almost no overseas broadcast revenue in 1998, to one raking in £1.7bn per season some 25 years later. Rights sales have plateaued in Asia over recent years as China fell out of love with English football and with the cooling of pay-TV battles in south-east Asia. However, this has been more than compensated for by the growth coming out of the United States, which in 2010 yielded only £14m for Scudamore. With support from his growing cohort of American owners, 'cracking the States' became an important strategic play for the league and, supported by David Beckham, Wayne Rooney and Steven Gerrard all ending their careers in the Major League Soccer (MLS), the courtship worked, with the ultimate prize handed over in 2013 when NBC signed a three-year/$250m deal to become home to the Premier League in the US. The contract was subsequently renewed for a further six years at a rights fee of $1bn and extended again at a whopping $2.7bn valuation to run through to the end of the 2027/28 Premier League season.

Further significant growth also came from Scandinavia with pay channel NENT placing a monster £330m bet on Premier League coverage to turbo-charge their subscriber numbers, which represented a tenfold increase on Scudamore's first Nordics deal: together, the United States and Scandinavian countries now therefore account for half the overseas media rights revenue the Premier League generates – or 25 per cent of its total revenue if domestic sales are included. Don't therefore be surprised to see the likes of New York, Boston, Copenhagen and Stockholm regularly featuring on future summer tours and maybe one day there will even be a round of Premier League matches played overseas to resurrect the '39th game', which was one of the few ideas their CEO had during his tenure in office that he failed to push through.

Richard Scudamore thus breezes into our Hall of Fame for having the confidence to ditch the broking agencies; for executing a determined growth plan to build the Premier League brand overseas; and for brilliantly riding the worldwide football bull-run as overseas rights sales hit £1.4bn in the 2010 auction before arcing upwards to £2.2bn in 2013. Three years later they reached £3bn and during the 2022–25 cycle will generate a mind-blowing £5bn. Which means the Premier League now makes more money from selling its overseas broadcast rights than it does from selling in the domestic market.

We should also doff our flat caps to his predecessor Rick Parry for negotiating the original Sky deal and his supporting cast of club executives, including David Dein, Phil Carter, Irving Scholar and Martin Edwards, who pushed hard for the breakaway from the Football League. Plus, of course, the array of talented colleagues Scudamore had working on his team during his tenure, including Phil Lines, Paul Moliner and Richard Masters. We should also never forget the real hero in all this was the brilliant football product he was given to sell and the box-office appeal of the rivalries between Sir Alex Ferguson, Wenger, Mourinho, Pep Guardiola and Jürgen Klopp.

'Glory Glory Man United. And the Reds go marching on'

I remember the first time I went to watch live sport in America and being blown away by what a fabulous experience it was. We were at Madison Square Garden and the Nicks were playing the Lakers. We waltzed in without queuing. Had a tasty burger. Sat in a comfy seat.

Had a great view. Found it easy to get into the washroom and were somewhat disoriented by the good humour as we laughed with the Nicks fans on our right and the Lakers to our left.

The country's first state-of-the-art stadium was the Houston Astrodome, an air-conditioned indoor venue which hosted the Battle of the Sexes in 1973 and was paid for by Texan oil money when the Houston Astros were awarded an MLB expansion franchise in the 60s. What made the Astrodome so revolutionary was that it was built with only one thing in mind: for fans to have a great time. There were therefore three private dining clubs, 50 corporate boxes and two huge restaurants, plus the 120-foot-long dugout which fans could pay to sit behind to get up close and personal with their heroes. The Astrodome, therefore, became the blueprint for the next generation of sports venues.

The next city to raise the bar was Toronto, which in 1989 opened its 50,000 all-seater stadia as the new home of its beloved Blue Jays. It was called the Sky Dome and had 168 luxury boxes, 7,000 club seats, an onsite hotel with 350-rooms, plus the biggest McDonald's franchise in North America. In order to pay for it, the Blue Jays received $30m of state funding and the support of 30 Canadian companies who happily signed up to buy long-term sponsorship packages to offer security to the bankers providing the loans.

Back in Manchester, Martin Edwards looked on longingly and knew radical change was needed in English football, which, when compared to the US fan experience, could best be described as 'basic'. His idea was therefore to increase Old Trafford's capacity by 10,000 seats and to target a new supporter demographic willing to spend money on enjoying a premium entertainment experience, like Astro and Blue Jay fans were. Post-flotation, he also powered-up the club's merchandising operation by hiring licensing guru Edward Freedman from Spurs and Umbro boss Peter Kenyon as his new CEO. Both appointments coincided with the arrival of Eric Cantona at United and the 'you'll win nothing with kids' Class of '92 (who of course went on to win six league titles, three FA Cups, the League Cup, and European Cup in 1999).

Success breeds success, and so it was for United off the field of play as club turnover hit £88m in 1997, which was five times higher than the pre-IPO (Initial Public Offering of shares) base. Four years later, the financial gap between United and their Premier League rivals then widened even further with the club generating £150m in another trophy-winning season with 15 per cent of their turnover coming from the sale of those extra seats. The Freedman merchandising machine was also in full flow by now with the new megastore selling £20m of replica jerseys, which had new sponsor Vodafone's logo on the front, and superstar player names like Beckham, Giggs or Van Nistelrooy printed on the back.

David Dein knew Arsenal had to expand if they wanted to keep up with United and so he hatched a plan to relocate the club from its 100-year-old home to a new 60,000 all-seater stadium half a mile up the road. An essential part of the funding involved selling the naming rights to the new ground, which coincided with Dein opening talks with a potential new US investor called Stan Kroenke, who knew a thing or two about selling naming rights since he owned the Denver Nuggets of the NBA and Colorado Avalanche of the National Hockey League, who both played at his Pepsi Center stadium. However, Denver is not north London, and the idea of changing the name of the home they'd played at since 1908 was considered sacrilege by some Arsenal fans. The BBC compliance department didn't like it either and told their reporters to think of other names to describe grounds like the one Bolton Wanderers played at, after they became the first club in England to change the name of their stadium. When asked for guidance on how to refer to the new Reebok Stadium, BBC staff were subsequently told to get creative, or simply ignore the new name and carry on calling it Burnden Park. It must have therefore amused the Arsenal board thinking what name BBC commentators might come up with for their own brand-new stadium. However, the bottom line was that there were no rich Texans willing to pay for this stadium and no queue of north London companies willing to sign long-term sponsorship deals like there were in Toronto. Dein therefore needed to find a naming partner as securitisation for the chunky bank loans he was taking out and, after unveiling the biggest sponsorship deal in Premier League history, argued there were only new memories to be made at the Gunners' new home. It was therefore goodbye Highbury and hello to the Emirates, who agreed to pay Dein £100m over the next ten years to become Arsenal's new shirt and stadium naming partner.

Tobacco and Sport

By 1920, most of the top baseball teams had a cigarette sponsor. Even fitness fanatic Stanley Matthews endorsed smoking with the following copy supporting an image of him holding a fag in his Blackpool strip: 'Stan takes his training very seriously and soon discovered the cigarette that suited him best. "It wasn't till I changed to Craven A," he says, "that I learned what smooth smoking was."' During the 1970s, F1, rugby, cricket, and tennis became hooked on tobacco money too, while the advertising industry had been addicted for years, with Leo Burnett developing the tough cowboy image for Marlboro and CDP winning multiple awards for the softer image they created for the Silk Cut brand. Like your Air Jordans in the 90s, the brand of cigarette you smoked was therefore an important personal lifestyle statement.

However, by the late 1960s, Western governments were coming under intense pressure from the medical profession to ban tobacco advertising on television, which happened in America in 1970 and soon followed in the UK. Curiously though, sports sponsorship was exempt from the ban and so during the 70s and 80s millions of pounds of tobacco marketing money found a home in sports marketing. We spoke earlier, for example, about the first one-day cricket league which was sponsored by John Player cigarettes, who also sponsored the knock-out cups of both codes of rugby and the iconic black Lotus driven by Mario Andretti and Emerson Fittipaldi. In 1970, Marlboro then started their 40-year association with Ferrari and quite soon the majority of the F1 grid were promoting cigarette brands. Other sports joined in too with the 1989 Whitbread Round-the-World Yacht Race a duel between Rothmans and Fortuna Extra Lights, and the snooker and darts boom was bankrolled by Embassy, who handed out branded ash trays for players to use as they puffed away live on primetime.

Most of these events were also broadcast on the BBC with their compliance department confusing everyone on a regular basis over what branding was/wasn't acceptable under their in-house advertising rules. My mum, for example, was a keen showjumping fan and I'll never forget the look on her face when horses called Hitachi Music Centre and Everest Double Glazing trotted out on to the Hickstead showground. However, the BBC's top brass knew these events would only take place if they were funded by sponsorship, which was also a convenient way to avoid having to put their hand in their own pocket to pay rights fees. Their producers were subsequently told to limit brand exposure wherever they could. Which of course was fine if a player is standing behind a branded interview backdrop, since you ask the camera operator to zoom in a bit closer. But not so easy if a horse is named after replacement windows.

In 1986, there was a fierce debate in the House of Commons to decide whether to ban cigarette sponsorship, with Labour MP, Frank Dobson summing up the mood of the house like this: 'The industry's investment in sport sponsorship is aimed at recruiting new smokers, especially new young smokers.

'Its success is shown by the surveys that have been undertaken in Manchester and other areas, to which the hon. Member for Chislehurst, referred. The industry has found an ace way of skirting the restrictions which Parliament has placed on its right generally to advertise.'

This stand-off rumbled on for a few more years until 1992 when a EU directive tabled a motion to ban sponsorship by tobacco brands across the region. Bernie Ecclestone and Max Mosely understood the dire consequences such a ban would have for their sport and so lobbied Tony Blair to support a UK opt-out from this EU directive, arguing the devastating damage it would do to the industry and the threat to 50,000 UK jobs. As we now know, Bernie usually had a nuclear threat up his sleeve when entering tense negotiations and he said he would relocate the sport to Asia if an EU ban was imposed. However, despite a lengthy debate, and even media allegations that Bernie had contributed £1m to New Labour to convince Blair to block the ban, he eventually caved in to mounting EU pressure and in November 2002 tobacco sponsorship was banned under the auspices of the Tobacco & Advertising Act.

The F1 teams were subsequently given a short runoff period to replace the estimated $750m of tobacco sponsorship money swirling around the sport and they did a brilliant job of targeting the booming financial, IT and telco sectors: Ferrari therefore signed with Vodafone, Williams partnered with Compaq, and ING Bank were recruited as Renault's principal partner.

However, not all teams were so fortunate, with Team Prost out of business after failing to replace Gauloises, and

Eddie Jordan's team also folding after not being able to replace Benson & Hedges. Jordan's exit from the sport also became a box-office event when he sued Vodafone for £150m with the allegation that they'd pulled out of a verbal contract with him to sponsor his team and switched to Ferrari at the last minute. However, the big problem for Eddie's QC was that he couldn't actually produce any concrete evidence to support his claim, with the case hinging on an alleged call he had with the Vodafone marketing director.

The *Irish Times* followed the case of their countryman closely and reported the following opening statement from Alan Boyle QC who was representing Jordan: 'The case in a nutshell raises two questions. One, did David Haines of Vodafone say to Eddie Jordan on March 22, 2001, "You've got the deal"?' It was a scene the *Drive to Survive* team would have paid good money to set up.

- - - - -

#34 THE BAHRAIN GRAND PRIX
(Bahrain, 4 April 2004)

Bernie Ecclestone was one of the first sports leaders to recognise how valuable hosting events could be for cities. Not only did television deliver millions of eyeballs to boost a destination's image, but there were millions of dollars of economic impact to be gained from the high rollers who came to town over race weekends. Plus, of course, the political kudos of being able to stick the ceremonial middle finger up to your neighbours.

Over time, Ecclestone therefore managed to significantly increase the price circuits were willing to pay to bring the F1 circus to town with other events following his lead, and Dubai, one of the Emirates, leading the way by hosting international golf, tennis, rugby, boxing and horse racing.

By 2002, I'd joined AIM-listed Sports Resource Group, and my boss Chris Akers asked me to join him at a meeting in Qatar. This was my first experience of doing business in the Middle East, and after the usual pleasantries our host asked whether we could help him organise a three-day sports showcase on behalf of His Excellency Sheikh Tamim bin Hamad Al Thani to test the region's ability to host the 2006 Asian Games. On his wish-list was a friendly match between AC Milan and the Qatar national football team, Haile Gebrselassie and Paula Radcliffe leading the field in a 10k road race, Michael Schumacher driving his Ferrari around the Doha corniche, and for Shaggy to play an open-air concert.

To which Chris replied, 'No problem.'

Our trip to Qatar took place six months before contractors started work on the new Bahrain International Circuit after the Kingdom had been chosen by Bernie to host the region's first Grand Prix. Here's how the Bahrain Grand Prix website explains how it all came about, and the chance involvement of Sir Jackie Stewart: 'His Royal Highness Prince Salman bin Hamad Al Khalifa, Crown Prince, Deputy Supreme Commander, and First Deputy Prime Minister's passion for motorsports enabled him to have a vision for raising the profile of the Kingdom of Bahrain internationally. The Crown Prince had also wanted to bring Formula One to the island. In a chance meeting with former Formula One world champion Sir Jackie Stewart on a Concorde flight, the seeds for this idea were planted.'

The relationship between sport and the Gulf States has since become deeply intertwined as the region looks to diversify away from reliance on oil and gas and towards tourism, and this regional Grand Prix was one of the key accelerators. The expansion of the Emirates airline was undoubtedly another as the rulers of the United Arab Emirates (UAE) discovered what Vodafone had recently come to know, which is that an association with high-profile sports property is a brilliant way to build rapid global brand awareness. The Arsenal partnership was the flag-carrying deal, but soon Emirates was visible at many other top sports events including the 2006 America's Cup, 2006 FIFA World Cup and 2007 Rugby World Cup.

In 2007, sovereign wealth strategy for the UAE then pivoted from passive sponsorship to the active ownership of sports assets and the hosting of major events, as deputy prime minister Sheikh Mansour paid £200m to buy Manchester City and eyebrows were raised when Qatar were awarded the hosting rights to the 2022 FIFA World Cup. The growing profile and cultural relevance delivered by these premium associations proved to be significant for the region with Sheikh Mansour then agreeing to pay Bernie $50m per race so Abu Dhabi could stick a similar royal finger back at their neighbours, and expanding his football interests by creating City Football Group, which has since acquired 12 football clubs around the world. Not wanting to get left behind, in 2011 Al Thani acquired Paris Saint Germain and launched a dedicated sports channel called beIN Sport, which delighted Richard Scudamore when they paid him $225m for the regional broadcast rights to the Premier League.

As for our events in Doha? Well, we managed to secure AC Milan to play Qatar, who beat the hosts 4-0 with Paulo Maldini and Roberto Carlos subbed off at half-time to keep the score respectable. Shaggy performed a memorable open-air concert for the people of Qatar, and while Schumacher didn't make it, the *Scuderia* did send two of their impressive Challenger road cars to Doha, which performed doughnuts up and down the corniche. Paula was injured, but Haile arrived with his pace-setting team, which meant he was taking the race seriously – very seriously – and was subsequently presented with a cheque for $1m at the prize-giving for breaking his own 10k road-race world record.

#35 THE GLAZER FAMILY BUY MANCHESTER UNITED
(12 March 2005)

As news of its blockbuster TV deals spread, foreign owners started to get interested in the Premier League, with Roman Abramovich blazing the trail in 2003 when he bought the club from Ken Bates for £132m. Next in line were the Glazer family, who owned the Tampa Bay Buccaneers of the NFL and were descendants of Abraham Glazer who arrived in America from Lithuania in the 1870s. His grandson, Malcolm, inherited the family watchmaking business in the 1950s and went on to expand its interests into shopping malls, real estate and healthcare products. In 2002 he briefed his lawyers to find an investment opportunity in European soccer and in the autumn of that same year therefore bought 2.9 per cent of Manchester United.

By February 2004, the family increased their shareholding to 16 per cent and two years later they launched a full takeover of the club with their bid of $1.4bn, introducing the new phrase of the 'leveraged buy-out' to the world of sports marketing: a financial instrument invented on Wall Street during the 1980s to help ambitious entrepreneurs raise money they didn't have to buy assets they otherwise couldn't afford.

Which, in United's case, meant loading its balance sheet with institutional loans of £716m that were secured against future earnings, such as season ticket sales and the Nike kit deal. The coupon on the debt was an eye-watering 14.25 per cent, which in one season alone cost the club £66m to service. How the Lancashire and Yorkshire railway engineers would therefore have marvelled at a very different kind of engineering going on at Old Trafford some 100 years later.

> *'As a friend of mine once said to me, America and sports is like France and cooking'* –
> Phil Knight, Nike

In 2007, with Arsenal settled into their new home, Stan Kroenke bought 9.9 per cent of the club. He was the son of a soybean farmer from Illinois – the 70th wealthiest man in America and so, unlike the Glazers, had no need of elaborate financial instruments to fund this investment. Neither did Ellis Short, a Dallas-based private-equity billionaire who specialised in 'distressed real estate' and somewhat ironically bought Sunderland FC, or fellow billionaire, Randy Lerner, who bought Aston Villa that same year from 'deadly' Doug Ellis for £65m.

Lerner's father created the MBNA credit card empire and when he died his son inherited the famous Cleveland Browns NFL franchise and saw romantic similarities between Cleveland and Birmingham. Over the next ten years he therefore handed his own personal credit card to manager Martin O'Neill, who was more than happy to make a serious dent in it by buying players to try to bring back the glory days to Villa Park. A lively year then concluded after US investors George Gillet and Tom Hicks borrowed £237m to buy Liverpool FC from the Moores family and managed to persuade Rick Parry to leave the Premier League to become their CEO. Within a decade, 27 of the 44 clubs in the top two divisions of English football ended up with foreign investors, and who could have predicted that these working men's clubs which were established as offshoots of pub, church and works teams would emerge as trophy assets for the world's rich and famous?

However, the involvement of these new owners didn't always go smoothly, with both Villa and Sunderland eventually relegated from the Premier League and *Forbes Magazine* estimating that Lerner lost $369m during his ten-year ownership of the club. The costly error he (and others) made was that they didn't grasp quickly enough that owning an English football team is a totally different ball game to owning an American sports franchise, most of which have operated since the 1920s as protected cartels. In Cleveland, the Browns' big rivals are the Steelers, who play 149 miles away in Pittsburgh and both teams will play in the NFL the following season even if they lose every single game they play. Aston Villa, on the other hand, compete in the West Midlands with six other clubs and if relegated will drop into a league generating ten times less TV revenue than the Premier League and with 71 other clubs all wanting a slice of it.

A few miles up the M6 motorway, Gillet and Hicks knew the chances of Liverpool getting relegated were slim. It had only happened once, in 1955, and never from the Premier League. Therefore, this duo's problem wasn't fear of relegation but fear of running out of money since the magic of the leveraged buy-out only works if you can generate enough cash to service the debt. Liverpool fans subsequently gave these two men the full Scouse treatment after the promise of high-profile signings failed to materialise, with the Kop dreaming of Alan Shearer but instead getting handed Milan Jovanović and Christian Poulsen. It was therefore a short tenure for the Gillett and Hicks show, ending up in court, with the owners of the Boston Red Sox swooping in to buy the club for £300m as it teetered on the brink of administration.

Back in north London, life was equally lively as Kroenke steadily increased his shareholding in Arsenal FC and infuriated their fans along the way by insisting Arsène Wenger operated under strict financial controls until the stadium loan was paid off. He also pushed up ticket prices and introduced 'the Marco Pierre White fine dining experience' to cater for the monied fans of the new millennium. In what became a toxic atmosphere at the Emirates we therefore used to have great fun shouting at the Arsenal fans, 'Is this a library?' with one angry fan amusingly shouting back, 'No, it's a chuffing restaurant.'

'When the sun goes down and the band don't play. I'll always remember you this way'

We can of course look back dewy-eyed at a time before Sky, foreign ownership and VIP dining. But the reality was that going to watch football in the early 80s was often a grim life experience. We'd stand in run-down (often dangerous) stadia, eat terrible food and put up with seriously antisocial behaviour. As a young kid, I remember, for example, being taken by my dad to watch the Saints play Manchester City at The Dell and being terrified as City's 'Maine line crew' ran wild in Southampton's city centre. The way the first black players in the league were treated during this era was appalling too, with former Spurs player Garth Crooks talking about how every time he touched the ball on his debut for Stoke he was greeted by deafening monkey noises. In 2024, working in football is considered a prestigious job, although Graham Kelly tells a very different story of his time as FA CEO between 1978 and 1989 and being introduced to the Duke of Edinburgh who asked him, 'What have you done to deserve that?' Let's also remember that football finances were on the floor until Rupert Murdoch came along and fast forward to the 2022/23 season when Premier League clubs spent a record £1.9bn to attract some of the best players in the world to play in England.

When the Glazers bought Manchester United in 2005, the club's two biggest commercial deals were their £9m Vodafone shirt sponsorship and £24m Nike kit deal. Within 15 years the club was generating $776m, with Team Viewer paying £47m to have their name on the front of United's shirt and Adidas signing a ten-year deal worth £750m for the right to sell them. The conclusion we can therefore draw is that lack of trophies under the Glazers' ownership has yet to dent the club's commercial revenue, which hit $343m in 2024 and accounted for 44 per cent of its turnover. By comparison, the average commercial revenue for the other Premier League clubs was $114m, which means United generate three times more commercial revenue than the league average. People often ask me why this is, and in addition to the club's rich history, the reason is the success the club has had introducing a new business model to the world of sports marketing. An idea the club came up with post the Glazer acquisition and was a smart twist on the official partner concept, by awarding marketing rights on a geographic rather than worldwide basis. This meant the sales team could sign multiple deals with brands operating in the same business category. So, while you could still be the exclusive airline of Manchester United, unlike with a TOP package, you were only exclusive in Malaysia – unless you wanted to pay additional rights fees to expand your footprint further.

Patrick Nally and his graduates would have been impressed and so, regardless of your personal opinion of the Glazers, it's hard to argue with the commercial success United have had under their ownership, even for Sir Alex, who with a twinkle in his eye said this about the club's commercial strategy: 'We had Turkish Airlines, telephone companies in Saudi Arabia, Hong Kong, Thailand, beer companies in the Far East. That sucked in tens of millions and helped service the debt. The 76,000 crowd helped a great deal too.' However, what irritates United fans the most is the feeling that 'their' club is being messed about with by foreign moneymen: people who don't love the club in the same way that they do and who rarely show up at Old Trafford to watch a game. For them, this is not therefore about celebrating having 48 worldwide sponsors or paying down debt. It's about the traditions of the club they care deeply about: the memories of Charlton, Best, Beckham, Rooney and Sir Alex; 20 League titles; 13 FA Cups; five League Cups and two European Cups.

The reality though, is that the modern Manchester United has little to do with the working men's club of Newton Heath. It's no longer the family affair of the Edwards dynasty, who fans could openly shout abuse at on Saturday afternoon in the directors' box. Nor is it the Class of '92, or Fergie's fiefdom. We'll explore the role of private equity investors in sports in the final chapter of the book, but the new reality for the modern football fan is that United, Chelsea, Liverpool, Palace and even Wrexham FC are global entertainment businesses that are increasingly part of 'multi-club' sports franchises and are expected to deliver a return on capital for their investors. Let's also remind ourselves that most fans only protest about foreign ownership when their team are doing badly on the pitch or aren't buying marquee signings in the transfer window. Few City and Newcastle fans have therefore complained that much about their new owners and most Liverpool fans seem perfectly happy (for now) with Fenway's ownership. Meanwhile, as Arsenal spend modestly in the transfer market, United lose their crown to their noisy neighbours and Spurs once again end the season trophy-less, it's all down to greedy foreign owners. Football fans, eh.

'You better you better you bet'

The concept of a wager has been part and parcel of sport for years, although at the turn of the 20th century the link between gambling and the outcome of sports events took a sinister turn when crime gangs in cities like Chicago tried to knobble MLB players to fix the outcome of certain games. Even Liverpool and Manchester United were implicated in 1915 when some of their players were accused of fixing a relegation decider and banned for life. The highest-profile incident occurred four years later when eight Chicago White Sox players were accused of taking bribes from a betting syndicate and throwing the 1919 World Series. When one heartbroken young fan heard the news, he confronted his hero Joe di Maggio and uttered the infamous words, 'Say it ain't so Joe.' But sadly, it was, with the White Sox players blaming low wages and the Reserve Clause as the reason they went rogue.

Back in Britain, the increased mobility offered by the railways enabled punters to enjoy a day at the races, which was one of the few legal places they could go to place a bet. If you couldn't get to races then the other way to bet was via the thousands of illegal betting dens that operated in city tenements, and for everyone else there was always the Football Pools, which was a national sweepstake that by 1960 had ten million people trying to guess the score of Saturday's games and claim a slice of the winners' pool.

With pressure building from the horse racing industry and the Conservative government eyeing a lucrative new source of tax revenue, the Betting and Gaming Act then legalised betting in 1961 with 6,000 licences issued to bookies, which allowed them to set up shop on Britain's high streets. The final path to respectability then happened eight years later when ITV started to cover live horse racing, with their marketing team coming up with the idea of the ITV Seven, which was an accumulator linking your seven bets to the seven races they were televising that day. When ITV tired of racing in 1984, Channel 4 picked up the rights and we used it as daytime filler content, although it needed to get packaged up with other airtime since the downmarket audience it attracted wasn't at all easy to sell to advertisers.

In 2005, the UK government passed the Gambling Act, which, amongst other things, allowed betting companies to run advertising campaigns and sponsor sports events. The freedom to associate with sports content and faster internet speeds subsequently paved the way for the next generation of digital sports entrepreneurs to offer punters the chance to place bets during live sports and two of the first movers were Peter Coates of Bet365 and a group of digital pioneers in Vienna calling themselves Bwin.com.

The product soon became known as 'in-play' betting and wasn't straightforward to take to market since it demanded the seamless integration of live video and live score data – in real time – to respond to the immediate happenings on, say, a football pitch or tennis court. The good news, however, was that historical event data was now readily available from companies like Opta to help bookmakers create a competitive sportsbook, while the dotcom era had helped train an army of skilled techies who could build robust trading platforms. Access to live score data was also now possible thanks to a Swiss company called Running Ball, and another based in Austria called Sport Radar, who had both developed proprietary tech making it possible to send live score updates directly from venues to the trading desks of the online betting companies. Having previously worked at Bwin, the founder of Sports Radar, Carsten Koel, also understood the danger of litigious sports lawyers and so offered to pay a licence fee to sports properties so his data scouts were officially accredited like the journalists and left the lawyers to chase down the data bandits operating in the black market.

Another phoenix to rise from the dotcom flames was a company called Premium TV, which was part of the cable group NTL whom we met trying to kick-start the UK cable industry in the early noughties. It was run by Ollie Slipper whose team had developed a proprietary streaming platform they were licensing to sports properties. He had also established an informal partnership with Simon Dwyer who was one of the 90s rights traders we heard all about in the previous chapter, and the two men followed what was going on in the betting world and realised that together they had the skills to help the betting industry solve the final piece in the in-play jigsaw puzzle. Slipper had the streaming platform, Dwyer had the rights-holder contacts.

The betting companies were willing to pay good money to stream live video on their websites and rights holders were always interested in hearing about new revenue streams.

After running the idea past a few online bookmakers and friendly rights holders, the feedback from both sides was positive, although Coates et al. made it clear that if this was going to be worth their while getting involved with, then Premium TV needed to supply them with thousands of hours of live content. Plus, exclusivity to provide them with a competitive advantage over the burgeoning number of companies trying to enter the in-play space. The sports events supplied also had to be the ones their customers wanted to bet on, which meant hours and hours of live football, cricket, basketball, volleyball and tennis.

With that as their brief, Slipper and Dwyer set to work and quickly grew into a crucial supplier of online content to the rapidly expanding in-play market: the betting sites wanted the content, sports properties liked the new revenue stream and the TV stations were happy so long as the 'home' market was geo-blocked and didn't cannibalise the TV audience. With growth funding secured from the owner of London's *Evening Standard* the duo then carried out a management buy-out and rebranded the company as Perform: the rights arbitrage model which had been invented in Hamburg in the 1990s was back, but this time with a digital twist.

'Insufficient data coming through'

Back in California, the head coach of the Oakland As lived on the other side of the Oakland Bay Bridge to Jack Dorsey but, even though he was living at the epicentre of a digital revolution, he was more preoccupied by the fact that his team salary budget was three times less than the Yankees and the Red Sox. The days of three straight World Series for this storied team were long gone as Billy Beane tried to deal with the consequences that free agency had forced on to his sport. He therefore began experimenting with a concept author Michael Lewis called 'Moneyball': a methodology created by his 30-year-old general manager to help analyse player performance data with the goal of building a team that could optimise the opportunity to efficiently get on base. Unlike Beane, Paul De Podesta hadn't played pro baseball, and his Harvard education would in fact have made him feel much more at home working for Dorsey or Zuckerberg. However, while he may not have known how to hit a home run, he did know how to write a probability program, which is what Beane deployed to recruit a band of seemingly misfit players who made it to the 2002 World Series. Here's an amusing extract from the book written by Lewis describing player scouting before the data revolution: 'In the scout's view, you found a big-league baseball player by driving 60,000 miles, staying in 100 crappy motels, and eating God knows how many meals at Denny's. Whilst with Moneyball, you invested in a top of the range Mac, sat through hours of player video, and surfed the internet for compelling narrative.'

Three years after Moneyball was first published, I received a call from a headhunter with news of a brief he was working on to find a part-time chair for a Swedish start-up client. It was the brainchild of Robert Hernadi who had secured the worldwide licence to adapt the optical tracking algorithms SAAB had developed for their Gripen fighter jet in the world of sports. Hernadi was an ex-referee, and his idea was that if this state-of-the-art software could track a missile from 30,000 feet then it must be capable of tracking a football and thereby solve the offside problem. He therefore started a company called TRACAB, teamed up with a Stockholm-based TV production company to do the heavy lifting and found Swedish venture capital to fund the research and development. By 2005, the consortium had invented a groundbreaking technology that could track in real time the position of the ball and all 22 players on the pitch. I was working at WPP at the time and was excited by the potential of this technology, but needed to be convinced there was money to be made from solving the offside problem. My instinct was therefore that TV held the key to monetisation and the good news was that Robert and his colleagues were coming around to the same way of thinking.

In the early days people thought we were a bit mad, with the head of one of Europe's top football leagues telling me, 'This is not our bag, David.' However, the truth was that by now the world of sports rights had become so complex that few people we spoke to knew how to start having a conversation with us. Was this a broadcast rights opportunity for Richard Scudamore? A sponsorship idea for Vodafone? A betting conversation with Peter Coates? More sports data for Opta to sell, or new scouting data Arsène Wenger needed to know about? However, the one rights holder that didn't have this dilemma were UEFA and their head of TV production, Alexandre Fourtoy, who immediately got our project and said he'd been trying for years to find a technology that could track objects in real time. We were therefore invited to track a number of his Champions League games and prove to him we'd found the secret sauce.

The tests proved successful and in 2005 Fourtoy handed us a three-year contract to integrate TRACAB into the production workflow of later-stage Champions League games.

We therefore had our proof of concept, and what a brilliant one it was, since now any market showing UEFA matches on Wednesday nights was exposed to new on-screen graphics powered by our technology which showed how fast a player had run or what distance they had covered. If it was good enough for UEFA, it was good enough for La Liga, who then signed a five-year deal with us to install our cameras at all 42 Liga 1 and Liga 2 grounds, which caught the eye of Barney Francis at Sky, who was looking to refresh *Monday Night Football*. He therefore saw how player tracking could fit into the plan and ordered a giant touchscreen for his revamped *MNF* studio and signed a three-year deal with us to track all 380 Premier League games. So, even if it was a goalless first half on a wet and windy Monday night at Selhurst Park, Gary Neville could fire up telling stats to keep viewers interested: 'Look how fast Zaha runs, a top speed of 36km/h, and the shape of the Palace back four has been awesome,' – well, words to that effect anyway. *Monday Night Football* on Sky had just got better and Roone Arledge and Peter Rozelle would have loved every second of it.

What quickly transpired was huge interest in our data from many of the people in the football ecosystem who had looked so bemused in the early days. Betting companies were eyeing up new data points to set smarter odds and invent new gamification products. We helped Castrol power their Euro 2008 and 2010 World Cup sponsorships as they became the official performance partner of both tournaments and created bespoke graphics and 3D animations for the likes of Fox and Sky to integrate into their live productions. Most top club coaches also wanted access to our data to help them evaluate new transfer targets and see if they could unlock the marginal gain that Billy Beane had uncovered in baseball. We then had our own Moneyball moment when we adapted the technology for baseball and signed a ten-year deal with the MLB. Now Beane could use our data to track the acceleration of his players and train them to perfect the optimum running technique between bases.

The London-based recruiter who rang me described this company as 'a bunch of crazy Swedes who have invented the coolest tech but have no clue where the market is for it'. And he was right – they were indeed crazy, but also some of the hardest-working, most understated and impressive people I've ever had the pleasure of working with: Swedish rainmakers who pioneered a data revolution that helped reimagine America's national game.

- - - - -

#36 THE LAUNCH OF THE IPL
(Mumbai, 18 April 2008)

The first game of competitive cricket was played in England in 1787 and it soon developed into something far more important to Britain and its Empire than simply being a fun summer bat-and-ball game. It was a sport that demanded fair play ('that's just not cricket'), discipline ('walk if you think you're out'), and, as historian Richard Holt puts it, was part and parcel of the nation's soft power: 'British sports served overwhelmingly to express and enhance the solidarity of colonial society ... sport was not so much a luxury as a necessity, a means of maintaining morale and a sense of shared roots, of Britishness, of lawns and tea and things familiar.'

While cricket was one of the standard-bearers for upholding gentlemanly values, some teams quietly paid working-class 'players' to strengthen their side, although these ringers were treated very differently to their 'gentlemen' team-mates and often asked to use separate changing rooms and entrances. They were also usually told to bowl rather than bat to avoid gents enduring the shame of being smashed around the pitch by someone they regarded as their social inferior. The best bit, though, was that 'gentlemen' had their names printed differently on matchday scorecards, with author C. Brookes telling a hilarious story concerning Fred Titmus who was the 1950s equivalent of Freddie Flintoff. An all-rounder who played 53 times for England and scored 21,508 first-class runs for Middlesex, although regardless of his sporting brilliance,

Fred had no clue how to use a butter knife and was therefore regarded as a 'player' in the eyes of the cricketing establishment. Imagine the shame, therefore, when during one county game his initials were wrongly printed on the Middlesex scorecard and the MCC were forced to correct their error with the following announcement over Lord's public address system: 'Your cards show, at number eight for Middlesex, F.J. Titmus; that should read of course, Titmus F.J.' Oh, how the Barmy Army would've loved that one.

The MCC then had an even bigger shock in 1977 after Aussie media entrepreneur Kerry Packer had his offer for Channel 9 to broadcast the Australian domestic league rejected by the cricketing authorities. Packer was furious, since he was convinced Cricket Australia had taken an inferior offer to the one he'd made, and so decided to get even by setting up a rival international league. He called it World Series Cricket and at the launch unveiled 35 international players, including England captain Tony Greig and the Australian skipper Ian Chappell in his player line-up. When the action started he then horrified the traditionalists even further by playing his games under floodlights, with players wearing coloured cricket clothing, and playing with a white ball. The fans loved it, but the cricketing authorities were outraged and swiftly closed ranks to end the circus by announcing that any player taking part in the World Series would be banned from playing international cricket. This was followed by the sacking of Greig by England, with the competition dead and buried after just two seasons.

Building on the need for innovation and declining attendances at county games, the next shock for the regulars of St John's Wood happened in 2003 and in their own backyard, when the ECB announced their plan to jazz up English cricket and launch a new 20-over format they were calling Twenty20 Cricket (T20). It was the brainchild of John Carr, Adam Acfield and ECB marketing manager

Stuart Robertson, who had been tasked to find out why it was that audiences were turning their backs on cricket. Like all good marketers, Robertson ran a series of focus groups to talk to people about their concerns and presented his findings to the first-class counties with the headline that two-thirds of people in England had no interest in cricket, and many found cricket grounds intimidating – especially young people.

Some in the room felt the quickfire nature of T20 would ruin the tradition and technique of the game. However, the research findings were clear: people would be far more likely to watch the game if it was wrapped up in under three hours and played on weekday evenings. The group then added further weight to their argument by telling colleagues that Sky liked the format and were willing to buy the TV rights for decent money and give it good exposure. The competition was thus approved by 11 votes to seven, with the MCC abstaining.

After the first game, Sky interviewed England all-rounder Ed Giddins and asked him for his thoughts about T20. He gushed, 'That was the best game of cricket I've ever played in. The atmosphere was amazing,' and the fans agreed too, with attendances in the first season of the new competition three times higher than the old Benson & Hedges Cup, which it had replaced in the English cricketing calendar. As Robertson told *ESPN Cricinfo*, 'These figures demonstrate that there is a healthy appetite for watching county cricket. We have produced a form of the game which not only seems to be appealing but also, is being played at convenient times for people to come and watch. We are delighted by the response we have had so far.'

The success of T20 in England attracted the attention of our next rainmaker, Lalit Modi, who was vice-president of India's Board of Cricket Control (BCCI) and working on a business plan to launch a new 50-over Indian Premier League (IPL). His business model was to sell eight city-based team franchises to private investors and invite the world's best players to put themselves up for auction to play for one of these teams. Like Packer, Modi planned to crank up the entertainment factor and pay players serious money to take part (although his voltage and cheque size was far bigger than those on offer 30 years earlier).

However, when Modi saw T20 he decided this was the format he wanted to go with and the first game took place in April 2008 with the *Adelaide Sunday Mail* describing the game as, 'A Bollywood carnival of jangling music, dazzling light shows and extravagantly clad performers ... Amid the razzmatazz and glitz of a cricketing revolution, it was easy to lose sight of the circus in the middle.' Roone Arledge would have been impressed, and so was Phil Knight who signed Nike up as clothing supplier. Sahara and Pepsi snapped up the sponsorship rights, Sony committed to a ten-year/$1bn broadcast deal and all before a ball was bowled.

If we fast forward 16 years, the IPL generated $4.7bn in 2023 and its latest two franchises were auctioned a year earlier for a combined enterprise value of $1.8bn. On a per-game basis, the competition therefore generates $13.4m per match, which places it second in yield to only the NFL. However, the ironic twist to its success was that Modi made enemies along the way and three years after the launch of the IPL was found 'guilty' by the BCCI on charges of 'financial irregularity' and banned from working in cricket for life. This, however, takes nothing away from his right to be included in this book – along with the fact that he takes no credit, either, for inventing the T20 format, since that honour lies squarely with the ECB. Nor can he claim to have come up with the idea of auctioning off team franchises, or the draft, both of which have been integral to the workings of the American sports franchise model since the 1920s. Finally, the idea of hyped-up night cricket and funky cricket gear came gift-wrapped courtesy of Kerry Packer. What Lalit Modi does therefore take credit for (and is the reason why he makes it on to my All-Star team) is that he had the vision to pull these ingredients together to create what is now the sixth most-attended competition in the global sporting calendar. As for the ECB and Robertson? Well, for some reason they chose not to trademark the intellectual property (IP) of the Twenty20 format and so they don't receive licence fees from leagues like the IPL to play the game they invented. But then neither did Ebenezer Morley, who gifted us the idea of the beautiful game; nor Dr James Naismith, who came up with the idea of shooting hoops; nor Walter Camp, who tweaked the rules of football to invent American football.

Robertson subsequently told the *Daily Mail*, 'There was never an opportunity to make money and I wasn't in it for that. Instead, I take a huge amount of pride in my input, along with many others, into the advent of Twenty20 and where it is today.' You should, Stuart. This innovation transformed cricket and has persuaded the IOC that it's the format that can ignite India's interest in the Olympics, with cricket to be included in the 2028 Games calendar for the first time since 1900.

PART EIGHT
An Ocean Full of Change

'Man help me out, I fear I'm on an island in an ocean full of change. Am I losing touch? Am I losing touch now?' –
George Ezra

Recent History

London 2012. Netflix. The Lionesses.

EVERY 30 years a new generation comes along and tells the current generation they're out of touch, which is a truth that surely has never been more relevant than with today's youth, a cohort referred to as GenZ who are the most progressive since young Americans took to the streets in the 60s with placards and loudhailers championing for change. Today's young people use very different tactics to the children of the revolution with X (Twitter) and YouTube their mouthpiece and their anger targeted at causes relating to climate change and social inclusion, but they're just as ferocious with their campaigning as their grandparents were.

Some of the historians I spoke to during my research told me they felt 20 years needs to pass before an event could be described as 'historic', although my feeling is that in years to come the past few years will be remembered as a pivotal time for humanity. Not only as a result of how we chose to respond to the big issues of our time, but because of the speed at which radical societal change impacted our lives. It will also be remembered for the outbreak of Covid-19, a dystopian time when Boris Johnson told us to stay at home and with the only small ray of good news during these torrid times for the world of sport being that most were insulated from economic collapse due to the nature of their commercial agreements. However, to get paid most events still had to complete their fixture list and so played in soulless empty stadia to fulfil their contractual commitments to brands and broadcasters; and thank goodness they did, or we'd now be discussing the biggest meltdown the world of sport had ever experienced. There were still a few casualties, such as rugby clubs Wasps and Worcester, who both failed to recover from the loss of ticketing revenue, but thankfully most leagues and their clubs managed to survive through a combination of dipping into reserves, government loans, shareholder loans, the furlough scheme and cutting costs.

Despite these turbulent headwinds, the TV rights bull-run continued unabated as TV viewing went through the roof during periods of lockdown, with the NFL once again coming out on top and commissioner Roger Goodell unveiling a breathtaking set of TV deals in July 2022 worth $110bn over ten years, which represented an 80 per cent increase on the previous 2014 deals.

Football continued its strong growth too, with the Premier League generating $4bn that year from selling their television rights, and UEFA posting sales of $3bn. In the post-Bernie era F1 was also motoring along and burst through the $1bn media rights barrier for the first time in its history, adding a further $1bn from sponsorship and circuit deals.

Sports Marketing 3.0 – 'hello, can we tell you why we're here?'

I spent seven years between 2005 and 2012 on the board of a company called Clipper Ventures, which was founded by legendary yachtsman Sir Robin Knox Johnston (RKJ) whom we first met in 1969 when he became the first solo sailor to circumnavigate the globe without stopping. He went on to create the Clipper Round-the-World Yacht Race, which was one of the 90s 'pay-to-play' sports ventures that offered everyday people the extraordinary opportunity of sailing around the world onboard one of his ten identical yachts.

Each boat was skippered by a professional sailor and crewed by an eclectic mix of bankers who were escaping the rat race, mums enjoying the fact their kids had left home and they could finally do something for themselves, and others who had sold their house to pay for the adventure of a lifetime. In addition to charging crew fees, we borrowed from the Bernie Ecclestone bid book and invited international cities to tender for the right to be included on the race route, and, if selected, one of our boats was then named after that city, with the likes of Liverpool, New York and Qingdao battling it out. It was a brilliant business model and exciting to watch, as thousands of well-wishers lined the sea walls to cheer the boat named after their city back into her home port.

In February 2007, I found myself in Spain with RKJ to agree a deal with the city of Bilbao to host the start and finish of the Velux 5-Oceans. This was our other event; a pro, solo round-the-world race we ran every four years and featured the rock stars of ocean racing. A few months earlier we'd also signed Danish company Velux as our new $6m race sponsor and so everything was looking great as we retired to a Basque bar to congratulate ourselves on a job well done. However, the inner peace with RKJ rarely lasts long, and so it was that sunny day in Bilbao when he whispered in my ear, 'David, I have news: I've found a boat, and I'm going to enter the race.' He was 68 years old, cut from Irish granite, and I knew him well enough to know he was deadly serious and so replied quizzically, 'OK, but how will you fund the campaign, and do you have enough time to prepare?' He smiled back: 'That's where you come in, and "yes", is the answer.'

I stepped outside in a mild state of shock to break the news to William Ward who was the CEO of Clipper. 'I know,' he said with a sigh. I then called Henry Chappell of Pitch PR to ask him if he could work his magic and get us some coverage for the story to drum up sponsor interest (page four of the *Sunday Times*, as it turned out). And finally, I spoke to WPP's sponsorship sales team Morgan Chennoeur and Fredrik Ulfsater to ask if they were up for it. They were. After half an hour I then returned to take RKJ through the plan and he quickly cut through my marketing speak and suggested the WPP guys spoke to Saga, (a company selling insurance and cruises to the over-50s) and tell them he was willing to become their poster child: 'Tell them just because you're 68 doesn't mean your brain turns to porridge.' As luck would have it, Saga loved the idea, since they were about to embark on an IPO and a campaign promoting the active lifestyle of older people was a perfect fit. However, these were risk-averse insurance people and as our conversations progressed, they explained they were concerned RKJ wouldn't make it round the world. I pointed out he was one of the most accomplished sailors in living memory: the first to circumnavigate alone, a previous holder of the Jules Verne round-the-world speed record and twice World Yachtsman of the Year. But they were good negotiators, and we were running out of time, so I agreed to ask Robin if he'd consider receiving funds on a 'leg-to-leg' basis.

'Bloody cheek,' was his obvious reply when I relayed the news.

'OK but tell them to budget for the full sponsorship fee.'

In the end, this extraordinary man finished third in the race as younger contestants in much faster boats dropped out like flies. The tortoise and the hare. Meanwhile, Saga found themselves with PR gold on their hands as their branded boat became the centre of a six-month global news story with RKJ's own version of 'Just Do It' resonating with millions. He also had the time of his life and played 'Don't stop me now, I'm having such a good time' every time he left port and so his PR team contacted Queen's drummer Roger Taylor to ask if he would come to the finish in Portsmouth to greet RKJ. And there he was dockside at Gunwharf Quay along with thousands of adoring fans.

Robin is one of the best storytellers I've ever met, and I can't think of many other people who would have had the same grit, determination and balls to pull off what he did. To be fair, though, we (and Saga as it turned out) got lucky with this deal, since by 2007 most brands were looking at sports sponsorship very differently to these smash-and-grab style deals. Sports marketing had matured into a $40bn global business with campaigns now rigorously evaluated and measured like all other forms of brand marketing and with a new generation of experts including Steve Martin at M&C Saatchi, Tim Crow at Engine and Andy Sutherden at Hill & Knowlton talking the new language of 'brand storytelling'. In 2010, Omnicom joined in too by hiring David Pinnington from Vodafone to launch FUSE: an internal start-up staffed by a crack team Pinnington recruited from his Vodafone world, including Louise Johnson, Mark Bullingham and Ros Robinson. David sadly passed away at the tender age of 39 but left behind him a legacy that people who knew him care not to forget. A brilliant agency which I now proudly chair and with a client list, culture and reputation that's the envy of the industry.

#37 LONDON 2012 OLYMPICS
(27 July to 12 August 2012)

Anyone lucky enough to have experienced the London Olympics during the summer of 2012 knew they'd witnessed something special. Londoners were being polite to tourists on the tube, Team GB and Paralympic GB were winning medals galore, and the venues in London's revitalised East End were full of Union Jack-waving fans. The London Organising Committee (LOCOG) ticketing strategy was also a huge success generating £659m of revenue as we high-fived each other after being allocated £50 tickets in the ballot to watch the table tennis.

In the run-up to the London Games I remember also sitting through a brilliant presentation from a London ad agency responding to a creative brief we'd given them and thinking how far up the marketing snakes and ladder board sports marketing had come. We used to be called the 'toys and games department' at one agency I worked at in the 90s, but here was one of the hottest shops in town putting their best creative brains on to an Olympic marketing brief. This was the challenge we set them: 'Brands on the track like Adidas have an easy enough job explaining why they're there. While brands that are part of the fan experience like TVs, snacks and beer also have an obvious link to watching live sports. Everyone else – like us – must, however, earn the right to be involved and to be welcomed we have to give fans something they'll thank us for. It might be the chance to win a ticket, meet someone famous, have a fantastic experience, watch brilliant content, or maybe simply give them a laugh. But we'll not be thanked for turning up without a gift.'

> *'It takes a strong person to make a strong person, thank you Mum'* – P&G.

Considering the financial crash of 2007, the ability of the LOCOG team to raise $1.1bn of domestic sponsorship revenue was also extraordinary, especially since so many business categories were out of bounds to them after TOP X1 had already mined $950m from brands. One of them was P&G who were a new commercial partner in 2012 and one that had to work hard to find an authentic link between its products and the values of the Olympic Games. They were also launching their partnership amongst the competitive clutter of 50 other official partners who were all going to fight hard for share of voice, along with the ambushers who would try to muscle in on the action.

In search of inspiration P&G turned to the master storytellers of Wieden+Kennedy who came up with a 'gift' any creative team would have been proud to have on their showreel; the heart-warming 'Thank you Mum' campaign, which was an idea that worked beautifully across their global product portfolio. Here's the W+K website explaining their thinking: 'At first blush, P&G doesn't have an obvious connection with the Olympics. But every Olympic athlete has, or had, a mom. And P&G loves moms. That became the connection that drove the creation of a powerful idea that would play out across a broad range of content and experiences. We didn't make the athletes our heroes; we celebrated their moms. We created a fully integrated Thank You Mom campaign that acknowledged a mom's rightful place in these Games. The tagline, "P&G, Proud sponsor of Moms" was used to tie in all elements of the campaign.'

By 2012, not only were brands and their agencies therefore confident about placing sports assets at the heart of their global marketing strategy, but they were getting increasingly excited too about digital media's ability to deliver value. After numerous false dawns, the London 2012 Games therefore claims its place in history as the first truly mega digital sports event, posting record engagement of 431 million website visits, 109 million unique users, 15 million app downloads, and 4.7 million followers across LOCOG's social media channels. Hill & Knowlton were tasked by P&G to translate 'Thank you Mom' into 'Thank you Mum' and came up with the genius idea of signing up mums of British Olympians to tell the story of their sons' and daughters' success through a series of beautiful online films. I was invited to attend the launch of this campaign and loved listening to Mrs Hoy, Mrs Ennis and Mrs Brownlee talking about their kids:

'Were Alastair and Johnny competitive growing up?' someone asked.

'Of course they were. They'd even race up the stairs at bedtime,' replied Mrs B.

It was storytelling gold for the journalists in attendance that day, who were much more used to listening to media-trained athletes giving very little away about their personal lives.

#38 'FIFA-GATE'
(Zürich, 28 May 2015)

FIFA was created in a small room rented out by Pierre de Coubertin to the founding executive committee (EXCO) who wrote the following manifesto for their new organisation: 'To develop the game; touch the world; build a better future.'

When Sepp Blatter walked up to the FIFA podium in Zürich on 2 December 2010 it was, however, clear that the Class of 2010 had not read the memo as he uttered the following 11 words which would eventually cost him his job, his reputation and send the world of football into freefall: 'The winner to organise the 2022 FIFA World Cup is ... Qatar.' Blatter looked uneasy when he opened that FIFA-branded envelope but not as uneasy as Bill Clinton did, sitting in the audience that day as part of the USA bid team and fully expecting to walk on stage and lift the World Cup triumphantly above his head. Like Clinton, the media were gobsmacked and with the USA having lost decisively by eight votes to 14 were asking how a country with a population half the size of Yorkshire and an average temperature in July of 43 degrees could get chosen to host a summer World Cup. Harold Mayne-Nicholls was FIFA's chief inspector for bidding cities and was asking himself the same question: 'Honestly, I never thought Qatar would win, they don't have a football tradition, and, in the report, they don't have the best marks. They had to virtually rebuild the city, build all the stadiums, they didn't have a single stadium which could host a single match. But the insurmountable obstacle was how to play in May, June, and July.' With so many red lines against Qatar, Mayne-Nicholls also commented that he found it strange none of the EXCO members had chosen to speak with him to discuss his concerns, especially when it was made abundantly clear in his report that international football could not be played in the searing heat of a Middle Eastern summer. But there it was: 14 of FIFA's EXCO had voted for Qatar to host the World Cup (there were, in fact, 24 board members, although two had been previously disqualified from voting due to earlier misdemeanours).

It took five years, and another presidential term of office for Mr Blatter, until the FIFA chickens came home to roost, when FBI officials arrived in Lausanne during their 2015 Congress and escorted seven of his most senior officials out of their five-star hotels in handcuffs. Meanwhile, at a dramatic New York press conference timed to coincide with the raid, the FBI's lead investigator Loretta Lynch claimed long-term corruption was endemic within FIFA and read out a lengthy charge sheet with her central allegation as follows: 'The indictment alleges corruption that is rampant, systematic and deep-rooted, both abroad and here in the United States. It spans at least two generations of soccer officials who, as alleged, have abused their positions of trust to acquire millions of dollars in bribes and kickbacks.' Most of the FBI's anger was directed at fellow US citizen Chuck Blazer and FIFA vice-president Jack Warner, who both represented the CONCACAF group of nations across North/Central America and the Caribbean. This group of 31 national federations had an informal agreement to vote together to extract maximum value out of FIFA, and for over 25 years Warner had their mandate to decide how to weaponise the three FIFA votes CONCACAF had at their disposal. When Qatar won the right to host the 2022 World Cup they beat the USA by six votes. For the 2010 finals, South Africa saw off Morocco by four votes, while Germany defeated South Africa by a single vote to win the right to stage the 2006 World Cup. Having Warner onside therefore really mattered, and boy did he know it.

The FBI went on to charge Warner with 'wire fraud, racketeering and money laundering' and estimated $24m was unaccounted for. His punishment was a life ban from having any further involvement in football – he was 68 years old. They then widened the investigation to include 14 other FIFA executives, five of whom sat on the main FIFA board, including Sepp Blatter and Michel Platini, who both eventually lost their presidential jobs. The commercial fall-out was significant too with Sony, Emirates, Castrol and Continental terminating their FIFA marketing contracts, which led to an 18 per cent drop in sponsorship revenue for the next World Cup quadrennial.

Having described earlier how the sports right arbitrage model evolved in the 1990s it should come as no real surprise that the market became so open to abuse, since Blazer, Warner et al. found themselves in key positions of influence at a time when football was uncorking billions of dollars of unregulated TV and sponsorship cash. I've myself had an international job for many years and it's fair to say the Anglo-Saxon way is different to how the wheels of business go around in other corners of the world. As trading borders widened, and people from different cultures learned to do business with one another, there were plenty of willing third parties offering their services to help resolve blockages. Some were even family relatives, with João Havelange's former son-in-law one of those eligible to vote in 2015 (and subsequently indicted) in his capacity as head of the Brazilian FA.

Football wasn't alone either in experiencing family misdemeanours and five years later the 87-year-old president of the IAAF, Lamine Diack, was prosecuted for taking bribes to cover up alleged doping offences by Russian athletes. The go-between this time was his son, Papa Diack, who was sentenced to five years in prison. As Judge Rose-Marie Hunault commented as she read out the guilty verdict to his father, who had run the sport of athletics for 16 years, 'The money was paid in exchange for a program of "full protection",' adding, 'The scheme allowed athletes who should have been suspended purely and simply to escape sanctions. You violated the rules of the game.'

'Catch me or I'll go Houdini'

What's so depressing about these two high-profile incidents is that in many ways Blatter and Diack both did an excellent job. Sure, in Blatter's case, football became highly desirable for brands and broadcasters during his tenure in office. But to increase FIFA's revenue from $1.7bn when he took over from Havelange to $4.8bn by the time of the 2014 World Cup took great skill and business acumen. Let's also remember that the national FAs who sit underneath FIFA were more than happy to bank their share of the FIFA billions and play the vote-winning game when it suited them. In 2015, David Conn wrote a fascinating book called *The Fall of the House of FIFA* and in it he describes Blatter's leadership qualities like this: 'He was always considered exceptionally smart in a formidably complex web of global sport, huge money flows, intricate power politics and personal alliances.' However, Conn is also critical of how Blatter used cronyism to shore up the support of his lieutenants and turned a blind eye to things that went on which he should've stopped.

What the FIFA and IAAF investigations therefore highlighted were the poor checks and balances that had been allowed to seep into the highest echelons of world sport as it grew into a self-regulated and self-appointed world with those in the inner sanctum increasingly aware of the influence they had and loving the attention they received. This was a problem many working inside the sports industry talked openly about for years but most knew they would get ostracised if they spoke out, since the system of backscratching dated so far back that those inside the FIFA circle of trust became bulletproof. If you were on the outside and wanted to get in you therefore had to get comfortable with leaving your moral compass at the door and accepting that if you can't beat them, you must join them. Many did too, with the English FA agreeing that England would play a friendly match in Trinidad and offered up David Beckham to run personal coaching classes in the Caribbean. As the *Daily Mirror* commented at the time, 'The sight of David Beckham paying respect to Jack Warner in Trinidad this weekend makes me queasy ... Warner is a loathsome character who won't pay his players what they are due. But he must be kept onside for the sake of England's 2018 World Cup bid. It is natural to wonder whether the prize is worth such an indignity.'

It is unclear precisely what the FBI's real motive was for making such a song and dance outside the Baur au Lac hotel but nevertheless they did sport a big favour that day and so their actions are deserving of a place in our top 40 game-changing moments of all time with 28 May 2015 the day when sports leaders were forced to take a long hard look at themselves and recognise it was not OK to abuse their position of trust and influence; that awarding commercial contracts without consulting independent auditors and expert advisors represented poor governance; and that the protocol for electing sports leaders and determining their remuneration needed root and branch overhaul. When dealing with the Salt Lake City scandal, Juan Antonio Samaranch said this: 'No revolution has been possible without a scandal,' and under the steady ongoing leadership of Jacques Rogge and Thomas Bach, the IOC has managed to shake off its 'cash for votes' scandal. They saw what had gone wrong inside their organisation and dealt with it decisively.

Let's hope, therefore, that Giovanni Infantino, the current FIFA president, (and whoever takes over from him in 2027) has the same appetite for change.

#39 SUNDERLAND TILL I DIE
(London, 14 December 2018)

On 14 April 1998 an American duo based in Scott's Valley, California launched a subscription film business called Netflix that posted movies to your home. However, with the world going digital at a rapid rate of knots, its founders Marc Randolph and Reed Hastings quickly realised this was an idea which would soon be well past its sell-by date and so pivoted the business towards online streaming. Part of their plan was to commission original content, with *House of Cards* starring Kevin Spacey their first big hit, which was followed three years later by a foray into the world of sports and from a very unlikely source.

Leo Pearlman and Ben Turner were lifelong Sunderland FC fans who owned a production company called Fulwell 73, which they set up in partnership with James Corden, and had successful sports documentary credits to their name including *I am Bolt* and *The Class of '92*. Their beloved club had just been relegated from the Premier League and so their pitch to Netflix was to commission them to produce an eight-part fly-on-the-wall series called *Sunderland Til I Die*, which would capture the story of the Black Cats' triumphant return to the top flight. Well, that was the pitch which secured the support of owner Ellis Short, who clearly liked the rights fee on offer, along with the idea that eight hours of TV exposure would shine a positive light on his club and rustle up a buyer to end his Wearside nightmare.

However, as we've learned by now, events rarely go according to script in the world of sport and Sunderland suffered a torrid year in the Championship that ended in a second successive relegation, this time to League One. The good news, though, for Netflix subscribers was that Fulwell had negotiated unrestricted access to film what ended up as a horror show for Ellis and Sunderland fans, with boardroom bust-ups, managerial sackings and their top player trying to engineer a move away from the club during the January transfer window. However, for the rest of us it was TV gold, especially for fans of Newcastle and Middlesbrough who fell about laughing in the pubs of the north-east and then raced home to binge-watch the series on a loop.

It might feel strange including this random show as our penultimate game-changer, but it makes the cut, since it debuted a pioneering new genre of documentary-style sports programming on a platform that has fundamentally altered the way we watch TV. And it presented the likes of Sky and ESPN with potentially their most ferocious competitor since they themselves broke the network TV cartel in the 1990s. Three months later, a behind-the-scenes look at the 2018 F1 World Championship then dropped on Netflix called *Drive to Survive*. In the post-Bernie era, it was a big bet from Liberty Media allowing the Box-to-Box film crew to have access to the F1 paddock but, unlike Short, they were skilled media folk and negotiated co-production rights which meant they retained editorial control.

The decision paid off handsomely too by delivering new audiences to F1 who previously had no interest in the sport. Many of them were also watching in the US, which had avoided Bernie's charm during his time running the real F1 show, and *Drive to Survive* has subsequently been credited with helping the new owners to land new circuit deals in Miami and Vegas, increasing the female audience to 40 per cent and reducing the average age of those interested in the sport from 40 to 37 years old. A ten-part series called *The Last Dance* then followed, which was produced by ESPN Films, who accessed their extensive NBA archive to tell the Michael Jordan story and became the fifth most-watched show on Netflix.

Today, Netflix has 290 million subscribers around the world, boasts a market value of $270bn and in 2023 spent $17bn on commissioning original programming to keep us hooked. Randolph and Hastings have changed our viewing behaviour and nine out of ten people in the elusive 16–24-year-old demographic are now ignoring linear television altogether and heading straight for streaming platforms and social video. Even baby boomers have caught the streaming bug and spend much of their time watching content on-demand with sports-related documentary series some of the highest rated shows.

#40 THE LIONNESSES
(London, 28 July 2022)

My daughter Charlie and I were two of the lucky ones who had tickets to the UEFA Women's European Championships Final in 2022: a moment in time when the whole country knew something special had just happened and the final rainmaking moment of this story. Not only had an England football team won their first major football tournament since 1966, but it had been achieved in front of a domestic TV audience of 17.4 million and at a sold-out Wembley Stadium. There was a joyous atmosphere, created by young families wearing bucket hats who proudly waved the flag of St George, sang their hearts out and ate ten tons of sugar.

The eagle-eyed amongst you have doubtless noted how few female rainmakers have so far made it into our Hall of Fame and please don't think this has anything to do with male author bias. Here's Richard Holt providing context: 'The history of sport in modern Britain is a history of men … sport has always been a male preserve with its own language, its initiation rites and models of true masculinity, its clubbable, jokey cosiness.' What he means by this is that back in the day it wasn't on the male radar for women to participate in team sports, with some men believing women would harm themselves if they took part in rigorous exercise. That was a view that even the forward-thinking Pierre de Coubertin held, asserting that women should be excluded from the Olympics. This attitude briefly changed when men's football was suspended during the First World War with the fixture void filled by games played by women's teams and 53,000 people showing up at Goodison Park to watch St Helens play Dick, Kerr Ladies FC. However, the strong turnout for this game so spooked the FA leadership that one year later women's football was outlawed, with the game deemed to be 'quite unsuitable for females', although the truth was more likely that the men who ran the FA were terrified the women's game was getting too popular. The ban remained in place until 1972.

'I was far too scared to hit him, but I would hit him in a heartbeat now'

My three daughters find this whole story mad, which through the lens of 2024 it of course is, but it was symptomatic of the gender stereotyping that used to exist in everyday society, and Diane de Navacelle de Coubertin, a descendent of Pierre, offered the following recent explanation to *Le Parisien* for the views of her relative: 'We reduce him to writings that are shocking from today's perspective. They were not shocking at the time.' There it is again. These were different times. It subsequently took until 1981 for Flor Isava Fonseca and Pirjo Häggman to be elected as the IOC's first female members, then in 1984 the first women's Olympic Marathon was run and women had to wait until 2005 before being allowed to box. Here's what journalist Simon Barnes had to say as he watched Ellen MacArthur's triumphant return to Plymouth in 1994 after breaking the round-the-world sailing speed record: 'For it is a matter of fact that extreme records tend to be held by women. Alison Streeter had by then swum the Channel 43 times. The unrelated Tanya Streter has dived 112m, 400ft, on a single lungful of air … Rosie Swale-Pope was halfway round the world, running all the way … Women. Bless 'em. Fragile things.' Barnes, of course, is being ironic, since having met Ellen, I would say 'fragile' is not a good word to describe her.

If we fast forward, the good news is that this growing push and pull pressure has started to break down many of the barriers that have stood in the way of women playing and influencing competitive sports – especially over the past five years. There is, of course, still considerable work to do with the behaviour of the president of the Spanish FA at the 2023 Women's World Cup a recent case in point – along with the access to opportunity, resources, quality of sports kit, quality of sports science and the underground drumbeat of misogyny. However, let's for a moment put that frustration to one side and acknowledge how far women's sport has come and applaud the fearless women who have played such an important part in helping women smash through sport's glass ceiling. In my female Hall of Fame, I would therefore include Ellen, Billie Jean, Sue Campbell, Liz Nichol, Barbara Slater, Karen Earl and Megan Rapinoe. The WTA has also continued to build on BJK's legacy, with female tennis players now amongst the highest-profile and best-paid athletes in world sport. More and more boards also now have a statutory commitment to gender balance, with the English FA appointing Debbie Hewitt in 2021 as chair of both the men's and women's games and pushing brands and broadcasters hard to get behind women's football. Despite our earlier amusement at how members of the MCC used to behave, there are also new leaders at Lord's starting to move with the times and agreeing equal pay deals for England's male and female players, a breakthrough moment for cricket.

'Russo's on fire. Your defence is terrified'

All this positive momentum therefore came together over two memorable weeks in the summer of 2022 with the touchpaper lit after Chloe Kelly toe-poked home that extra-time winner and waved her Nike England shirt wildly above her head. She then summed up perfectly what we all felt in a breathless post-match interview with the BBC: 'I am speechless, I can't take it all in, I am still in shock. I can't believe we've won it, I just can't, it's mad.' Well said, Chloe. It was a mad moment for sure, but one which will hopefully lead to an ocean full of change for female team sports … Millimetres and timing, as a wise man once said.

I watched on admiringly as a smiling Dame Sue Campbell – at the time the FA's director of women's football – walked around the Wembley pitch that day, with her FA colleagues Kelly Simmonds and Marzena Bogdanowicz, who had both played such a massive part in England's success. Her joy was captured in this interview she later gave to *The Guardian*: 'My life has been dedicated to one simple mission – changing girls' and women's lives in sport and through sport. It has not been easy and there have been many setbacks, but the strength of my purpose has helped me to recover and continue the journey.' Congratulations therefore go to Sue, Kelly and Marzena for doing such an incredible job. Three female FA musketeers who kicked the door wide-open for the next generation of young women to charge through.

PART NINE

What Lessons Can Sporting History Teach Us?

'We don't make history; we're made by history' – Martin Luther King

---

Conclusions

COMING INTO the business of sport from the world of media in the 90s, I was somewhat taken aback by how unsophisticated the sales pitch was, with most of the talk about meeting famous people, enjoying VIP hospitality and how our clients would have their brand exposed to millions of eyeballs on TV. Where was the strategy? What was the big idea? Why was my client's brand such a good fit with the property? Where was the supporting data? And what kind of ROI (return on investment) might we expect? Some deals were also agreed because the CEO (or his wife) liked the sport and we were once fired mid-presentation for giving the client 'the wrong answer', which in his mind was cricket – even though the data showed his target market had very little interest in the sport. As Peter Ueberroth once said, 'For some reason, good, sound businessmen seem to waive all their business principle when they get involved in sports.'

To be fair, many of the people who found themselves running sport back in the day had little experience of media or marketing, with Lord Killanin an Old Etonian who saw active service at the Battle of Normandy. Bernie Ecclestone sold second-hand cars, Sepp Blatter sold Swiss watches, Richard Scudamore sold advertising and Michel Platini sold dummies to defenders. Then of course there was the army of ex-lawyers who somehow found themselves running sport, with McCormack, Stern and Bach having the perfect surnames to start a law firm together.

One of my objectives for writing this book was therefore to help people new to the world of sport business to understand why the industry behaves the way it does. For example, it should now hopefully be clear why there are different versions of football; how Sky and ESPN have managed to establish such dominant positions in sports broadcasting; and the complex journey brands have been on transforming sports sponsorship from chairman's whim to must-have content. The other conclusion we can confidently make is that the history of sports marketing is a short one – less than 40 years in fact – with Sepp Blatter inheriting a governing body that in 1998 employed only 12 people, who worked in a small house in Lausanne.

We've learned too that despite a slow start, our love affair with sport has always been closely pegged to the growth of television, which is presently going through the next stage of its evolution as audiences migrate online, at scale, and increasingly consume their content on demand. This final chapter will therefore look at the lessons we can learn from the past in order to identify the future challenges facing sport. Will broadcasters still be able to write the big cheques to buy rights? How do we keep young people interested when there are so many other things competing for their attention and their view of the world is so different to their parents? What skills will the industry's new leaders need to be able to navigate through our rapidly changing world? And who will be the new 'rainmakers' that will define sports next 40 years?

Adapt or die

We've come across numerous examples of how forward-thinking sports have innovated over the years to keep their fans interested. For example, the NBA introduced the 'shot clock' in the 1970s which increased the average number of points scored by 20 per cent, while baseball made its ballparks smaller to make it easier to hit home runs. However, the critical issue facing the modern sports industry is not how many goals or runs get scored but how it engages with the next generation of fans, and to help us understand the challenge we can lean on You Gov research that in 2012 concluded the average age of NBA fans was 40, that followers of the Olympics were 44, and fans of golf were nine years older than that. Their researchers then updated the survey in 2022 and concluded that the NBA had done a good job appealing to new audiences since the average age of their fans had only increased by two years, which was a result of how the sport has always looked to refresh its storytelling, to build the profile of the next crop of rookies and to weave fashion and lifestyle into the overall NBA experience. The sport was also one of the first to notice when young people started moving online and stayed relevant by continuing the conversation on Facebook and YouTube. However, the data for the other sports was far less encouraging, with the average age of Olympic sports fans having risen to 53 and those into golf now 62 years old. This therefore suggests that the millions of Boomers and Generation X fans who fell in love with sport during the 1980s and 1990s are not being replaced in sufficient numbers, an insight that would send up a flare in the marketing departments of customer-centric companies like Vodafone and P&G.

It would take deep interrogation of the data to explain why these sports properties are failing to connect well enough with young people, although one reason will be that, for many, following sports has simply become too expensive, with the cost of a season ticket at Arsenal now ranging from £1,200-2,050 and a basic Sky subscription with Sky Sports setting you back around £60 per month. For others, maybe the current sports experience falls short and the Shakespearean improv we discussed earlier is a bit too old-school. A bit too tribal. A bit too alpha, and in a world increasingly going digital perhaps young people have less inclination to attach themselves to analogue traditions of the past. Maybe also with so many screens and leisure choices competing for their attention, sport takes up too much time and, with attention spans getting shorter and shorter, their content gratification needs to be quicker. Some are even finding the virtual world more appealing than the real one.

Finally, there are also thousands of new storytellers competing for their attention and most don't preach and sensationalise like the 'old media' often does and are therefore viewed by young people as being more authentic, more in touch with what they're thinking, and people they can better relate to. TV producers, therefore, have a big part to play in ensuring they serve up content younger audiences want to watch: recognising they consume media very differently to their parents and wanting to snack, binge, chat, bet and multi-screen, or as the trade magazine *Sportspro* amusingly put it, 'Older fans might value the short walk from the sofa to the fridge, many spectators, especially younger ones, want to be able to access social media during live events, see data-driven insights and watch instant replays.'

Whatever the reasons for this loss of engagement, today's sports leaders need to carefully study the NBA's strategy of the past ten years, analyse what the Olympics did in the 1980s, learn from the actions of the Premier League in the 90s and embrace how F1 has used lifestyle programming to hook a whole new demographic. Otherwise, they will experience continued decline in their fan base, and the next survey could well be reporting that golf's remaining fans can no longer make it out on to the golf course.

It can't be left to the old boys anymore

Mark Schaeffer is the ex-marketing director of Unilever and defines the modern world like this in his book *Marketing Rebellion*: 'We live in the most prosperous age in history. The next thing we want to achieve is significance. What is our purpose? Are we making a difference? Do our actions matter and echo in the distance? Can we connect our choices to positive impact in our world?' Schaeffer goes on to underline the consequences of companies ignoring societal change by citing a report from Enso which ranked P&G

as the 12th most respected global brand for people over 55, but showed it came in a lowly 103rd amongst people aged 18-34. He also references other research from Edelman which suggests 67 per cent of younger consumers will try a brand because they agree with its position on a controversial subject. Aside from the battle for our attention, the other big 'adapt or die' question facing today's sports leaders is therefore whether those on the field of play, in the stands and in the boardroom are in step with the rapidly shifting values of society.

A look back in time isn't that promising either, since the world of sport is usually slow to respond to change and often prefers to react to media fires as they break out rather than leading from the front. As Graham Kelly once said, 'Nothing happens at the FA unless there's a committee,' and to get on to one of them your face needed to fit. You also needed to play the game to stay on it and if you did you were pretty much set for life. Which explains why the top jobs are usually filled by 50- and 60-somethings. Or, in the case of FIFA and the IOC, often by septuagenarians who plod on into their 80s, with João Havelange 80 when he handed the reins to Sepp Blatter and Lamine Diack six years older than that when he was sentenced by Judge Hunault in 2022.

This partly explains why sports governance has been so slow to react to the changing world, and if we were looking for a song to sum up sport's societal attitude over the years then 'Don't Worry About a Thing' by Bob Marley might do it. If sport's governing bodies are therefore serious about driving a progressive agenda, they'll need to reimagine their whole ecosystem and recruit new people on to their boards and management groups from outside of the 'old boys' club'. This observation isn't meant to be disingenuous towards people with experience – I'm no spring chicken myself – but the world is changing fast and if we look at the inbox of today's CEO, they're confronted by complex issues which many of the old boys are ill-equipped to handle, such as digital transformation, dealing with diversity and inclusion, taking sustainability seriously and understanding what young people are really passionate about. Surely, therefore, a mix of experience and those in touch with contemporary thinking is the right balance. Otherwise, if sport remains deaf to change then its leaders will wake up in ten years' time, read the latest YouGov report, and ask 'What happened?'

At FUSE, we've responded to the challenge by establishing an Innovations board, which anyone can put themselves forward to join. It sets its own agenda, has a regular slot on the main board and exists to make sure the issues that get missed by the senior leadership team are addressed. It's not an idea I suspect some of our rainmakers would have liked, although the good news is that some of sports new bosses are listening. The FA, for example, under the leadership of CEO Mark Bullingham and Gareth Southgate, hasn't been afraid to use the power of football to fight racism and homophobia. Under the guidance of Fran Connolly, England Netball is another forward-thinking governing body which is stimulating conversation about the blockages that get in the way of women and girls playing sport, such as puberty, periods, poor-fitting sports kit and the menopause. Neither of these initiatives has an overtly commercial agenda, although both organisations understand that evolving into places of purpose will win them new fans and commercial partners along the way. Having spoken to both Mark and Fran, they also believe deep down this is important work and is part of the moral compass that goes with doing their job.

However, it's not just the governing bodies of sport who can make a difference, since athletes are powerful role models and can connect with young people in a unique way. Surely, rowers, swimmers and sailors therefore want to campaign for cleaner oceans? Professional cyclists and

F1 drivers must feel strongly about making our roads safer. Boxers are brilliant role models to help tackle the danger of gang culture. And with millions of teenage girls dropping out of sport because they feel uncomfortable in their bodies, why aren't more female athletes leaning in with messages of reassurance and empathy? Perhaps, therefore, the carrot and stick of reduced funding might be needed to stir athletes from their sleepy slumber and with that in mind here's a wake-up call from Esther Britten who heads up the major events team at UK Sport and had this to say on the topic: 'Today's fans want multiple consumption options, and event experiences that are socially conscious, inclusive and showcase much more than just sport. UK Sport will now fund only events that consider equality, diversity and inclusion, sustainability, and social impact as key elements of their event delivery.'

The world of sport has, of course, come a very long way since the Washington Redskins owner refused to include black players in his team. Or women were banned from playing football, boxing and running marathons. However, if the question everyone's serious about tackling is how to win the hearts, minds and wallets of the next generation of sports fans, then there's a lot of work still to do and, for anyone out there crying 'woke', here's what Seb Coe, the president of World Athletics recently had to say on the subject: 'Does sport really, genuinely, understand the challenge that sits out there before it – its relevance, its salience, navigating the most complicated political landscape while holding out to its moral compass?'

No Seb, I'm not convinced it does.

The sports economy is built around television

The jazz singer Gil Scott Heron sang, 'The revolution will not be televised, brother', although he was wrong when it came to sport since one clear conclusion from this book is that the modern sports marketing industry has been shaped by TV. However, it wasn't always that way, with one of NBC's great pioneers, Harry Cole, saying in the early days it was actually the other way around: 'Television got off the ground because of sports; today, maybe sports need television to survive, but it was just the opposite when it first started. When you put on the World Series in 1947, heavyweight fights, the Army-Navy football game, the sales of television sets just rocketed.' The satellite revolution then made it possible to beam pictures of the Mexico City Olympics, Neil Armstrong's moonwalk, RKJ's homecoming and the 1966 World Cup live into our sitting rooms as sport grew into killer programming for TV networks to attract advertisers. Here's one of sport's greatest storytellers Mr Roone Arledge explaining the attraction in words that should really be delivered by Kenneth Branagh: 'Life condensed, all its drama, struggle, heartbreak and triumph embodied in artificial contests ... sports always contained the unexpected – a catch that should have been made and wasn't, a bar that shouldn't have been leaped and was. So did life – chaos intruding on the orderly patterns of civilisation. Sports could bring tears or laughter, in wonderment over its sometime absurdity.'

The revelation of colour TV was the next big innovation, with people watching on in amazement when they saw Pelé hand his bright yellow shirt to Bobby Moore at the 1970 World Cup. The stakes were then raised considerably on the incoming tide of TV advertising as America's networks went toe-to-toe with each other to secure sport's top broadcast contracts. When Peter Rozelle first pitched the NFL as a league-wide collective, CBS had to treble the licence fee to retain the rights and achieved it by counting on Ford's upfront ad dollars to get the deal over the line. The eminently quotable Jack Welch once said, 'If you don't have a competitive advantage, then don't compete,' and the network TV cartels were rudely disrupted in the 90s after Ruper Murdoch discovered live sport was the competitive advantage he'd been looking for to kick-start his failing satellite TV business. Sports rights subsequently skyrocketed in the UK, fuelled by the boom in pay-TV. Many observers then thought the rapid growth of digital platforms would lead to a third wave of disruption but, despite billions having been invested, few have yet succeeded in uncorking the digital sports dollar.

If we drill down into how the big sports properties make their money, it is broadly the same as it was in 1994. Yes, there's much more of it, but it's the same mix of linear broadcast rights fees, sponsorship, ticketing and merchandise that have fuelled its growth, with TV rights the economic scaffolding supporting the sports economy and 80 per cent of the $21bn the NFL, Premier League, NBA, F1 and UEFA Champions League collectively generate coming from the sale of their TV rights. The supply of exclusive and original audio-visual (A/V) content therefore continues to be critical for media companies and I don't believe the top sports should be unduly concerned about relying on A/V content as their primary source of future funding. That said, having heard earlier how quickly the media world is shifting from analogue to digital, sport's reliance on linear TV is at odds with the broader media industry and a warning sign flashed up recently when the last Premier League domestic TV contract announced the per match rights fee had fallen from £7.2m to £5.9m. Which is why the flurry of rights announcements in the summer of 2022 was noted with great interest as sports broadcasting moves towards its next inflexion point.

Amazon were first out the blocks by announcing they'd acquired the UK rights to the UEFA Champions League, the top tier of domestic football rights in France, plus the Thursday NFL game of the week. Days later, Apple+ then unveiled a ten-year/$2.5bn deal to stream MLS in the

United States and were followed by Google who made a $2bn offer for the rights to the NFL *Sunday Ticket*. Three heavily capitalised tech companies had therefore just made significant plays for live sports rights, outbidding the usual suspects with talk of connecting their massive subscriber base to the global sports audience. As commissioner Mark Abbot remarked when announcing his deal with Apple, 'I think it's huge. Our fanbase is young, digitally native, that's where they consume now. So, to be where they are, with the leading company in this area, is something that's really significant for us.'

If Rupert Murdoch had the subscription ace up his sleeve in the 1990s, then Amazon and Apple have a powerful card of their own to play moving forward, which is to view sports content as a Trojan horse to drive e-commerce on to their platforms. Here's *Sportspro* commenting on Amazon's debut telecast of the Chiefs v the Chargers on 15 September 2022: 'Amazon will be happy with the 13 million viewers that tuned in. But the real metric to consider isn't viewership – it's Prime subscriptions. Virtually everything Amazon does – except for its cloud services business – is designed to drive online retail sales, with the company's whole sports broadcasting strategy focused on acquiring more Prime sign-ups ... the initial results were promising with Amazon claiming internally they had secured more sign-ups over a three-hour period than any other day in the company's history.'

It's early days, but these first-mover streaming deals therefore signal we're entering the next evolution of the sports media and marketing business. During the last wave of disruption, neither ITV nor BBC could find a way to compete with Sky, while CBS had to throw in the towel against Fox and ESPN. Anyone who regards live sport as strategically important to their business model must therefore figure out how to compete with the deep pockets and multi-revenue business model of the tech giants, with even Channel 4 saying half their revenue will come from streaming by 2030. Let's not assume either that it will simply be a three-way battle of linear v pay v streamer. Look, for example, at the recent announcement from the LA Clippers that they were launching 'Clipper Vision': a dedicated direct-to-consumer streaming platform with augmented reality and six-stream options built into the production workflow, which was followed in February 2024 by ESPN and Warner Discovery announcing their own streaming collaboration in sports. Maybe the big sports properties like the NFL and Premier League will therefore take the advice of futurologist Carlo de Marchis and ditch their third-party broadcast deals altogether to launch their own dedicated streaming channels and thereby own the customer data: 'In my view, the end game for retaining fans is funnelling them into rich, engaging, high-value own-and-operated experiences where first-party data can be the foundation for a long-term mutual relationship.'

It's the jeopardy that keeps it interesting

There are many reasons why we follow sport. Maybe our dad was passionate about his team and took us to watch them from a young age. Perhaps the team are from our home town and so it makes us feel nostalgic to follow them. Possibly, when we were kids, we wanted to support a team that won things, loved a certain player or, like me, were excited about supporting a team with flashy kit and a flamboyant manager. Whatever it was that initially drew us into our tribe of choice, what keeps us drinking the Kool-Aid is the jeopardy of not knowing what's going to happen next. Can Matthews win the FA Cup? Will the America's Cup stay bolted down in the NYYC board room for another 132 years? How long will it be before an African team wins the World Cup? What was Christian Horner thinking of?

Conclusions

Another reason we get hooked on sport is the same as with all good drama, in that it has unpredictable twists and turns and all of them are unscripted. Even if nothing interesting is happening on the field of play, we're still entertained by funky graphics, interesting data, multiple camera angles and the inane chatter of pundits. As Ellis Cashmore once said, 'The risk in sports may be tiny, but its presence is what counts; and where it doesn't exist, we invent it.'

The Premier League is therefore one of television's best real-world dramas, which debuted in 1992 and celebrated its 30th anniversary on Sky by serving up one of its finest-ever episodes on the final day of the 2021/22 football season: ten games that kicked off in front of a global audience of 650 million and produced twisting plots and sub-plots and when the music stopped at 5.30pm ended in tragedy for fans of Burnley, Liverpool and Arsenal, and a psychedelic high for supporters of Manchester City, Leeds United and Tottenham Hotspur.

'Delirium at the Etihad'

The preshow hype from the Sky studio was how Aston Villa had nothing much to fight for and their players were already on the beach. Manchester City therefore simply needed to turn up at the Etihad, beat Villa, and pip Liverpool to the title. However, with 14 minutes to go, the plot was not going to script as the men in claret and blue found themselves 2-0 up, and it wasn't lost on the Sky commentary team that their coach Steven Gerrard had played for Liverpool his whole career and yet never won the title. When another ex-Liverpool player slotted in the second goal, Gary Neville therefore delivered the one-liner millions of us watching at home were thinking to ourselves: 'Oh my word. Gerrard, Coutinho, the story that people talked about all week may very well be coming true.'

However, as we know by now, good drama always carries an unexpected plot twist and so it was that spring afternoon in Manchester when two goals from İlkay Gündoğan and another from Rodri sent City fans wild as their team scored three times in ten crazy minutes. Sky's modern-day bard, Martin Tyler, was then once again left to sum up what had just happened with words William Shakespeare himself would have been proud to have delivered: 'It's gone right until the final whistle of the campaign: 93 points; 99 goals and three – in a rapid spell – turned a potential disaster into delirium at the Etihad.'

At the other end of the league table another Shakespearean improv was playing out at Turf Moor, which is the home of Burnley FC, one of the founding members of the Football League, who began life as a Victorian rugby club but were now owned by American private equity. Their jeopardy was that if they beat Newcastle, they would avoid relegation to the Championship, although their rivals for the drop, Leeds United, would themselves stay up if Burnley lost and Leeds beat Brentford away. By 5.30 pm both teams knew their fate, with Burnley fans suffering the double heartbreak of having a last-minute shot cleared off the line and Jack Harrison scoring a 94th-minute winner for Leeds. Burnley were subsequently relegated and lost ALK Capital a fortune, while Leeds announced new investment from the owners of the San Francisco 49ers.

As if this wasn't enough to take in, 200 miles down the M1 motorway another sub-plot was unfolding at the Emirates with the Sky pundits alive to the scenario that if Arsenal could beat Everton and their arch-rivals Spurs lost at Norwich then the Gunners would claim that crucial fourth-place spot that used to keep Arsène Wenger awake at night. They did win – 5-0 – but so did Tottenham, to claim both north London bragging rights and a fat cheque from UEFA.

Not even the collective brilliance of ESPN Films, Bill Bernbach and the entire Wieden+Kennedy creative department would have had the audacity to pitch such a far-fetched and complicated script to Sky's commissioning editor. But it did happen, and so did THAT shot from Michael Jordan, Johnny Wilkinson's drop-goal, Usain Bolt's lightning runs, Tiger's magical puts, Schumacher's five consecutive world championships, Van Nistelrooy's miss and Chloe's toe-poke. One of the companies I therefore love working with are the data wizards of Twenty-First Group who are black belts at understanding jeopardy and the probability of sporting outcomes. I asked their chief intelligence officer, Omar Chaudhuri, to simulate the likelihood of some of the sporting game-changers we've come across in this book actually happening. This is what his models predicted – based on actual historical data:

What was the probability of Ruud van Nistelrooy missing that penalty in 2003?
'Twenty-two per cent, since over the past five years only one in five penalties have been missed in the Premier League.'

What's the chance of playing an entire season in the Premier League without losing?
'Very slim – our models suggest just 0.3 per cent – and so it's no exaggeration to say that Arsenal team of 2002/3 were Invincible.'

How likely was it Blackpool would come back from 3-1 down to win the 1953 FA Cup?
'With only 22 minutes to go, and based on historical FA Cup data, we estimate no more than 9.4 per cent – so less than a one in ten chance – although in those days the unrivalled brilliance of Stanley Matthews would have doubtless shifted the odds.'

What was the likelihood of City beating Villa in that 2021/22 title decider?
'With only 14 minutes to go only three per cent of games have ended in a comeback like that.'

What a brilliant company. Data-led storytellers who are feeding the next generation of content producers with storylines that keep us on the edge of our seats and begging for more.

Surround sound keeps the conversation going

Being able to watch a few games on Sky isn't the only reason why football has become such a big part of our lives. The unscripted drama on TV might well be where the live matchday action plays out but our addiction goes much, much deeper than this and is fuelled by the constant provocation of newspaper gossip, talk-radio banter, in-play betting, and the 24/7 back and forth of social media. Is Ten Haag going to be sacked? Why don't Chelsea play with a back three? When will Arsenal buy a decent striker? For many, the narrative of sport has therefore replaced soap operas like *Coronation Street* as the modern-day water cooler conversation of choice. This obsessive behaviour is also amped up further if, like me, you get hooked on the endorphin rush of fantasy league: a parallel universe where a goalless draw between Brentford and Bournemouth takes on a whole new meaning. I used to sit on the board of Fantasy League Limited whose founder Andrew Wainstein introduced the idea to the UK in the 90s. For years he ran *The Sun* fantasy game which, in its heyday, had 500,000 players and I remember him telling me some players visited the site over 100 times a day to tinker with their team. I understand their obsession too, since one day I turned to my daughter after we lost to a late winner from Harry Kane

Conclusions

at Selhurst and said, 'Oh well, at least that's five points for my fantasy team.' She rightly told me to grow up (or words to that effect).

Meanwhile, since deregulation in 2005 the UK sports betting industry has developed into a £5bn marketplace with in-play appealing to a much younger demographic than the oldies who used to watch our horse racing coverage on Channel 4. The success of the gambling industry of course divides opinion, with those against arguing it's a dangerous addiction that should be banned and quoting a recent Public Health England report which estimated there were 246,000 people in the UK who were fighting gambling addiction, and a further 2.2 million were classified as problem gamblers. Those in favour, however, see things very differently and talk of the enormous tax revenue betting generates for the Exchequer, that sport and gambling have always been intrinsically linked, and that in a democracy what right does government have to rule what is and isn't fun?

However, if there was a league table for football-related addictions then the winner would surely be the FIFA video game. The first version of it was developed by Jian Tian in his small cubicle at the Electronic Arts office in Geneva and was released so quickly it had a strange software bug which meant that if your striker stood in front of the keeper then the ball rebounded off him into the net – a 'Gary Lineker' as we used to call it. There was also no time for the EA marketing team to agree a licence to use real player names in the game and so Tian asked his colleagues in the office to come up with imaginary names to describe the individual players, and bagged the famous Brazil #10 shirt for himself by naming the player Tiano.

Despite these glitches, FIFA International Soccer was a great success and sold one million copies, which was ten times the usual volume for a new release. With the coding issues resolved and the FIFA licence strengthened, 'FIFA'

95' kicked on to become one of the most successful video games of all time, with later iterations incorporating state-of-the-art motion-capture, lifelike avatars of players and in more recent times incorporating real-world data into the graphics. Since the launch of that first game in 1993, EA Sports have subsequently sold 325 million games with the 2022 version generating an astonishing $5.7bn of retail sales. A whole generation of young fans have thus grown up 'playing FIFA' and many of them have absolutely no clue what those four letters stand for. That said, in 2021 EA paid FIFA royalties of £158m and while there were extenuating circumstances that year (since it was a fallow one for the World Cup, and the boredom of lockdown fuelled a massive spike in gaming) as journalist David Owen wrote at the time, 'This might very well be the first instance in history of a traditional sport's governing body generating more in a year from video games than the underlying physical activity that is its *raison d'être*.' However, within weeks of his story, news broke that the relationship between EA and FIFA had broken down irrevocably and the reason was that EA wanted a sizeable reduction in the royalty payments, which was something FIFA was unwilling to accept. The CEO of their sports division Andrew Wilson therefore announced to his colleagues that EA were going to launch their own branded game called EA Sports FC and was quoted by the *Daily Mail* telling them what many had doubtless been thinking for years: 'What we get from FIFA, in a non-World Cup year, is the four letters on the front of the box.'

Football calls the shots

At Channel 4, we used to conduct quarterly research to find out what was influencing young people, and we used the insight to both demonstrate to advertisers how effectively our shows like *Friends*, *Cheers* and *The Word* reached youth audiences, and to guide producers over what type of shows they should be making for us. In the late 90s, the research told the story of declining respect for politicians, the professions and the media but growth in celebrity culture as footballers like David Beckham joined the Spice Girls, Britney and contestants on *Big Brother* as the people to follow. The launch of the Premier League, therefore, not only turbocharged the finances of English football, but played a big part in changing British popular culture, with players who once earned a few hundred quid a week and went home on the bus morphing into A-list celebrities driving Ferraris and finding themselves on the front page of the *News of the World* for their nocturnal indiscretions. Following the tribalism of the 70s and 80s, football therefore started to appeal to a new monied demographic attracted by the Champions League, video games, fantasy, Euro '96 and the constant drumbeat of the tabloid media.

As a result, the value of Premier League TV rights trebled in the second auction, to reach £3m per match and by 2013 had doubled again. Key to this extraordinary growth has been the skilful way the Premier League media team courted competitive tension between rival broadcasters and, like UEFA, gradually increased the number of games shown on TV. Sky, meanwhile, fought hard to retain the exclusivity of the first contract but were eventually thwarted by EU competition law in 2001, although despite solid attempts by NTL, Setanta, ESPN and ITV, only BT Sport ever managed to provide them with meaningful competition. The Premier League therefore made Sky and Sky made the Premier League.

The NFL's founding fathers would, however, now be looking down nervously with the original 60-match package expanded to incorporate 200 out of the 380 available fixtures and, while the Saturday afternoon kick-off time remains protected, games are now also scheduled on Saturday at 12.30pm and 5.30pm, on Sunday afternoon and Monday night to maximise the global audience. Fixture times also regularly move around to suit the schedulers, with the top clubs usually therefore playing on Sunday afternoon or Monday evening. This disruption won't be getting any easier for fans either with the next Premier League contract expanding to televise 270 matches, with 215 of them shown live on Sky. In return, clubs will share £1.68bn over the next four years and so, yes, football definitely calls the shots and, whilst this is of course fantastic for Premier League clubs, most of the other sports (including the 40 Olympic sports) are left fighting over the TV scraps and wondering where they went wrong.

The IOC has become an ATM for Olympic sports

If we analyse how the top sports properties make money, most now rely on a handful of commercial contracts to pay the bills. The finances of English football, cricket and rugby would be decimated without their Sky deals. I wonder, therefore, if some of the clubs who voted to break away from the Football League, like AFC Wimbledon, Coventry, Middlesbrough and Oldham, who all now languish outside of the riches of the Premier League, would vote the same way again. The learning from the past is that relying on a single TV deal, title sponsor or third-party subsidy is a risky old strategy and one that came into stark view for Olympic sports during the Covid pandemic. To illustrate this point, in 2022, David Owens wrote a fascinating blog analysing the published accounts of the IOC up to the Tokyo 2020 quadrennial with the headline that this Olympic cycle generated $5bn of revenue of which 73 per cent was raised from selling television rights. A further 18 per cent was then generated from the TOP sponsorship programme and a further $450m from licensing the Olympic brand. As for expenditure, Rio, the host of the 2016 Summer Games received $1.5bn towards their staging costs and

PyeongChang – the host of the 2018 Winter Olympics – received $900m. The IOC then retained 11 per cent of the $5bn towards their operating costs, allocated the same amount towards broadcast production and $800m was spent funding 'miscellaneous projects' including the world anti-doping agency, event cancellation insurance and running the Olympic channel. Which left a balance of $1.1bn to be shared between the 207 national Olympic committees and 38 international federations who had been selected to participate in Brazil and Korea.

In the same year that Owens conducted his analysis David Graham was appointed as the new chief executive of World Sailing and discovered he'd joined an organisation with a severe cash-flow problem. In his first few months in the job, he was therefore forced to ask Thomas Bach for an emergency loan of $3.1m without which he admitted World Sailing would have gone into liquidation. The sport of sailing was not alone in feeling the pain of the postponement of Tokyo 2020, with the IOC making similar 'solidarity payments' totalling $150m to a raft of Olympic sports. After decades of struggling with its own finances the IOC had thus emerged as the chief financier of Olympic sports, with many of them, in the words of Graham, having become 'unhealthily subordinate' to the IOC. As Owens commented, 'It is almost as if IFs are on the point of accepting that the only thing that really matters in international sport is the Olympic Games.' Sir Steve Redgrave went even further recently by telling the BBC that if the sport of rowing lost its IOC funding then 'our sport will die'.

History tells us it was never part of the De Coubertin plan for the IOC to govern and bankroll Olympic sports and if Samaranch and Dassler were alive today then I wonder whether they would be comfortable with the economic power shift away from the international federations that has been allowed to take place. As rainmaker Patrick

Nally commented, 'The Olympics is an event, made up of different sports, but it's become de facto the governing body of sport; everyone needs the IOC approval or IOC sanction and I think that's a danger.'

Let's hope, therefore, that the shock of the potential cancellation of Tokyo 2020 has acted as a wake-up call to Olympic sports and that those operating within the ecosystem take a far more proactive approach to sourcing their own funding in the future. The same is also true of Britain's NGBs, who some believe have become equally complacent and now rely heavily on the £336m of government funding UK Sport distributes to fund their high-performance programmes. It's time therefore for Olympic sport to wake up, since history shows gravy trains never last forever.

It's time to re-think the official partner

It took a while for brands to get their heads around how sport fitted into their marketing plans, but once they did, it started to play an increasingly important role.

The first generation of sponsors we met on our journey, like Coke and JVC, were attracted by the growing interest broadcasters were showing in sport and looked at logo exposure as a cost-effective media buy. They were then followed by a second wave who were fighting in cluttered markets like cars and finance and saw an association with a sports property as a good way to stand out from their competitors. Others were seeking to win the globalisation game and saw sport's IP as a differentiated brand-storytelling platform. If Heineken sponsors the best brand of football in the world, then it has to be one of the best beers, right? And if Ferrari and David Beckam love Vodafone then we should love them too.

The concept of the official partner has also played a significant role in financing the modern sports industry and has powered the sponsorship industry's extraordinary growth, with Omnicom estimating it's a market now worth north of $100bn, with the cost of putting your name on the front of the famous red shirt of Manchester United having increased from £500k in 1985 to the current market value of £52m per season.

However, as the world of sports marketing enters its fourth purposeful wave, brands are reappraising how they spend their marketing dollars with 'emotional connectivity' regarded by many as the new battle to fight. Modern marketing, therefore, goes way beyond logos, straplines and raising brand awareness and is concerned with making emotional customer promises that companies must keep, or consumers will walk elsewhere. Here's what Mark Schaeffer has to say: 'Having a relationship with customers is transactional. Having a relationship with fans is ongoing. Fans want to be part of what you do – they want to know the news before it happens, and you have to respond to that. Customers in the traditional sense are people who shop around and don't really care about your team and culture.'

This should all be music to the ears of the sports marketing industry since high-performance sport is powered by emotion and it is an association with these values that makes it such a compelling marketing platform. In a world where making meaningful connections with audiences is getting harder and harder, it is therefore a no-brainer, right, to partner with a sports team or league? Well, 'sort of' is the answer, since the bad news for sports marketers is that the emotional connectivity Schaefer speaks about is increasingly taking place via digital media channels with over half of global ad spend now directed at Meta, Google and TikTok and the global marketing director of Coke announcing in 2024 that 60 per cent of his future ad budget will be committed to digital media.

As far back as 2009, Rupert Murdoch gave the media industry the following wake-up call at the World Media Summit: 'Media companies know that if you do not respond intelligently and creatively to the digital challenge, your future will be bleak indeed. The presses are now silent at some of the world's most famous newspapers – they were supposed to report on their societies, but somehow failed to notice that those societies were changing fundamentally.' And herewith the current challenge for the sports marketing industry, since 15 years on from Murdoch's speech it continues to largely think in an analogue way, conditioned to bank the TV money and let broadcasters determine the narrative. There are of course a few exceptions, such as the NFL and NBA, who have invested heavily in their digital future, but most sports properties have yet to seriously lean into digital transformation and have either sold on their digital and data rights to third parties or left it to companies like Perform and Sports Radar to figure out the digital play. The knock-on for the sponsorship industry is that many rights holders have not moved with the times and, while a few vanity CEO deals do occasionally still get done, in the main they're few and far between. As long-standing supporters of the Olympics such as Toyota pull out and many other mid-tier properties struggle to attract sponsorship, the conclusion must be drawn, therefore, that brands are being sold the same stuff they've been sold since the 1980s, which, for many like Coke, is increasingly the wrong stuff.

It's therefore time to hit reset on the idea of the official partner: a pioneering concept which has served the industry brilliantly but has hardly evolved since Patrick Nally and Horst Dassler first came up with it in the mid-1970s. And, as the industry faces up to the opportunity presented by the next iteration of the sports marketing business model it should not be afraid to think differently – just like ISL did when it came up with TOP – and seek to link the power of emotional storytelling with the emerging potential of real, virtual and digital worlds. To show openness to mining their first-, second- and third-party data rights. To invest in their digital media capabilities and fully embrace the platform of driving purposefulness through sport. For many this will be a step into the unknown, but as the English author A.A. Milne once said, 'One of the advantages of being disorderly is that one is constantly making exciting discoveries.'

It's time the ambushers paid up

There have been few more influential voices in developing the business of sport than the athletic-wear brands. I would go even further and say Adidas, Nike, Puma and Converse invented modern sports marketing, with their segment of the market now worth $330bn and forecast to grow at an average rate of 6.4 per cent compound annual growth rate (CAGR) across the next ten years. The first movers were Adolf and Armin Dassler and their 30-year boot war. Followed by Phil Knight, who turned the sneaker into a personal lifestyle statement and rewrote the playbook for how brands unlock value from associating themselves with athletes.

Adidas was confronted by significant challenges following the death of Horst Dassler but has evolved into a highly successful lifestyle business with global sales of $22bn and the idea of aligning with top sports properties remaining strategically important to the company. For example, they still supply the match balls to FIFA and UEFA, fit out Team GB, and are the official kit supplier to three of the top four best-selling football shirts, with Bayern Munich the top seller on 3.2 million jerseys during the 2022/3 season and United fourth with sales of 1.95m. Horst would have been delighted with that and also that a three-striped team has featured in all but one of the past ten World Cup finals. However, he would be furious that Nike now generate twice as much revenue and five times the profits of his old company, and apoplectic with the news that broke earlier this year that in 2027 Nike are going to replace Adidas as kit supplier to the team whom his father lovingly made boots for in the 1950s and has ever since been a jewel in the Adidas endorsement crown – the German national team.

Surprisingly, Nike was slow getting involved in football after their first boot was developed for the 1970 World Cup and proved to be a big disappointment. There were then a few random forays, with Aston Villa wearing Nike on their way to their 1982 European Cup triumph until 1994 when Phil Knight declared, 'We will only truly understand football when we see the game through the eyes of Brazilians,' and unveiled a ten-year deal with the Brazil national team worth $160m: cue the music for Wieden+Kennedy to do their thing, and they didn't disappoint either, creating one of the greatest sports commercials of all time which was timed to ambush France '98 and featured the (90s version) of Ronaldo playing an impromptu game of football at Galeao International Airport. In other sports, Roger Federer, Le Bron James and Venus Williams are also long-term Nike brand ambassadors – along with a stable of maverick athletes like John McEnroe and Eric Cantona, who few of their competitors would have touched with a barge pole.

When you see a Nike ad, it therefore has an attitude all of its own and even before the swoosh appears you just know it's from Nike. Who else would get away with staging an impromptu tennis match between Pete Sampras and Andre Agassi on the streets of Manhattan? Or ask Tiger Woods to play keepy-uppy with a golf ball? But my favourite Nike ad of all time has to be a vintage press ad from the 1988 'Just Do It' campaign featuring an 80-year-old-runner from San Francisco saying this: 'I run 17 miles every morning. People ask me how I keep my teeth from chattering in the wintertime. I leave them in the locker.' Partnering with gifted individuals of course also carries risk and Nike had to ride the media roller-coaster of the Tiger Woods sex addiction scandal in 2009 and watch on in horror as the Lance Armstrong odyssey unravelled three years later. Unlike almost all his other sponsors, Nike stuck by Tiger, (although to be fair he had single-handedly grown the sale of their golf equipment tenfold in less than three years), but not even Knight could shrug off the Armstrong scandal when the depth of the doping deception became known. Celebrating troubled genius is one thing but associating the brand with cheats is quite another.

Phil Knight gave a rare interview to *The Guardian* in 2023 and commented: 'Part of our success is that we know who we are.' He goes on, 'We defined ourselves. It is our job to provide inspiration and aspiration for everyone interested in sports in the world.' And this, Phil, despite all your genius, is where your company falls a bit short, in my opinion, since the brand significantly underinvests in support of grassroots sport. Up to now, it's worked spectacularly well riding on the coattails of the big sports events and athletes, but as we now know, the new purposeful consumer expects far more from the products they buy and regardless of how much they love your brand, the danger is that many may well choose to shop elsewhere unless Nike adapts to the changing consumer landscape. In the year to May 2023, for example, Nike Inc made net income of $5bn. Imagine, therefore, the difference reinvesting one per cent of these profits into meaningful grassroots projects could make. A fighting fund of $50m to build 4G football pitches and inner-city basketball courts in disadvantaged communities and a war chest to gift free kit to families who can't afford to buy shoes or shorts for their kids. In *Shoe Dog* (first published in 2016), Knight tackles the criticism Nike received from a scandal that blew up after his company sourced product from Asian sweatshops. He also talked about the company's investment in 'Girl Effect' – a campaign to help improve the lives of young girls, and how hard Nike

The 2023 Forbes Money List

RANK	1992	Total $m	2002	Total $m	2012	Total $m	2023	Total $m	On-Field
1	Jordan	36	Woods	67	Mayweather	85	Ronaldo	136	33%
2	Holyfield	28	Schumacher	67	Pacquiao	62	Messi	130	50%
3	Senna	22	Jordan	36	Tiger	59	Mbappe	120	83%
4	Mansell	14.5	L. Lewis	28	Le Bron	43	Le Bron	120	38%
5	A.Palmer	11.1	S O'Neil	24	Federer	53	C. Alvarez	110	91%
6	Agassi	11	G. Hill	24	Bryant	52	D Johnston	107	95%
7	Montana	9.5	Tyson	23	Mickelson	48	Mickelson	106	98%
8	S. Ray L	9.2	Garnett	23	Beckham	46	S. Curry	100	48%
9	Courier	9	Bryant	22	Ronaldo	42	Federer	95	0
10	Seles	8.5	Villeneuve	20	Manning	42	Durrant	89	49%

has worked to improve their supply chain. He writes, 'We told ourselves: "we must do better".' Yes, Phil, many would agree and we're not talking about better PR, but a long-term commitment to 'Provide inspiration and aspiration' … oh and committed dollars for those who need help too, please. I'm not singling just Nike out for criticism either, for hitching a free ride on the back of sport's IP. Some of their competitors do the same. As do Facebook, TikTok, Twitter, betting companies and the search engines who use sports content as click-bait to drive customer engagement. Time to lean in folks, to pay your dues and help fund the eco-system that creates the IP which helps to fuel your business.

Power now lies with the top talent

Our journey through sporting history began in the era of 'gentlemen and players' when many believed there was more honour competing in sport as an amateur – and losing – rather than behaving as a professional and trying to win. Or as author DJ Taylor somewhat harshly put it, 'The amateur, formerly the symbol of fair play and a stout heart, became the watchword for terminal second rate-ness and lower rung incompetence.' When Kevin Keegan joined Liverpool from Scunthorpe he was offered £45 per week and said this in his autobiography: 'I wanted to sign there and then, but remembered that my father had told me not to sell myself cheap.' Ultimately, Keegan and his manager Bill Shankly agreed on a starting wage of £50 a week, which meant with top-up win bonuses of £80, he was on £6,730 a year.

As we've seen, the game moved on in the early 80s with acceptance of the Athlete Reserve Fund allowing track and field athletes to collect their career earnings once they'd retired, pro-baseball allowing its players to earn a living from the game by scrapping the Reserve Clause and intense pressure applied on sport's governing bodies by the top stars of tennis, golf and football, with threats of breakaway tours and strikes unless change was forthcoming. If we fast-forward to the new millennium, the pendulum of power has swung firmly towards athletes and their agents, with the average salary of a Premier League player now standing at £3.1m, with Kevin De Bruyne taking home £20m a year. American sports wages have spiralled upwards too, with the average player in the NBA now on an annual salary of $10m, an NFL wide receiver paid $2.3m, and a starting pitcher in the MLB taking home $5.2m.

That said, the playing field is an uneven one and so if you play in the top flight of English rugby, you might take home £100k per year, while a county cricketer might expect to receive £40k, and if you're a potential Olympian you'll need to get by on around £40k of lottery funding. This swing towards the top talent and a handful of sports is further highlighted in the Forbes Money List with Cristiano Ronaldo their top earner on $136m, closely followed by Messi, Mbappé, Le Bron and Alvarez. Eight of the top ten earners therefore play either football, basketball or golf, which compares to the 1992 rankings which included two F1 drivers, two boxers, three tennis players, Joe Montana,

Arnold Palmer and Michael Jordan. Interestingly, Forbes also break down on/off-field earnings, with Roger Federer still in their top ten despite having retired from playing competitive tennis, and the extent to which LIV golfers Phil Mickelson and Dustin Johnston are benefiting from the huge salaries on offer from the Kingdom of Saudi Arabia shows, with each of them getting paid $100m+ to compete in the 2023 LIV golf tour and neither generating much money away from their appearance money.

Investing in sport can be a risky business

As Mark McCormack once said, 'Sport is not something you can buy your way into as you can in other industries.' By which he refers to its unique governance, having the old boys' network to deal with and the emotional energy of investing in something millions of people care so deeply about. The first to try his luck was Sir Henry Norris, a property developer who bought Woolwich Arsenal FC in 1907 and sourced a patch of land in north London for his team to play on. He then set up a company to own the assets and offered investors the opportunity to buy one of 7,000 shares at £1 per share. It was significantly undersubscribed.

History is littered with similar warnings to would-be investors in sport, with hundreds of team franchises failing, unsuccessful stock market listings, billions invested in ambitious dotcom investments, agencies overpaying for rights contracts, and the regular 'spin the bottle' jeopardy of promotion and relegation. There have of course been a few big hits, like the four-time multiple CVC received from selling F1 to Liberty Media, and the Glazer family recently selling 25 per cent of Manchester United for the same price they paid for the entire club back in 2005. Many working in the business of sport have, however, become wide-eyed at the recent interest being shown by private equity funds in sporting properties.

This is an industry that in 2022 raised $727bn from the capital markets with the objective of delivering above-average returns for their investors. And up until five years ago showed very little interest in sport. However, the Deloitte 2024 Investment Report highlighted how this has changed, with 62 per cent of the investment they identified sourced to funds headquartered in the United States and leading to much head-scratching by many working inside the European sports ecosystem who are asking themselves what have they missed? In search of answers, I therefore asked one of them – off the record – to explain why sports leagues and clubs fit the investment profile of his fund. 'I look at many sports properties as an undervalued asset class. What makes them attractive is they generate steady cash flow through the longevity of their TV and sponsorship contracts and the rhythm and predictability of their season-ticket and merchandise sales. Furthermore, many of these businesses haven't started to uncork the value of their data and digital assets so I usually feel confident of our ability to unlock value if the deal is set up right.'

Since a large chunk of this new private equity money has been raised in the United States, deals usually involve a cohort of investors with previous experience of buying and selling American sports franchises and most have experienced rapid inflation over recent years, with the average enterprise value of an NFL franchise now $6bn, which is an increase of 34 per cent on 2022. As prices in US sports rise, some of these investors have therefore turned their attention to Europe and one of the biggest deals involved Chelsea FC, a club established 117 years ago in the Rising Sun pub in Belgravia by two brothers who wrote their business plan on the back of a beer mat. One of the new investors in Chelsea is Jonathan Goldstein who had this to say to the *Sunday Times* when asked to explain the attractiveness of the club to his investor group: 'There's the global base, the media rights, the merchandising, the broadcasting rights – the brand.' If I sat in the same pub today – armed with another beer mat and a copy of the Deloitte annual football survey – I could therefore construct the following argument for why Goldstein and his colleagues felt buying Chelsea was such a bargain.

> *'The greater fool theory is someone with the perfect blend of self-delusion and ego to think he can succeed where others have failed'* –
> Aaron Sorkin

The club was bought for £2.5bn with a further £1.75bn pledged in development capital. This was a multiple of five on the turnover the club generated the previous year with £71m of its revenue coming from matchday activities. Getting planning permission to expand Stamford Bridge in the next five years is going to be tricky, so let's assume this revenue stream grows by only three per cent (CAGR) over the same period. The club also made £239m from broadcast sales, and with the new domestic Premier League deals in place, and overseas sales still growing, let's estimate Chelsea's media rights grow by five per cent CAGR over the next five years. Meanwhile, the £180m the club made from their commercial activities punches well below United's at £266m and Liverpool's at £237m, and Goldstein told us he sees much more scope to unlock commercial value from the Chelsea brand, so let's estimate ten per cent CAGR is do-able through strengthening this revenue line. Finally, in our baseline year the club had a transfer embargo imposed on it during the complex sale process and so made a modest £11m net transfer surplus during that financial year.

Through better contract management and mining their impressive academy in Cobham, let's therefore assume it is possible to drive 15 per cent CAGR growth from future player trading. Which means that if the above scenario materialised, the club would be turning over £671m and on a similar multiple of five would have grown its enterprise value to £3.35bn, making a profit on the purchase price (before amortisation) of £1bn.

However, what if we factor in the club winning the Champions League in year five of the business plan, and selling the naming rights to Stamford Bridge? This would add £50m to the top line and £250m to its asset value. And what if the European Super League became a thing during this timeframe, and/or the Premier League allowed Chelsea to sell the games excluded from the current UK TV package direct to their fans? And how about sourcing and selling merchandise direct and/or refusing to pay excessive agent fees? If any of these material factors occurred then the exit profit for this Californian investor group could climb to three or four times what they paid for the club (although I'd need another beer mat to be more precise).

In search of quick momentum, within a few months the new owners of Chelsea spent £1bn bringing in new young players on long-term contracts and while the league form was up and down, the team did eventually finish sixth, make it to the Carabao Cup Final and the semi-final of the FA Cup. Not where the club has been in the modern era under the ownership of Roman Abramovich, but not a horrendous start. However, if you spent any time at Stamford Bridge during the 2023/4 season you'd have seen how unhappy their fans were and the reason why is summarised in the following statement from the Chelsea Supporters' Trust: 'Supporters are saying that there currently seems a fast-growing lack of trust from much of the fan-base, especially match-goers, towards the board, partially due to severely limited communication. Many supporters have significant concerns about the short and long-term future of our football club.'

The next few years are therefore going to be interesting

for Chelsea and for sport in general as it ceases to be reliant on wealthy benefactors, as it was in the past, and is run like most other businesses with a close eye on the bottom line and focus on growing asset value. Some observers are cynical about whether private equity and sport can cohabit comfortably, with blogger Roger Mitchell one of the most sceptical: 'Sport, as an asset and a set of cashflows, is often too volatile, too emotional and too correlated to the media sector, for PE to get the quick return it needs. Not a good fit in the first place, and then the full "stakeholder risk" is underpriced.' But as TV rights plateau and the axis of power in world sport shifts to New York and Riyadh, the money to fund sports digital transformation journey has to come from new sources and I'm therefore optimistic about the potential of successfully aligning the sporting objectives of cautious governing bodies with the economic objectives of private equity investors who take a medium-term view on ROI, invest in the right things, respect the traditions of what it is they've bought into and appoint boards who take fans with them on the journey.

Politics plays a big part

When David Conn interviewed Sepp Blatter for his book he asked him if he knew why Michel Platini had voted for Qatar. This was his reply, 'Platini later admitted that he changed his mind following lunch at the Elysée Palace in November 2010 with his country's president, Nicolas Sarkozy, and the son of Qatar's Emir, Tamim bin Hamad Al Thani.'

Whether this is the case or not, it wouldn't be the first-time political pressure has been applied to influence sporting outcomes. We've seen, for example, how the Olympic Games has been used as a political football for decades; how the issue of apartheid haunted the world sport; and that during the Cold War sporting success was a big part of the Soviet propaganda machine. It took a report in 1964 by Lord Wolfenden for the British Government to realise how far British sport had fallen behind the rest of the world and then the humiliation of Atlanta '96 and John Major's passion for sport to seriously do something about it.

In that same year there was great national pride too when England hosted Euro '96 and Tony Blair started to recognise the economic and societal benefit of hosting the Olympics in London.

A change in government attitude and a more vibrant policy towards sport, media and advertising has therefore played a significant part in shaping Britain's modern sports industry, with the Broadcasting Act of 1990 giving ITV and BBC new competition to think about, and legislation permitting sport to swap cigarettes for gambling as its guilty secret. The actions of European politicians have also had a profound impact, with agreement in 1975 to allow migration between member states and the Bosman ruling offering free agency to Europe's footballers. I therefore wonder what new legislation could be on the horizon which will shape sport's future? Might advertising from betting companies get banned like tobacco? Will there be a new football regulator, who will reel in the insurgency of the top clubs and ensure a fairer distribution of TV money down the footballing pyramid? Will social media activity get better controlled? Will support for UK Sport and Sport England get dialled down? Is the Listed Events legislation fit for purpose? And how can government ensure a step change in growing female sports?

Rainmakers get stuff done

Through the lens of 2024 some of what used to pass for acceptable behaviour in the workplace was extraordinary. When I worked in the world of television, for example, I had one boss who needed a drink before our first meeting and would creep round the back of a small hotel near our office at 9am to get the bar staff to serve him a beer. We'd then go to a meeting, often have lunch where he'd down half a bottle of wine, then he'd down a few pints in the pub at 5.30pm before going home to see his much-maligned wife and kids. On another occasion, an agency media buyer turned up unannounced in our reception wanting to punch my lights out because he didn't believe the cost I was quoting him to buy a spot in our late-night football coverage. 'Get Stubley down here now,' he screamed at poor John on the desk, who called me from the safety of upstairs and said there was a gentleman downstairs to see me who seemed quite cross.

'Gentleman or player, John?' I should have replied.

It was also totally fine to shove people out of the way or ignore them to get what you wanted. Here's Greg Dyke explaining the 1980s BBC management style in relation to his head of sport, John Bromley: 'He was uneasy about doing a side deal with the big clubs, so I didn't take him to the next one [meeting]. That's a tactic I discovered was widely used at the BBC … if someone doesn't agree, hold the next meeting without them.'

Yep, that was about it; we put on our thick skins when we got out of bed in the morning to enter the lion's den of the 1980s workplace. One hour for lunch to catch your breath and straight into the pub at 5.30pm to blow off some steam and laugh about the madness that had just unfolded. The world of sport experienced its fair share of bad behaviour too and here's Mihir Bose describing what he witnessed when writing for the *Daily Telegraph* in the 1990s: 'Sports organisations behaved as if the world was still governed by the ethics of 19th-century American capitalism. The modern corporate world had long recognised the need to embrace transparency and disclosure, but sport behaved as if it was above and beyond such considerations.' In an interview after FIFA-gate, Sepp Blatter explained his take on that era to David Conn: 'You can't judge the past on the basis of today's standards ... otherwise it would end up with moral justice.' His secretary general, Jerome Valcke went further: 'The old world was the system of commission. Twenty years ago ... you were giving commissions to people in order to get market or to get product or whatever. Today the legal system has changed. I don't know if it's an improvement or not, just say it has changed. You can't do it anymore.'

It's easy to look down your nose at commission payments, but Valcke was right that receiving a clip from deals was how many people were (and often still are) paid in the world of sports rights. As they were/are in real estate, financial services and all manner of other service-based sectors. However, where the wheels came off sport's governing bodies in the 1990s was that these commissions were rarely declared. And they were sometimes paid to individuals who had worked their way into trusted positions of influence and were abusing it for personal gain. So, to avoid doubt, let's repeat what Valcke said, 'You can't do it anymore.'

Looking for explanations as to why some went rogue, we've discussed the previous lack of money in the sports ecosystem and the poor commercial governance dating back to the 1970s. However, another reason was that as sport emerged from its amateur slumber, few of those holding down the top jobs had much experience of handling politicians and skilled businesspeople and so, as world leaders and global brands started to aggressively chase sports deals, is it any wonder some had their heads turned? In 2004, for example, a frail Nelson Mandela took a nine-hour flight to Trinidad to win Jack Warner's vote for South Africa to host the 2010 World Cup and five years later President Obama arrived in Copenhagen on a six-hour stopover to lobby for Chicago to host the 2016 Olympics. The following year, David Cameron joined in the gladhanding and invited Sepp Blatter to Number 10, treating him like a head of state with the following flattery: 'Mr President, you have done a huge amount for football during your whole life. The decisions you have made have been instrumental in taking the game to new heights, breaking new boundaries and reaching new people, culminating in what we were just discussing together – bringing the hugely successful World Cup to Africa ... I hope you see that England has got what it takes to host the greatest tournament on earth. I hope you can see how much our country wants this.' The leaders of these once amateur sports organisations were therefore feted like kings and Vladimir Putin even suggested that Sepp Blatter received a Nobel Peace Prize. Why were they elected in the first place? Why did they stay so long? Why didn't others around them try to change things? Where were the checks and balances? How could they live with themselves? All are fair questions and in search of an explanation I'll default to Tony Collins, who is one of sport's most respected historians and said this about the shifting standards of public life: 'The old codes of gentlemanly conduct had dissolved and been replaced, in some cases by a "culture of moral vagueness".'

What Collins is therefore saying is that the way business was conducted changed significantly between 1960 and 1990, as it has in subsequent years, and the safest thing to say (once again) is that these were 'different times', when people learned their moves in a different era, fought different fights and against opponents who used different tactics and had very different reference points. For example, if you were touched by the war years, like some of our rainmakers, then you quite obviously saw the world differently to people who were not and did not grow up in a world with social media and 24-hour news which therefore made it easy to be vague. As ex-A&R man David Hepworth amusingly wrote in *Uncommon People*, 'It's unimaginable that a band today would be able to behave as

Led Zeppelin and David Bowie did during their early 70s tours. All their misbehaviour would be webcast live. They would be regularly required to do the one thing the stars of yesteryear never did – apologise. Rock fans like to feel that their heroes misbehave but wouldn't really wish to see the evidence.'

Whatever we think of the behaviour of some of our rainmakers, what we can say about them, for sure, is that they acted decisively. That doesn't mean we need to agree with the decisions they made, the way they went about their business or that we should even like these people. However, inertia rules without strong leadership and these people certainly got stuff done. Lennart Johansson, for example, kept Europe's clubs together after the first threat of a Super League breakaway in the late 90s. Meanwhile, Rupert Murdoch, Ted Turner and Roone Arledge made their networks successful by doing whatever it took to secure the contracts they wanted, and Peter Rozelle, David Stern and Richard Scudamore kept their owners happy through regularly visiting the TV rights cash machine. As Lalit Modi explained in an interview with the *Daily Telegraph*, 'Yes, my style is different, but styles of different entrepreneurs are different, whether it's a Bernie Ecclestone, a Rupert Murdoch, or a Donald Trump. They may upset people, but they should be judged by the results.'

The final word on what makes a good rainmaker must, however, be left to one of the best in the business: our smooth operator, Mr Peter Ueberroth, who showed the world of sport how to make money from LA to Chicago: 'Practising good leadership and striving for excellence are not popularity contests. If I've learned one lesson from the Olympic experience, it is that when you take risks, you inevitably ruffle feathers.'

PART TEN:
The Sports Marketing Hall of Fame

'Well, maybe I'm just thinking that the rooms are all on fire. Every time that you walk in the room'–
Stevie Nicks

'I am the greatest, I said that even before I knew I was' – Ali.

SPORTS WERE never invented to make money. Which is lucky really since up until 1984 most clubs and sports franchises had to rely on generous owners to keep the lights on, until sport figured out its relationship with television and the advertising business.

If we fast-forward to 2024, brands are spending $100bn on sports sponsorship and media corporations are paying another $50bn for the right to show live sport on their platforms. Meanwhile, the global betting and gaming industry generates $50bn a year and humans spend another $335bn buying athlete-endorsed sports gear. If we throw in the billions spent buying tickets, branded merchandise and the value of stadium construction contracts, then the sports ecosystem is now easily worth over $1tn, or one per cent of global GDP. All this has happened in the space of just 40 years and, since Roone Arledge once told us sport is all about showbiz, the final question we must answer is who has been sport's greatest rainmaker of all time?

Arledge obviously makes the Hall of Fame for the bold bets he made on sports rights and for turning American television into a three-network race. Also, for being the first to get live sport to rate in primetime, for pioneering new production techniques and for ensuring his team were on standby to capture some of sport's greatest-ever TV moments, such as the Tommie Smith interview in Mexico City; Franz Klammer's breathtaking downhill run in Montreal; the 'Rumble in the Jungle' and the 'Battle of the Sexes'.

Horst Dassler, meanwhile, was sport's Don Corleone, who ranks high up the list for showing international sports properties how to package up their rights to appeal to global brands and for building Adidas into one of sport's most influential companies. Along with his brother Rudolf, who kept him awake at night, and Phil Knight who 'just did it'. It wasn't always a smooth ride with these three men, but they certainly got the job done. So did João Havelange and Sepp Blatter, who can't be airbrushed out of history for their obvious misdemeanours since on their watch they turned the World Cup into the most watched event in the sporting calendar. Mark McCormack and his IMG colleagues have also played a starring role since they were the first to identify the role for a marketing agency dedicated to managing the careers of sportsmen and women and for building the chosen few into household names. And what about the ultimate sporting ringmaster who turned the Corinthian sport of F1 into a commercial juggernaut which in 2024 will generate turnover of $2.2bn for its new owners? Uniquely amongst the top sports properties F1 also makes one-third of its revenue from circuit fees as the emerging nations we spoke about earlier bask in the glow of having the F1 circus coming to town. Love him or loathe him, you therefore can't argue with Bernie Ecclestone's achievement of turning F1 into the sixth most valuable franchise in world sport.

There are other sports administrators we must call out too for the skilful way they handled the complex politics of their sports. David Stern, for example, who turned the NBA from a laughing stock into an economic powerhouse with individual team franchises now changing hands for an average of $3.85bn. And what about Peter Rozelle who turned the Superbowl into the most important day in the advertising calendar and drove through the idea of his teams collectively selling their rights, which now generates $10bn a year for the current cohort of NFL franchises? Rozelle was also the first to understand the power of emotional storytelling and transformed the NFL into a personal passion for millions that goes way beyond watching live games at the weekend. He realised too that keeping fans interested in the sport meant games had to remain competitive, which meant sharing revenue fairly and resulted in 13 different teams winning the championship final over the course of his 25-year tenure.

Peter Ueberroth was another determined leader who makes my top ten for showing the IOC how to make money from the Olympic Games and for using these learnings to turn around the commercial fortunes of MLB, his success coming from doing what many entering the business of sport often forget to do – which is to not get too carried away by all the emotion and understand he had a responsibility to deliver value to his backers, owners, investors, athletes, politicians and commercial partners, while taking the fans with him on the journey.

Dame Sue Campbell also makes my dream team for her tireless work transforming British Olympic sports and, more recently, for pushing the FA and the British media to get behind women's football. Speaking of which, we can't exclude the architects of the Premier League with Rick Parry, David Dein and Martin Edwards the three names that came up most often in my research. Plus, Lennart Johansson and Richard Scudamore, who oversaw the rapid growth of the UEFA Champions League and Premier League, which together now generate $7bn a year for the clubs participating in these two competitions.

Then there are our TV barons, including Ted Turner, who pioneered the distribution of television pictures via satellite, while Bill Rasmussen's idea for a 24-hour cable sports network may well have been scoffed at in the early days, but ESPN has had the last laugh and gone on to dominate and define sport in the United States, investing $4bn a year in sports rights and generating revenue for its current owner Disney of $14.4bn. What also of the ultimate disruptor, Rupert Murdoch, and his News Corp colleagues who pioneered pay-TV in Europe and Asia with their Sky, Fox and Star brands? Without them, English football, cricket and both codes of rugby would look very different;

and their cash has led to a stampede of foreign players into English football, which has vicariously uncorked billions of pounds of overseas TV rights fees.

After television, the sponsorship of clubs, leagues and content has been the other principal economic driver for the world of sport with Coca-Cola, Gillette, Vodafone, Ford and Adidas my five greatest sports sponsors of all time. The involvement of marketing groups like Omnicom and Dentsu should also not be underestimated since they turned the sponsorship decision from a 'nice to have' into a crucial strategic marketing play for big brands. And, if we're voting for people motivated not by money, but for their deep passion for driving fairness through sport, then it's hard to look beyond Billie Jean King for her unwavering commitment to driving equality and inclusivity; although world champions Ed Moses and Seb Coe also deserve a seat at the top table after helping to end shamateurism and with Coe now trying to fix the broken sport of athletics. Marc Hodler, Loretta Lynch and James Comey also deserve a mention for calling out some of the bad behaviour that had been allowed to form around the governance of world sport.

As for more recent rainmakers? Matt Rogan and Gareth Baulch were often name-checked during my research for creating Two Circles: an agency championing the idea that sports properties should better monetise their data. Ollie Slipper, Simon Dwyer, Carsten Koel, Aidan Cooney, Johan Apel and Peter Coates were the early pioneers of the digital data revolution. Meanwhile, social networks and gamers have provided the ongoing surround sound – although EA Sports, along with Sony, are two of the few who pay their sporting dues.

Then there are the less-feted rainmakers whom we've met on our journey through time who maybe didn't benefit from the same fame and fortune as others. This includes the founding fathers of the NFL, and the talented executives working at West Nally, ISL and IMG. A special mention also to the rainmakers of TEAM Marketing for creating the blueprint for what I believe to be the finest sports brand ever created – the UEFA Champions League.

Lalit Modi and the ECB class of 2003 also deserve a place on our All-Stars Team for reimaging what cricket could look like, along with the city of Tokyo for preventing a total meltdown within Olympic sports by managing to stage the Olympic Games during a global pandemic. And finally, while this book is centred on the black belts of sports marketing, we cannot ignore the gifted individuals who have supplied those unforgettable moments that get us so excited. The sporting legends who go faster, higher, stronger, like Babe Ruth, Stanley Matthews, Ali, Pelé, Eusébio, Borg, McEnroe, the Class of '92, the Invincibles, Senna, Jordan, Tiger, Schumacher, Serena, Bolt, Federer and the Lionesses, et al. who make Super Bowls, Super Leagues and Super Sundays, simply – super.

However, when all is said and done, there can only be one winner at any sports award ceremony, so I'm going to cast my vote for sport's most valuable rainmaker to Señor Juan Antonio Samaranch, an unassuming Spaniard who inherited an organisation in total disarray and used his political skill and determination to transform the Olympic Games into one of sport's most powerful marketing platforms, while simultaneously working hard to stay true to the original values laid down by Pierre de Coubertin.

The decision to introduce a competitive auction for the sale of Olympic TV rights and hiring ISL to introduce the TOP marketing programme arguably saved the IOC from ruin, with TV rights fees up from $80m when he was elected president to reach $1.3bn and with sponsorship revenue increasing tenfold to $2bn by the time he stepped down. Unlike his predecessors, Samaranch was willing to embrace the Olympics as a commercial marketing platform and to seek ways for athletes to earn an honest living from playing sport and so end the double standards that had existed for years in Olympic sports.

This analysis is, however, clearly a subjective one and so I'd be interested to know what you think – so please cast your vote at www.gamechangersandrainmakers.com and let me know who your top sporting rainmakers of all time are and why. Here are my 40 runners and riders (in no particular order).

	THE SPORTS MARKETING HALL OF FAME	**FOR ...**
1	**Ebenezer Morley**	*Establishing the Football Association and gifting us the FA Cup*
2	**Pierre de Coubertin**	*Creating the modern-day Olympic Games*
3	**Bill Bernbach**	*Inspiring a generation of creative people*
4	**Stanley Matthews**	*Kick-starting Britain's interest in watching live sport on TV*
5	**The NFL founding fathers**	*Creating sport's most valuable property*
6	**Mark McCormack**	*Inventing the idea of a sports marketing agency*
7	**Peter Rozelle**	*Introducing collective selling/the Superbowl*
8	**Billie Jean King**	*Fighting so hard for equal rights*
9	**Marvin Miller**	*Ensuring fairness in player contracts*
10	**Phil Knight**	*Creating one of the most loved brands on the planet*
11	**Patrick Nally**	*Inventing the official partner model*
12	**Tadayuki Ito**	*For saving Nike*
13	**Horst Dassler**	*Creating Adidas and setting up ISL – the first sports rights agency*
14	**Jao Havelange**	*For turning FIFA and world football into a global powerhouse*
15	**Juan Antonio Samaranch**	*Saving/modernising the Olympic Games*
16	**Roone Arledge**	*Being the first to truly understand the power of live sport on TV*

Gamechangers and Rainmakers

17	Jay Chiat	Putting the Superbowl on the map
18	David Stern	Re-inventing the NBA
19	Michael Jordan	Creating the blueprint for the pop-culture styled superstar
20	Peter Ueberroth	Showing us how to make money from the Olympics
21	Ted Turner	Helping build the cable industry in America
22	Bernie Ecclestone	Building F1 into an $8bn sporting powerhouse
23	David Dein et al	Creating the Premier League
24	Bill Rasmussen	Creating ESPN
25	Rupert Murdoch and Sam Chisholm	Creating Sky Sports and Fox Sports
26	Lennart Johansson and TEAM Marketing	Creating the UEFA Champions League
27	The Vodafone Class of 2000	Showing how to use sponsorship strategically
28	Jian Tian	Creating the first FIFA videogame
29	John Major	Creating UK Sport
30	Sue Campbell	Making UK Sport a success/ driving women's football forwards
31	Richard Scudamore	Turning the Premier League into sport's second most profitable property
32	Wieden + Kennedy	Being sport's best brand storytellers
33	Billy Beane	Making sports data cool
34	Ollie Slipper and Simon Dwyer	Being the catalyst to help unlock in-play betting
35	Carsten Koel	Being the first to make money from live sports data
36	Marc Randolph and Reed Hastings	Creating Netflix
37	Peter Coates and Norbert Teufelberger	Coming up with the idea of in-play betting
38	Lalit Modi	For creating the IPL
39	Matt Rogan and Gareth Baulch	Inventing the idea of data-driven sport
40	Loretta Lynch and James Comey	Helping clean up sport

Epilogue

> *'I demand a better future, or I might stop loving you'* — David Bowie.

IF 1984 was the year when sports marketing came of age, then I wonder how its 40th anniversary will be remembered in years to come? Will Paris '24 be seen as the high-water mark for the industry? The moment when anyone under the age of 24 turned their backs on the hyperbole of the sports media and the rising cost in time, money and energy of getting involved. Or maybe 2024 will be the year when, funded by private equity, sport moves into the next stage of its evolution, which revolves around virtual worlds, connected commerce, direct-to-consumer video streaming, content marketing, NFTs and artificial intelligence, which together power sport on to greater riches and recruit an army of new digital native fans?

It's often easy to look forward in life through rose-tinted glasses but in an age where attention spans are getting shorter and shorter, one of the few things that keeps us engaged (and together) is the drama of live sport. The pair I'm wearing, therefore, point towards a bright future for those willing to adapt, look forward and respect the important traditions of the past.

The Baby Boomers hankering after 'jumpers for goalposts' won't enjoy the ride for sure, but could it be that Amazon emerges as the 'new ESPN', with Jeff Bezos anointed as Rupert Murdoch's natural successor, and looks at sports content as compelling click-bait to drive e-commerce to his platform? And maybe Adam Silver, the current commissioner of the NBA, will disrupt the market like David Stern did back in the 1990s when he dumped the networks to go all-in with cable, but this time doing what everyone else is talking about, which is launching a dedicated streaming platform which cuts out broadcasters from sport's ecosystem.

What too of Andrew Wilson and his colleagues at EA Sports, who, free of FIFA red tape, can now offer gamers the chance to play live virtual football with real-time stats, augmented reality and personal avatars? And maybe Nick Clarry of CVC, one of the largest private equity investors in sport, will emerge as the new Horst Dassler, wielding great power over the sports he invests in and, like Sepp Blatter, deciding the rules of the game and who gets to play.

And what about the next generation of rainmakers, who we know nothing about yet and are busy inventing new ideas that will help sport make its next leap forward, just like Roone Arledge, Rupert Murdoch and Billy Beane did back in the day? Companies like Eleven Sports who are helping to put the lost community spirit back into clubs or Twenty First Group who are turning jeopardy into sport's new storytelling currency. As I write, look also at the billions of dollars the Kingdom of Saudia Arabia is throwing at sport with the objective of using it as a shiny shop window through which its economy can be transformed. And could the English FA, once derided for its antiquated and misogynistic behaviour but now under the astute leadership of Debbie Hewitt and Mark Bullingham, be writing the blueprint for what a modern, profitable, responsible, diverse and purposeful NGB should look like? While Tim Hollingworth, the CEO of Sport England reminds us that it's not all about money and medals and urges the nation to get active and for sport to remember its moral compass.

Epilogue

Whatever the future holds I hope you've enjoyed this ride through sporting history and reliving what I consider to be 40 of sport's most decisive moments. I hope you've also enjoyed getting to know our rainmakers: a group of extraordinary men and women who had the vision and energy to spot new opportunities and whose actions have combined to invent a vibrant new segment of the global entertainment business which unleashes unexplainable emotion deep inside of us. A personal passion that makes us laugh, cry, angry, confused and ecstatic in equal measure. Entertainment of magnificent triviality bringing humans together like nothing else and something that matters so deeply to us because it doesn't really matter at all.

Acknowledgements

ONE OF my main motivations for writing this book was to explain to the next generation of sports marketeers coming into the industry how this brilliant business was created. Not that there were specific business plans to analyse since if you've got this far you will know by now that much of what led us to where we are today happened totally by chance. That cannot, however, be said of the team at Pitch Publishing who have guided me through my first book with great skill and patience. Thank you, therefore, to my publisher Jane Camillin for taking a chance on this Palace fan. To my editor, Katie Field, who worked so hard knocking the manuscript into shape, to Duncan Olner for capturing the spirit of the book through his clever cover design and to Graham Hales for his great care and skill typesetting the book. I also need to say a big thank you to the many people who helped me with my research and to all our rainmakers without whom there wouldn't have been much to write about. Thank you also for the amazing support and encouragement from friends and colleagues who checked, challenged, told stories, bought beer, and contributed so much. I've been lucky to meet some extraordinary people during my career, you know who you are and thanks for the good times. Finally, a massive thank you to Team Stubley: my wife Alison for her unswerving love and support and our three fearless daughters Georgie, Annie and Charlie who provided so much encouragement and inspiration. Thank goodness for Vitbe bread.

Selected Bibliography

Anstiss, Sue, *Game On* (Unbound, 2021)
Arledge, Roone, *Roone* (Harper Collins, 2003)
Barnes, Simon, *The Meaning of Sport* (Short Books, 2006)
Beam, George, *The Sun King* (Hardie Grant 2012)
Bose, Mihir, *Gamechangers* (Marshall Cavendish, 2012)
Bowman, Tom, *No Angel* (Faber and Faber, 2012)
Brookes, C, *English Cricket* (Littlehampton Book Services Ltd, 1978)
Cashmore, Ellis, *Making Sense of Sports* (Routledge, 2010)
Coggan, Philip, *More* (Profile Books, 2020)
Collins, Tony, *A Social History of English Rugby Union* (Routledge, 2009)
Collins, Tony, *Rugby League: A People's History* (Scratching Shed Publishing Ltd, 2020)
Conn, David, *The Fall of the House of FIFA* (Yellow Jersey Press, 2017)
Dallaglio, Lawrence, *Rugby Tales* (Headline, 2010)
Davies, Barry, *Interesting, Very Interesting,* (Headline Publishing Group, 2007)
Dyke, Greg, *Inside Story* (Harper Perennial, 2005)
Ferguson, Alex, *My Autobiography* (Hodder & Stoughton, 2013)
Futterman, Matthew, *Players* (Simon & Schuster, 2016)
Garton Ash, Timothy, *Homelands* (Penguin, 2023)
Gorn, Elliot J. & Warren Goldstein, *A Brief History of American Sports* (Farrar, Strauss, and Giroux, 2013)
Grothe, Philip, *The Sports Entrepreneur Podcast*, 23.3.21

Heffer, Simon, *The Age of Decadence* (Penguin, 2017)
Helyar, John, *Lords of the Realm* (Random House, 1994)
Hepworth, David, *Uncommon People* (Bantam Press, 2017)
Higham, John, *The Reconstruction of American History* (Praeger Publishers, 1980)
Holt, Richard, *Sport and the British* (Oxford University Press, 1989)
Hopcraft, Arthur, *The Football Man* (Penguin, 2014)
Isenberg, John, *The League* (Basic Books, 2019)
Izenberg, Jerry, *Rozelle* (University of Nebraska Press, 2014)
Keegan, Kevin, *My Life in Football* (Macmillan, 2018)
Kelly, Graham, *Sweet FA* (Collins Willow, 1999)
Kelner, Martin, *Sit Down and Cheer* (Bloomsbury Publishing, 2012)
King, Billie Jean, *All In* (Penguin Random House, 2021)
Knight, Phil, *Shoe Dog* (Simon & Schuster, 2016).
Levitt, Theodore, *Harvard Business Review*, 1983
Lewis, Michael, *Moneyball* (W.W. Norton & Company 2004)
MacCambridge, Michael, *America's Game* (Anchor Books, 2005)
Miller, David, *Igniting the Games* (Pitch Publishing, 2022)
Miller, David, *Olympic Revolution* (Pavilion Books, 1992)
Payne, Michael, *Olympic Turnaround* (London Business Press, 2005)
Polley, Martin, *Moving the Goalposts* (Routledge, 1998)
Robinson, Joshua & Jonathan Clegg, *The Club* (John Murray, 2018)
Rogan, Matt, *All to Play For* (Ebury Press, 2021)
Schaefer, Mark, *Marketing Rebellion* (Amazon, 2019)
Scragg, Steven, *The Undisputed Champions of Europe* (Pitch Publishing, 2021)
Smit, Barbara, *Pitch Invasion* (Penguin, 2006)
Smith, Ed, *What Sport Tells Us About Life* (Penguin, 2008)
Smith, Rory, *Expected Goals*, (Mudlark, 2022)

Syed, Matthew, *Black Box Thinking* (John Murray Publishers, 2015)

Tungate, Mark, *Adland* (Kogan Page Limited, 2007)

Turner, Ted, *Call Me Ted* (Turner Works, 2008)

Ueberroth, Peter, *Made in America* (Ballantine Books, 1985)

Vogan, Travis, *ESPN, The Making of a Sports Media Empire* (University of Illinois, 2015)